NEED A LITTLE HELP?
Call me.

I'M HERE TO HELP

Stop banging your head against the wall! The LSAT and law school admissions aren't as mind-boggling as you might think. If there's a type of LSAT question that's bothering you, or you're really confused by the whole "sufficient vs. necessary" thing, or you want to know how to negotiate for law school scholarships... please let me help! I'm a nerd about this stuff, and I love to show students how easy it can be. Email me any time at **nathan@foxlsat.com**, or just pick up the phone. I'm generally available to talk between 9 am and 7 pm PST.

ONLINE LSAT COURSE

If you like my books, I think you'll love my online LSAT class. It includes the exact same tests, quizzes, and lectures as my 12-week "Extended-Length" Class in San Francisco. Students pay $1495 for the 12-week classroom experience, but the class video is yours to watch and rewatch at your own pace from anywhere in the world for just $595. All materials included. And you're always encouraged to call or email me directly if you have any questions during the course. Like I said, I'm a nerd.

www.foxlsat.com/online-lsat-course

No confusing jargon, no pulled punches, no bullshit.
LSAT made simple.

@nfox
facebook.com/FoxTestPrep
foxlsat.com/lsat-blog
linkedin.com/in/foxlsat

CALL NATHAN TODAY
415-518-0630

Copyright 2012 by Nathan Fox

Design by Christopher Imlay

Published by Avocado Books,
Los Angeles, California

ISBN: 978-0-9838505-1-9

Breaking The LSAT:
The Fox Guide to
a Real LSAT, Volume 2

by Nathan Fox

TABLE OF **CONTENTS**

Fox LSAT

www.foxlsat.com
372 West Portal Ave. #4
San Francisco, CA 94127
415-518-0630
nathan@foxlsat.com

**BREAKING THE LSAT:
THE FOX GUIDE TO
A REAL LSAT, VOL. 2**

by Nathan Fox

Welcome

(or, "Breaking the LSAT")

The purpose of this book is to break the spell that the LSAT has over the typical unwary student. Yes, at first, the LSAT can look like a big, mysterious, omnipotent monster. But once we pull back the curtain, we're going to find a pathetic little old man with a smoke machine and a couple mirrors. Good news, test-takers! This shit just ain't that hard. I promise.

Logic Games: Breaking it Down

Everyone struggles with Games at first, but this is actually the easiest, most learnable section of the test. My students improve by an average of five to six questions on this section alone, and I've even seen jumps of 15 questions or more. It definitely looks like black magic if you go too fast and miss something. But when you slow the tape down to normal speed, you'll see the illusion dissolve into a series of bite-sized and totally manageable baby steps. There's nowhere else on the test that you can answer questions with 100 percent certainty. You're about to see how.

Reading Comprehension: Breaking the Boredom

There's absolutely no magic here. Instead, there are a series of horrifically boring passages that you 1) must read, and 2) must *comprehend*. I'm sorry to say that there is no shortcut. But there are a couple simple techniques that will help you stay awake, grasp the main point of the passages, and get dramatically more correct answers. I won't bullshit you though: The other sections will be more fun.

Logical Reasoning: Breaking Balls

Go watch *Goodfellas* and *Casino* and *Reservoir Dogs* and *Pulp Fiction*—and any other gangster movies you can find. Notice how the characters never take anybody's word for anything. Instead, they're always arguing. *My Cousin Vinny* is also perfect—the only character to ever trump Joe Pesci at breaking balls is his girlfriend, Marisa Tomei's "Mona Lisa Vito." As you do Logical Reasoning questions, you need to take this same attitude. *The speaker is always wrong.* Your job is simply to articulate why. If you want to do it with a Jersey accent in your head, more power to you.

Logical Reasoning is, by far, the most fun section of the test to teach and write about. If you're doing it right, it's also the most fun section of the test to take. The great news here is that there are *two* of these sections on every LSAT test. This is where we're really going to break the LSAT down. And like gangsters in a coffee shop, we'll have fun doing it.

Meet Your Guide

I took the official LSAT in February of 2007, and scored 179. In 2008, I enrolled at UC Hastings College of the Law. It was the best school within biking distance from my home in San Francisco's Mission District. I was 32 years old at the time, and I had no idea what I wanted to do with my life. I already had a Master's degree in journalism. I already had an MBA. I'd already held, hated, and supremely sucked at a succession of jobs.

Now I'm 35. And as I write this introduction—with a glass of wine in hand—my law career is mercifully over. I will never be a lawyer, and I couldn't be happier about that. Because the same year I started law school, I discovered my true passion and obvious calling in life. It wasn't law. I'm a teacher.

I know it's my calling because, for the first time in my life, I'm doing the thing that 1) I'm good at, 2) I love, and 3) I can get paid for. If this describes you at your current occupation, then please put down this book and walk away from the LSAT. For good. Seriously. Because professionally, that's about as good as it gets.

For the rest of you (and polls would suggest that's most of you), I'll assume you haven't yet found your calling. I'll assume that a J.D. will move you toward your calling, whether as a lawyer or in some other career. For taking the risk, for wanting to better yourself, and for not settling for unhappiness, I commend you. Law may or may not turn out to be your thing. But you'll have no way of knowing until you try.

Thank you for picking up this book. Before we get started, here's how you can reach me: My cell phone number is 415-518-0630. My email address is nathan@foxlsat.com.

Your questions, comments, and concerns—not just about the LSAT, but about law school and career counseling in general—are the lifeblood of my business. If you've made it this far, then I consider you my student. I wouldn't be here without you. Let me know how I can help.

How to Use This Book

The fastest way to learn to ride a bike is to crash. A lot. The technique seems mysterious at first. How the hell do the other kids make it look so easy? You skin your knees, you shed a few tears, you get back up, and you try it one more time. And then one day—maybe when you're on the verge of giving up—you don't crash. Suddenly, before you even realize it, you're halfway down the block. You've done it!

And, of course, as soon as you make this realization, you panic and you crash once more.

You never stop crashing, really. But the crashes become less and less frequent, until they're almost nonexistent. You're never a perfect rider, but you never stop getting better. The more you practice, the better you become.

The LSAT is exactly the same. There is no amount of abstract theory that can help you learn. (*The Theory of Bicycle Physics* would be worthless to a kid.) Instead, you need to try, and fail, and learn from your mistakes. That is the purpose of this book, with emphasis on the last part there, of course.

The instructions are simple:

1. **Do one section of the December 2010 LSAT.** Time yourself, 35 minutes per section. When time is up, check your answers.
2. **Read the strategy introduction.** At the beginning of each section, you'll find a brief primer on my general strategies for that set of questions.
3. **Read the explanations.** And not just for the ones you got wrong. The LSAT is notorious for allowing students to choose the right answer for the wrong reasons. The explanations in this book will help you answer future questions with more certainty.
4. **Repeat.**

Don't focus too intently on any one question. Perfection is not a useful, or even reasonable, goal on the LSAT. Time yourself, but remember that most people don't finish each section. Most people randomly guess on a few questions at the end of each section—there's no penalty for guessing. Focus on repeatedly nailing the easier questions instead of occasionally getting the harder ones correct, because some of the harder ones are so convoluted that little can be gained from studying them, something I'll point out in the explanations. (Easier questions tend to appear near the beginning of each section.)

The goal here is to try to eliminate your repeated, systematic mistakes. Eventually, just like riding a bike, you'll start to get a feel for it.

Until then, put 35 minutes on the clock—and have fun crashing.

THE DECEMBER 2010 LSAT

SECTION I

Time—35 minutes

27 Questions

<u>Directions</u>: Each set of questions in this section is based on a single passage or a pair of passages. The questions are to be answered on the basis of what is <u>stated</u> or <u>implied</u> in the passage or pair of passages. For some of the questions, more than one of the choices could conceivably answer the question. However, you are to choose the <u>best</u> answer; that is, the response that most accurately and completely answers the question, and blacken the corresponding space on your answer sheet.

To study centuries-old earthquakes and the geologic faults that caused them, seismologists usually dig trenches along visible fault lines, looking for sediments that show evidence of having shifted. Using radiocarbon
(5) dating, they measure the quantity of the radioactive isotope carbon 14 present in wood or other organic material trapped in the sediments when they shifted. Since carbon 14 occurs naturally in organic materials and decays at a constant rate, the age of organic
(10) materials can be reconstructed from the amount of the isotope remaining in them. These data can show the location and frequency of past earthquakes and provide hints about the likelihood and location of future earthquakes.
(15) Geologists William Bull and Mark Brandon have recently developed a new method, called lichenometry, for detecting and dating past earthquakes. Bull and Brandon developed the method based on the fact that large earthquakes generate numerous simultaneous
(20) rockfalls in mountain ranges that are sensitive to seismic shaking. Instead of dating fault-line sediments, lichenometry involves measuring the size of lichens growing on the rocks exposed by these rockfalls. Lichens—symbiotic organisms consisting of a fungus
(25) and an alga—quickly colonize newly exposed rock surfaces in the wake of rockfalls, and once established they grow radially, flat against the rocks, at a slow but constant rate for as long as 1,000 years if left undisturbed. One species of North American lichen, for example,
(30) spreads outward by about 9.5 millimeters each century. Hence, the diameter of the largest lichen on a boulder provides direct evidence of when the boulder was dislodged and repositioned. If many rockfalls over a large geographic area occurred simultaneously, that
(35) pattern would imply that there had been a strong earthquake. The location of the earthquake's epicenter can then be determined by mapping these rockfalls, since they decrease in abundance as the distance from the epicenter increases.
(40) Lichenometry has distinct advantages over radiocarbon dating. Radiocarbon dating is accurate only to within plus or minus 40 years, because the amount of the carbon 14 isotope varies naturally in the environment depending on the intensity of the radiation
(45) striking Earth's upper atmosphere. Additionally, this intensity has fluctuated greatly during the past 300 years, causing many radiocarbon datings of events during this period to be of little value. Lichenometry, Bull and Brandon claim, can accurately date an
(50) earthquake to within ten years. They note, however, that using lichenometry requires careful site selection

and accurate calibration of lichen growth rates, adding that the method is best used for earthquakes that occurred within the last 500 years. Sites must be
(55) selected to minimize the influence of snow avalanches and other disturbances that would affect normal lichen growth, and conditions like shade and wind that promote faster lichen growth must be factored in.

1. Which one of the following most accurately expresses the main idea of the passage?

(A) Lichenometry is a new method for dating past earthquakes that has advantages over radiocarbon dating.

(B) Despite its limitations, lichenometry has been proven to be more accurate than any other method of discerning the dates of past earthquakes.

(C) Most seismologists today have rejected radiocarbon dating and are embracing lichenometry as the most reliable method for studying past earthquakes.

(D) Two geologists have revolutionized the study of past earthquakes by developing lichenometry, an easily applied method of earthquake detection and dating.

(E) Radiocarbon dating, an unreliable test used in dating past earthquakes, can finally be abandoned now that lichenometry has been developed.

2. The passage provides information that most helps to answer which one of the following questions?

(A) How do scientists measure lichen growth rates under the varying conditions that lichens may encounter?

(B) How do scientists determine the intensity of the radiation striking Earth's upper atmosphere?

(C) What are some of the conditions that encourage lichens to grow at a more rapid rate than usual?

(D) What is the approximate date of the earliest earthquake that lichenometry has been used to identify?

(E) What are some applications of the techniques involved in radiocarbon dating other than their use in studying past earthquakes?

GO ON TO THE NEXT PAGE.

3. What is the author's primary purpose in referring to the rate of growth of a North American lichen species (lines 29–30)?

(A) to emphasize the rapidity with which lichen colonies can establish themselves on newly exposed rock surfaces

(B) to offer an example of a lichen species with one of the slowest known rates of growth

(C) to present additional evidence supporting the claim that environmental conditions can alter lichens' rate of growth

(D) to explain why lichenometry works best for dating earthquakes that occurred in the last 500 years

(E) to provide a sense of the sort of timescale on which lichen growth occurs

4. Which one of the following statements is most strongly supported by the passage?

(A) Lichenometry is less accurate than radiocarbon dating in predicting the likelihood and location of future earthquakes.

(B) Radiocarbon dating is unlikely to be helpful in dating past earthquakes that have no identifiable fault lines associated with them.

(C) Radiocarbon dating and lichenometry are currently the only viable methods of detecting and dating past earthquakes.

(D) Radiocarbon dating is more accurate than lichenometry in dating earthquakes that occurred approximately 400 years ago.

(E) The usefulness of lichenometry for dating earthquakes is limited to geographic regions where factors that disturb or accelerate lichen growth generally do not occur.

5. The primary purpose of the first paragraph in relation to the rest of the passage is to describe

(A) a well-known procedure that will then be examined on a step-by-step basis

(B) an established procedure to which a new procedure will then be compared

(C) an outdated procedure that will then be shown to be nonetheless useful in some situations

(D) a traditional procedure that will then be contrasted with other traditional procedures

(E) a popular procedure that will then be shown to have resulted in erroneous conclusions about a phenomenon

6. It can be inferred that the statements made by Bull and Brandon and reported in lines 50–58 rely on which one of the following assumptions?

(A) While lichenometry is less accurate when it is used to date earthquakes that occurred more than 500 years ago, it is still more accurate than other methods for dating such earthquakes.

(B) There is no reliable method for determining the intensity of the radiation now hitting Earth's upper atmosphere.

(C) Lichens are able to grow only on the types of rocks that are common in mountainous regions.

(D) The mountain ranges that produce the kinds of rockfalls studied in lichenometry are also subject to more frequent snowfalls and avalanches than other mountain ranges are.

(E) The extent to which conditions like shade and wind have affected the growth of existing lichen colonies can be determined.

7. The passage indicates that using radiocarbon dating to date past earthquakes may be unreliable due to

(A) the multiplicity of the types of organic matter that require analysis

(B) the variable amount of organic materials caught in shifted sediments

(C) the fact that fault lines related to past earthquakes are not always visible

(D) the fluctuations in the amount of the carbon 14 isotope in the environment over time

(E) the possibility that radiation has not always struck the upper atmosphere

8. Given the information in the passage, to which one of the following would lichenometry likely be most applicable?

(A) identifying the number of times a particular river has flooded in the past 1,000 years

(B) identifying the age of a fossilized skeleton of a mammal that lived many thousands of years ago

(C) identifying the age of an ancient beach now underwater approximately 30 kilometers off the present shore

(D) identifying the rate, in kilometers per century, at which a glacier has been receding up a mountain valley

(E) identifying local trends in annual rainfall rates in a particular valley over the past five centuries

GO ON TO THE NEXT PAGE.

While courts have long allowed custom-made medical illustrations depicting personal injury to be presented as evidence in legal cases, the issue of whether they have a legitimate place in the courtroom
(5) is surrounded by ongoing debate and misinformation. Some opponents of their general use argue that while illustrations are sometimes invaluable in presenting the physical details of a personal injury, in all cases except those involving the most unusual injuries, illustrations
(10) from medical textbooks can be adequate. Most injuries, such as fractures and whiplash, they say, are rather generic in nature—certain commonly encountered forces act on particular areas of the body in standard ways—so they can be represented by
(15) generic illustrations.

Another line of complaint stems from the belief that custom-made illustrations often misrepresent the facts in order to comply with the partisan interests of litigants. Even some lawyers appear to share a version
(20) of this view, believing that such illustrations can be used to bolster a weak case. Illustrators are sometimes approached by lawyers who, unable to find medical experts to support their clients' claims, think that they can replace expert testimony with such deceptive
(25) professional illustrations. But this is mistaken. Even if an unscrupulous illustrator could be found, such illustrations would be inadmissible as evidence in the courtroom unless a medical expert were present to testify to their accuracy.
(30) It has also been maintained that custom-made illustrations may subtly distort the issues through the use of emphasis, coloration, and other means, even if they are technically accurate. But professional medical illustrators strive for objective accuracy and avoid
(35) devices that have inflammatory potential, sometimes even eschewing the use of color. Unlike illustrations in medical textbooks, which are designed to include the extensive detail required by medical students, custom-made medical illustrations are designed to
(40) include only the information that is relevant for those deciding a case. The end user is typically a jury or a judge, for whose benefit the depiction is reduced to the details that are crucial to determining the legally relevant facts. The more complex details often found
(45) in textbooks can be deleted so as not to confuse the issue. For example, illustrations of such things as veins and arteries would only get in the way when an illustration is supposed to be used to explain the nature of a bone fracture.
(50) Custom-made medical illustrations, which are based on a plaintiff's X rays, computerized tomography scans, and medical records and reports, are especially valuable in that they provide visual representations of data whose verbal description would
(55) be very complex. Expert testimony by medical professionals often relies heavily on the use of technical terminology, which those who are not

specially trained in the field find difficult to translate mentally into visual imagery. Since, for most people,
(60) adequate understanding of physical data depends on thinking at least partly in visual terms, the clearly presented visual stimulation provided by custom-made illustrations can be quite instructive.

9. Which one of the following is most analogous to the role that, according to the author, custom-made medical illustrations play in personal injury cases?

(A) schematic drawings accompanying an engineer's oral presentation

(B) road maps used by people unfamiliar with an area so that they will not have to get verbal instructions from strangers

(C) children's drawings that psychologists use to detect wishes and anxieties not apparent in the children's behavior

(D) a reproduction of a famous painting in an art history textbook

(E) an artist's preliminary sketches for a painting

10. Based on the passage, which one of the following is the author most likely to believe about illustrations in medical textbooks?

(A) They tend to rely less on the use of color than do custom-made medical illustrations.

(B) They are inadmissible in a courtroom unless a medical expert is present to testify to their accuracy.

(C) They are in many cases drawn by the same individuals who draw custom-made medical illustrations for courtroom use.

(D) They are believed by most lawyers to be less prone than custom-made medical illustrations to misrepresent the nature of a personal injury.

(E) In many cases they are more apt to confuse jurors than are custom-made medical illustrations.

11. The passage states that a role of medical experts in relation to custom-made medical illustrations in the courtroom is to

(A) decide which custom-made medical illustrations should be admissible

(B) temper the impact of the illustrations on judges and jurors who are not medical professionals

(C) make medical illustrations understandable to judges and jurors

(D) provide opinions to attorneys as to which illustrations, if any, would be useful

(E) provide their opinions as to the accuracy of the illustrations

GO ON TO THE NEXT PAGE.

12. According to the passage, one of the ways that medical textbook illustrations differ from custom-made medical illustrations is that

(A) custom-made medical illustrations accurately represent human anatomy, whereas medical textbook illustrations do not

(B) medical textbook illustrations employ color freely, whereas custom-made medical illustrations must avoid color

(C) medical textbook illustrations are objective, while custom-made medical illustrations are subjective

(D) medical textbook illustrations are very detailed, whereas custom-made medical illustrations include only details that are relevant to the case

(E) medical textbook illustrations are readily comprehended by nonmedical audiences, whereas custom-made medical illustrations are not

13. The author's attitude toward the testimony of medical experts in personal injury cases is most accurately described as

(A) appreciation of the difficulty involved in explaining medical data to judges and jurors together with skepticism concerning the effectiveness of such testimony

(B) admiration for the experts' technical knowledge coupled with disdain for the communications skills of medical professionals

(C) acceptance of the accuracy of such testimony accompanied with awareness of the limitations of a presentation that is entirely verbal

(D) respect for the medical profession tempered by apprehension concerning the tendency of medical professionals to try to overwhelm judges and jurors with technical details

(E) respect for expert witnesses combined with intolerance of the use of technical terminology

14. The author's primary purpose in the third paragraph is to

(A) argue for a greater use of custom-made medical illustrations in court cases involving personal injury

(B) reply to a variant of the objection to custom-made medical illustrations raised in the second paragraph

(C) argue against the position that illustrations from medical textbooks are well suited for use in the courtroom

(D) discuss in greater detail why custom-made medical illustrations are controversial

(E) describe the differences between custom-made medical illustrations and illustrations from medical textbooks

GO ON TO THE NEXT PAGE.

Passage A

Because dental caries (decay) is strongly linked to consumption of the sticky, carbohydrate-rich staples of agricultural diets, prehistoric human teeth can provide clues about when a population made the transition
(5) from a hunter-gatherer diet to an agricultural one. Caries formation is influenced by several factors, including tooth structure, bacteria in the mouth, and diet. In particular, caries formation is affected by carbohydrates' texture and composition, since
(10) carbohydrates more readily stick to teeth.

Many researchers have demonstrated the link between carbohydrate consumption and caries. In North America, Leigh studied caries in archaeologically derived teeth, noting that caries rates differed between
(15) indigenous populations that primarily consumed meat (a Sioux sample showed almost no caries) and those heavily dependent on cultivated maize (a Zuni sample had 75 percent carious teeth). Leigh's findings have been frequently confirmed by other researchers, who
(20) have shown that, in general, the greater a population's dependence on agriculture is, the higher its rate of caries formation will be.

Under some circumstances, however, nonagricultural populations may exhibit relatively
(25) high caries rates. For example, early nonagricultural populations in western North America who consumed large amounts of highly processed stone-ground flour made from gathered acorns show relatively high caries frequencies. And wild plants collected by the Hopi
(30) included several species with high cariogenic potential, notably pinyon nuts and wild tubers.

Passage B

Archaeologists recovered human skeletal remains interred over a 2,000-year period in prehistoric Ban Chiang, Thailand. The site's early inhabitants
(35) appear to have had a hunter-gatherer-cultivator economy. Evidence indicates that, over time, the population became increasingly dependent on agriculture.

Research suggests that agricultural intensification
(40) results in declining human health, including dental health. Studies show that dental caries is uncommon in pre-agricultural populations. Increased caries frequency may result from increased consumption of starchy-sticky foodstuffs or from alterations in tooth wear. The
(45) wearing down of tooth crown surfaces reduces caries formation by removing fissures that can trap food particles. A reduction of fiber or grit in a diet may diminish tooth wear, thus increasing caries frequency. However, severe wear that exposes a tooth's pulp
(50) cavity may also result in caries.

The diet of Ban Chiang's inhabitants included some cultivated rice and yams from the beginning of the period represented by the recovered remains. These were part of a varied diet that also included
(55) wild plant and animal foods. Since both rice and yams are carbohydrates, increased reliance on either or both should theoretically result in increased caries frequency.

Yet comparisons of caries frequency in the Early and Late Ban Chiang Groups indicate that overall
(60) caries frequency is slightly greater in the Early Group. Tooth wear patterns do not indicate tooth wear changes between Early and Late Groups that would explain this unexpected finding. It is more likely that, although dependence on agriculture increased, the diet
(65) in the Late period remained varied enough that no single food dominated. Furthermore, there may have been a shift from sweeter carbohydrates (yams) toward rice, a less cariogenic carbohydrate.

15. Both passages are primarily concerned with examining which one of the following topics?

(A) evidence of the development of agriculture in the archaeological record

(B) the impact of agriculture on the overall health of human populations

(C) the effects of carbohydrate-rich foods on caries formation in strictly agricultural societies

(D) the archaeological evidence regarding when the first agricultural society arose

(E) the extent to which pre-agricultural populations were able to obtain carbohydrate-rich foods

16. Which one of the following distinguishes the Ban Chiang populations discussed in passage B from the populations discussed in the last paragraph of passage A?

(A) While the Ban Chiang populations consumed several highly cariogenic foods, the populations discussed in the last paragraph of passage A did not.

(B) While the Ban Chiang populations ate cultivated foods, the populations discussed in the last paragraph of passage A did not.

(C) While the Ban Chiang populations consumed a diet consisting primarily of carbohydrates, the populations discussed in the last paragraph of passage A did not.

(D) While the Ban Chiang populations exhibited very high levels of tooth wear, the populations discussed in the last paragraph of passage A did not.

(E) While the Ban Chiang populations ate certain highly processed foods, the populations discussed in the last paragraph of passage A did not.

GO ON TO THE NEXT PAGE.

17. Passage B most strongly supports which one of the following statements about fiber and grit in a diet?

(A) They can either limit or promote caries formation, depending on their prevalence in the diet.
(B) They are typically consumed in greater quantities as a population adopts agriculture.
(C) They have a negative effect on overall health since they have no nutritional value.
(D) They contribute to the formation of fissures in tooth surfaces.
(E) They increase the stickiness of carbohydrate-rich foods.

18. Which one of the following is mentioned in both passages as evidence tending to support the prevailing view regarding the relationship between dental caries and carbohydrate consumption?

(A) the effect of consuming highly processed foods on caries formation
(B) the relatively low incidence of caries among nonagricultural people
(C) the effect of fiber and grit in the diet on caries formation
(D) the effect of the consumption of wild foods on tooth wear
(E) the effect of agricultural intensification on overall human health

19. It is most likely that both authors would agree with which one of the following statements about dental caries?

(A) The incidence of dental caries increases predictably in populations over time.
(B) Dental caries is often difficult to detect in teeth recovered from archaeological sites.
(C) Dental caries tends to be more prevalent in populations with a hunter-gatherer diet than in populations with an agricultural diet.
(D) The frequency of dental caries in a population does not necessarily correspond directly to the population's degree of dependence on agriculture.
(E) The formation of dental caries tends to be more strongly linked to tooth wear than to the consumption of a particular kind of food.

20. Each passage suggests which one of the following about carbohydrate-rich foods?

(A) Varieties that are cultivated have a greater tendency to cause caries than varieties that grow wild.
(B) Those that require substantial processing do not play a role in hunter-gatherer diets.
(C) Some of them naturally have a greater tendency than others to cause caries.
(D) Some of them reduce caries formation because their relatively high fiber content increases tooth wear.
(E) The cariogenic potential of a given variety increases if it is cultivated rather than gathered in the wild.

21. The evidence from Ban Chiang discussed in passage B relates to the generalization reported in the second paragraph of passage A (lines 20–22) in which one of the following ways?

(A) The evidence confirms the generalization.
(B) The evidence tends to support the generalization.
(C) The evidence is irrelevant to the generalization.
(D) The evidence does not conform to the generalization.
(E) The evidence disproves the generalization.

GO ON TO THE NEXT PAGE.

Recent criticism has sought to align Sarah Orne Jewett, a notable writer of regional fiction in the nineteenth-century United States, with the domestic novelists of the previous generation. Her work does
(5) resemble the domestic novels of the 1850s in its focus on women, their domestic occupations, and their social interactions, with men relegated to the periphery. But it also differs markedly from these antecedents. The world depicted in the latter revolves around children.
(10) Young children play prominent roles in the domestic novels and the work of child rearing—the struggle to instill a mother's values in a child's character—is their chief source of drama. By contrast, children and child rearing are almost entirely absent from the world of
(15) Jewett's fiction. Even more strikingly, while the literary world of the earlier domestic novelists is insistently religious, grounded in the structures of Protestant religious belief, to turn from these writers to Jewett is to encounter an almost wholly secular world.

(20) To the extent that these differences do not merely reflect the personal preferences of the authors, we might attribute them to such historical transformations as the migration of the rural young to cities or the increasing secularization of society. But while such
(25) factors may help to explain the differences, it can be argued that these differences ultimately reflect different conceptions of the nature and purpose of fiction. The domestic novel of the mid-nineteenth century is based on a conception of fiction as part of
(30) a continuum that also included writings devoted to piety and domestic instruction, bound together by a common goal of promoting domestic morality and religious belief. It was not uncommon for the same multipurpose book to be indistinguishably a novel, a
(35) child-rearing manual, and a tract on Christian duty. The more didactic aims are absent from Jewett's writing, which rather embodies the late nineteenth-century "high-cultural" conception of fiction as an autonomous sphere with value in and of itself.

(40) This high-cultural aesthetic was one among several conceptions of fiction operative in the United States in the 1850s and 1860s, but it became the dominant one later in the nineteenth century and remained so for most of the twentieth. On this
(45) conception, fiction came to be seen as pure art: a work was to be viewed in isolation and valued for the formal arrangement of its elements rather than for its larger social connections or the promotion of extraliterary goods. Thus, unlike the domestic novelists, Jewett
(50) intended her works not as a means to an end but as an end in themselves. This fundamental difference should be given more weight in assessing their affinities than any superficial similarity in subject matter.

22. The passage most helps to answer which one of the following questions?

(A) Did any men write domestic novels in the 1850s?
(B) Were any widely read domestic novels written after the 1860s?
(C) How did migration to urban areas affect the development of domestic fiction in the 1850s?
(D) What is an effect that Jewett's conception of literary art had on her fiction?
(E) With what region of the United States were at least some of Jewett's writings concerned?

23. It can be inferred from the passage that the author would be most likely to view the "recent criticism" mentioned in line 1 as

(A) advocating a position that is essentially correct even though some powerful arguments can be made against it
(B) making a true claim about Jewett, but for the wrong reasons
(C) making a claim that is based on some reasonable evidence and is initially plausible but ultimately mistaken
(D) questionable, because it relies on a currently dominant literary aesthetic that takes too narrow a view of the proper goals of fiction
(E) based on speculation for which there is no reasonable support, and therefore worthy of dismissal

24. In saying that domestic fiction was based on a conception of fiction as part of a "continuum" (line 30), the author most likely means which one of the following?

(A) Domestic fiction was part of an ongoing tradition stretching back into the past.
(B) Fiction was not treated as clearly distinct from other categories of writing.
(C) Domestic fiction was often published in serial form.
(D) Fiction is constantly evolving.
(E) Domestic fiction promoted the cohesiveness and hence the continuity of society.

GO ON TO THE NEXT PAGE.

25. Which one of the following most accurately states the primary function of the passage?

   (A) It proposes and defends a radical redefinition of several historical categories of literary style.
   (B) It proposes an evaluation of a particular style of writing, of which one writer's work is cited as a paradigmatic case.
   (C) It argues for a reappraisal of a set of long-held assumptions about the historical connections among a group of writers.
   (D) It weighs the merits of two opposing conceptions of the nature of fiction.
   (E) It rejects a way of classifying a particular writer's work and defends an alternative view.

26. Which one of the following most accurately represents the structure of the second paragraph?

   (A) The author considers and rejects a number of possible explanations for a phenomenon, concluding that any attempt at explanation does violence to the unity of the phenomenon.
   (B) The author shows that two explanatory hypotheses are incompatible with each other and gives reasons for preferring one of them.
   (C) The author describes several explanatory hypotheses and argues that they are not really distinct from one another.
   (D) The author proposes two versions of a classificatory hypothesis, indicates the need for some such hypothesis, and then sets out a counterargument in preparation for rejecting that counterargument in the following paragraph.
   (E) The author mentions a number of explanatory hypotheses, gives a mildly favorable comment on them, and then advocates and elaborates another explanation that the author considers to be more fundamental.

27. The differing conceptions of fiction held by Jewett and the domestic novelists can most reasonably be taken as providing an answer to which one of the following questions?

   (A) Why was Jewett unwilling to feature children and religious themes as prominently in her works as the domestic novelists featured them in theirs?
   (B) Why did both Jewett and the domestic novelists focus primarily on rural as opposed to urban concerns?
   (C) Why was Jewett not constrained to feature children and religion as prominently in her works as domestic novelists were?
   (D) Why did both Jewett and the domestic novelists focus predominantly on women and their concerns?
   (E) Why was Jewett unable to feature children or religion as prominently in her works as the domestic novelists featured them in theirs?

S T O P

IF YOU FINISH BEFORE TIME IS CALLED, YOU MAY CHECK YOUR WORK ON THIS SECTION ONLY.
DO NOT WORK ON ANY OTHER SECTION IN THE TEST.

SECTION II
Time—35 minutes
26 Questions

Directions: The questions in this section are based on the reasoning contained in brief statements or passages. For some questions, more than one of the choices could conceivably answer the question. However, you are to choose the best answer; that is, the response that most accurately and completely answers the question. You should not make assumptions that are by commonsense standards implausible, superfluous, or incompatible with the passage. After you have chosen the best answer, blacken the corresponding space on your answer sheet.

1. In a recent study, a group of young children were taught the word "stairs" while walking up and down a flight of stairs. Later that day, when the children were shown a video of a person climbing a ladder, they all called the ladder stairs.

   Which one of the following principles is best illustrated by the study described above?

   (A) When young children repeatedly hear a word without seeing the object denoted by the word, they sometimes apply the word to objects not denoted by the word.

   (B) Young children best learn words when they are shown how the object denoted by the word is used.

   (C) The earlier in life a child encounters and uses an object, the easier it is for that child to learn how not to misuse the word denoting that object.

   (D) Young children who learn a word by observing how the object denoted by that word is used sometimes apply that word to a different object that is similarly used.

   (E) Young children best learn the names of objects when the objects are present at the time the children learn the words and when no other objects are simultaneously present.

2. Among people who live to the age of 100 or more, a large proportion have led "unhealthy" lives: smoking, consuming alcohol, eating fatty foods, and getting little exercise. Since such behavior often leads to shortened life spans, it is likely that exceptionally long-lived people are genetically disposed to having long lives.

   Which one of the following, if true, most strengthens the argument?

   (A) There is some evidence that consuming a moderate amount of alcohol can counteract the effects of eating fatty foods.

   (B) Some of the exceptionally long-lived people who do not smoke or drink do eat fatty foods and get little exercise.

   (C) Some of the exceptionally long-lived people who exercise regularly and avoid fatty foods do smoke or consume alcohol.

   (D) Some people who do not live to the age of 100 also lead unhealthy lives.

   (E) Nearly all people who live to 100 or more have siblings who are also long-lived.

3. Medications with an unpleasant taste are generally produced only in tablet, capsule, or soft-gel form. The active ingredient in medication M is a waxy substance that cannot tolerate the heat used to manufacture tablets because it has a low melting point. So, since the company developing M does not have soft-gel manufacturing technology and manufactures all its medications itself, M will most likely be produced in capsule form.

   The conclusion is most strongly supported by the reasoning in the argument if which one of the following is assumed?

   (A) Medication M can be produced in liquid form.
   (B) Medication M has an unpleasant taste.
   (C) No medication is produced in both capsule and soft-gel form.
   (D) Most medications with a low melting point are produced in soft-gel form.
   (E) Medications in capsule form taste less unpleasant than those in tablet or soft-gel form.

GO ON TO THE NEXT PAGE.

4. Carol Morris wants to own a majority of the shares of the city's largest newspaper, *The Daily*. The only obstacle to Morris's amassing a majority of these shares is that Azedcorp, which currently owns a majority, has steadfastly refused to sell. Industry analysts nevertheless predict that Morris will soon be the majority owner of *The Daily*.

Which one of the following, if true, provides the most support for the industry analysts' prediction?

(A) Azedcorp does not own shares of any newspaper other than *The Daily*.
(B) Morris has recently offered Azedcorp much more for its shares of *The Daily* than Azedcorp paid for them.
(C) No one other than Morris has expressed any interest in purchasing a majority of *The Daily*'s shares.
(D) Morris already owns more shares of *The Daily* than anyone except Azedcorp.
(E) Azedcorp is financially so weak that bankruptcy will probably soon force the sale of its newspaper holdings.

5. Area resident: Childhood lead poisoning has declined steadily since the 1970s, when leaded gasoline was phased out and lead paint was banned. But recent statistics indicate that 25 percent of this area's homes still contain lead paint that poses significant health hazards. Therefore, if we eliminate the lead paint in those homes, childhood lead poisoning in the area will finally be eradicated.

The area resident's argument is flawed in that it

(A) relies on statistical claims that are likely to be unreliable
(B) relies on an assumption that is tantamount to assuming that the conclusion is true
(C) fails to consider that there may be other significant sources of lead in the area's environment
(D) takes for granted that lead paint in homes can be eliminated economically
(E) takes for granted that children reside in all of the homes in the area that contain lead paint

6. Although some nutritional facts about soft drinks are listed on their labels, exact caffeine content is not. Listing exact caffeine content would make it easier to limit, but not eliminate, one's caffeine intake. If it became easier for people to limit, but not eliminate, their caffeine intake, many people would do so, which would improve their health.

If all the statements above are true, which one of the following must be true?

(A) The health of at least some people would improve if exact caffeine content were listed on soft-drink labels.
(B) Many people will be unable to limit their caffeine intake if exact caffeine content is not listed on soft-drink labels.
(C) Many people will find it difficult to eliminate their caffeine intake if they have to guess exactly how much caffeine is in their soft drinks.
(D) People who wish to eliminate, rather than simply limit, their caffeine intake would benefit if exact caffeine content were listed on soft-drink labels.
(E) The health of at least some people would worsen if everyone knew exactly how much caffeine was in their soft drinks.

7. When the famous art collector Vidmar died, a public auction of her collection, the largest privately owned, was held. "I can't possibly afford any of those works because hers is among the most valuable collections ever assembled by a single person," declared art lover MacNeil.

The flawed pattern of reasoning in which one of the following is most closely parallel to that in MacNeil's argument?

(A) Each word in the book is in French. So the whole book is in French.
(B) The city council voted unanimously to adopt the plan. So councilperson Martinez voted to adopt the plan.
(C) This paragraph is long. So the sentences that comprise it are long.
(D) The members of the company are old. So the company itself is old.
(E) The atoms comprising this molecule are elements. So the molecule itself is an element.

GO ON TO THE NEXT PAGE.

8. A leading critic of space exploration contends that it would be wrong, given current technology, to send a group of explorers to Mars, since the explorers would be unlikely to survive the trip. But that exaggerates the risk. There would be a well-engineered backup system at every stage of the long and complicated journey. A fatal catastrophe is quite unlikely at any given stage if such a backup system is in place.

The reasoning in the argument is flawed in that the argument

(A) infers that something is true of a whole merely from the fact that it is true of each of the parts

(B) infers that something cannot occur merely from the fact that it is unlikely to occur

(C) draws a conclusion about what must be the case based on evidence about what is probably the case

(D) infers that something will work merely because it could work

(E) rejects a view merely on the grounds that an inadequate argument has been made for it

9. A retrospective study is a scientific study that tries to determine the causes of subjects' present characteristics by looking for significant connections between the present characteristics of subjects and what happened to those subjects in the past, before the study began. Because retrospective studies of human subjects must use the subjects' reports about their own pasts, however, such studies cannot reliably determine the causes of human subjects' present characteristics.

Which one of the following, if assumed, enables the argument's conclusion to be properly drawn?

(A) Whether or not a study of human subjects can reliably determine the causes of those subjects' present characteristics may depend at least in part on the extent to which that study uses inaccurate reports about the subjects' pasts.

(B) A retrospective study cannot reliably determine the causes of human subjects' present characteristics unless there exist correlations between the present characteristics of the subjects and what happened to those subjects in the past.

(C) In studies of human subjects that attempt to find connections between subjects' present characteristics and what happened to those subjects in the past, the subjects' reports about their own pasts are highly susceptible to inaccuracy.

(D) If a study of human subjects uses only accurate reports about the subjects' pasts, then that study can reliably determine the causes of those subjects' present characteristics.

(E) Every scientific study in which researchers look for significant connections between the present characteristics of subjects and what happened to those subjects in the past must use the subjects' reports about their own pasts.

GO ON TO THE NEXT PAGE.

10. Gigantic passenger planes currently being developed will have enough space to hold shops and lounges in addition to passenger seating. However, the additional space will more likely be used for more passenger seating. The number of passengers flying the air-traffic system is expected to triple within 20 years, and it will be impossible for airports to accommodate enough normal-sized jet planes to carry that many passengers.

Which one of the following most accurately states the conclusion drawn in the argument?

(A) Gigantic planes currently being developed will have enough space in them to hold shops and lounges as well as passenger seating.

(B) The additional space in the gigantic planes currently being developed is more likely to be filled with passenger seating than with shops and lounges.

(C) The number of passengers flying the air-traffic system is expected to triple within 20 years.

(D) In 20 years, it will be impossible for airports to accommodate enough normal-sized planes to carry the number of passengers that are expected to be flying then.

(E) In 20 years, most airline passengers will be flying in gigantic passenger planes.

11. Scientist: To study the comparative effectiveness of two experimental medications for athlete's foot, a representative sample of people with athlete's foot were randomly assigned to one of two groups. One group received only medication M, and the other received only medication N. The only people whose athlete's foot was cured had been given medication M.

Reporter: This means, then, that if anyone in the study had athlete's foot that was not cured, that person did not receive medication M.

Which one of the following most accurately describes the reporter's error in reasoning?

(A) The reporter concludes from evidence showing only that M can cure athlete's foot that M always cures athlete's foot.

(B) The reporter illicitly draws a conclusion about the population as a whole on the basis of a study conducted only on a sample of the population.

(C) The reporter presumes, without providing justification, that medications M and N are available to people who have athlete's foot but did not participate in the study.

(D) The reporter fails to allow for the possibility that athlete's foot may be cured even if neither of the two medications studied is taken.

(E) The reporter presumes, without providing justification, that there is no sizeable subgroup of people whose athlete's foot will be cured only if they do not take medication M.

12. Paleontologist: Plesiosauromorphs were gigantic, long-necked marine reptiles that ruled the oceans during the age of the dinosaurs. Most experts believe that plesiosauromorphs lurked and quickly ambushed their prey. However, plesiosauromorphs probably hunted by chasing their prey over long distances. Plesiosauromorph fins were quite long and thin, like the wings of birds specialized for long-distance flight.

Which one of the following is an assumption on which the paleontologist's argument depends?

(A) Birds and reptiles share many physical features because they descend from common evolutionary ancestors.

(B) During the age of dinosaurs, plesiosauromorphs were the only marine reptiles that had long, thin fins.

(C) A gigantic marine animal would not be able to find enough food to meet the caloric requirements dictated by its body size if it did not hunt by chasing prey over long distances.

(D) Most marine animals that chase prey over long distances are specialized for long-distance swimming.

(E) The shape of a marine animal's fin affects the way the animal swims in the same way as the shape of a bird's wing affects the way the bird flies.

13. Buying elaborate screensavers—programs that put moving images on a computer monitor to prevent damage—can cost a company far more in employee time than it saves in electricity and monitor protection. Employees cannot resist spending time playing with screensavers that flash interesting graphics across their screens.

Which one of the following most closely conforms to the principle illustrated above?

(A) A school that chooses textbooks based on student preference may not get the most economical package.

(B) An energy-efficient insulation system may cost more up front but will ultimately save money over the life of the house.

(C) The time that it takes to have a pizza delivered may be longer than it takes to cook a complete dinner.

(D) A complicated hotel security system may cost more in customer goodwill than it saves in losses by theft.

(E) An electronic keyboard may be cheaper to buy than a piano but more expensive to repair.

GO ON TO THE NEXT PAGE.

14. Music professor: Because rap musicians can work alone in a recording studio, they need not accommodate supporting musicians' wishes. Further, learning to rap is not as formal a process as learning an instrument. Thus, rap is an extremely individualistic and nontraditional musical form.

Music critic: But rap appeals to tradition by using bits of older songs. Besides, the themes and styles of rap have developed into a tradition. And successful rap musicians do not perform purely idiosyncratically but conform their work to the preferences of the public.

The music critic's response to the music professor's argument

(A) challenges it by offering evidence against one of the stated premises on which its conclusion concerning rap music is based

(B) challenges its conclusion concerning rap music by offering certain additional observations that the music professor does not take into account in his argument

(C) challenges the grounds on which the music professor generalizes from the particular context of rap music to the broader context of musical tradition and individuality

(D) challenges it by offering an alternative explanation of phenomena that the music professor cites as evidence for his thesis about rap music

(E) challenges each of a group of claims about tradition and individuality in music that the music professor gives as evidence in his argument

15. Speaker: Like many contemporary critics, Smith argues that the true meaning of an author's statements can be understood only through insight into the author's social circumstances. But this same line of analysis can be applied to Smith's own words. Thus, if she is right we should be able, at least in part, to discern from Smith's social circumstances the "true meaning" of Smith's statements. This, in turn, suggests that Smith herself is not aware of the true meaning of her own words.

The speaker's main conclusion logically follows if which one of the following is assumed?

(A) Insight into the intended meaning of an author's work is not as important as insight into its true meaning.

(B) Smith lacks insight into her own social circumstances.

(C) There is just one meaning that Smith intends her work to have.

(D) Smith's theory about the relation of social circumstances to the understanding of meaning lacks insight.

(E) The intended meaning of an author's work is not always good evidence of its true meaning.

16. Tissue biopsies taken on patients who have undergone throat surgery show that those who snored frequently were significantly more likely to have serious abnormalities in their throat muscles than those who snored rarely or not at all. This shows that snoring can damage the throat of the snorer.

Which one of the following, if true, most strengthens the argument?

(A) The study relied on the subjects' self-reporting to determine whether or not they snored frequently.

(B) The patients' throat surgery was not undertaken to treat abnormalities in their throat muscles.

(C) All of the test subjects were of similar age and weight and in similar states of health.

(D) People who have undergone throat surgery are no more likely to snore than people who have not undergone throat surgery.

(E) The abnormalities in the throat muscles discovered in the study do not cause snoring.

GO ON TO THE NEXT PAGE.

17. One should never sacrifice one's health in order to acquire money, for without health, happiness is not obtainable.

The conclusion of the argument follows logically if which one of the following is assumed?

(A) Money should be acquired only if its acquisition will not make happiness unobtainable.
(B) In order to be happy one must have either money or health.
(C) Health should be valued only as a precondition for happiness.
(D) Being wealthy is, under certain conditions, conducive to unhappiness.
(E) Health is more conducive to happiness than wealth is.

18. Vanessa: All computer code must be written by a pair of programmers working at a single workstation. This is needed to prevent programmers from writing idiosyncratic code that can be understood only by the original programmer.

Jo: Most programming projects are kept afloat by the best programmers on the team, who are typically at least 100 times more productive than the worst. Since they generally work best when they work alone, the most productive programmers must be allowed to work by themselves.

Each of the following assignments of computer programmers is consistent both with the principle expressed by Vanessa and with the principle expressed by Jo EXCEPT:

(A) Olga and Kensuke are both programmers of roughly average productivity who feel that they are more productive when working alone. They have been assigned to work together at a single workstation.
(B) John is experienced but is not among the most productive programmers on the team. He has been assigned to mentor Tyrone, a new programmer who is not yet very productive. They are to work together at a single workstation.
(C) Although not among the most productive programmers on the team, Chris is more productive than Jennifer. They have been assigned to work together at a single workstation.
(D) Yolanda is the most productive programmer on the team. She has been assigned to work with Mike, who is also very productive. They are to work together at the same workstation.
(E) Kevin and Amy both have a reputation for writing idiosyncratic code; neither is unusually productive. They have been assigned to work together at the same workstation.

19. In West Calverton, most pet stores sell exotic birds, and most of those that sell exotic birds also sell tropical fish. However, any pet store there that sells tropical fish but not exotic birds does sell gerbils; and no independently owned pet stores in West Calverton sell gerbils.

If the statements above are true, which one of the following must be true?

(A) Most pet stores in West Calverton that are not independently owned do not sell exotic birds.
(B) No pet stores in West Calverton that sell tropical fish and exotic birds sell gerbils.
(C) Some pet stores in West Calverton that sell gerbils also sell exotic birds.
(D) No independently owned pet store in West Calverton sells tropical fish but not exotic birds.
(E) Any independently owned pet store in West Calverton that does not sell tropical fish sells exotic birds.

20. Astronomer: Earlier estimates of the distances of certain stars from Earth would mean that these stars are about 1 billion years older than the universe itself, an impossible scenario. My estimates of the distances indicate that these stars are much farther away than previously thought. And the farther away the stars are, the greater their intrinsic brightness must be, given their appearance to us on Earth. So the new estimates of these stars' distances from Earth help resolve the earlier conflict between the ages of these stars and the age of the universe.

Which one of the following, if true, most helps to explain why the astronomer's estimates of the stars' distances from Earth help resolve the earlier conflict between the ages of these stars and the age of the universe?

(A) The stars are the oldest objects yet discovered in the universe.
(B) The younger the universe is, the more bright stars it is likely to have.
(C) The brighter a star is, the younger it is.
(D) How bright celestial objects appear to be depends on how far away from the observer they are.
(E) New telescopes allow astronomers to see a greater number of distant stars.

GO ON TO THE NEXT PAGE.

21. Most large nurseries sell raspberry plants primarily to commercial raspberry growers and sell only plants that are guaranteed to be disease-free. However, the shipment of raspberry plants that Johnson received from Wally's Plants carried a virus that commonly afflicts raspberries.

Which one of the following is most strongly supported by the information above?

(A) If Johnson is a commercial raspberry grower and Wally's Plants is not a large nursery, then the shipment of raspberry plants that Johnson received was probably guaranteed to be disease-free.

(B) Johnson is probably not a commercial raspberry grower if the shipment of raspberry plants that Johnson received from Wally's Plants was not entirely as it was guaranteed to be.

(C) If Johnson is not a commercial raspberry grower, then Wally's Plants is probably not a large nursery.

(D) Wally's Plants is probably not a large, well-run nursery if it sells its raspberry plants primarily to commercial raspberry growers.

(E) If Wally's Plants is a large nursery, then the raspberry plants that Johnson received in the shipment were probably not entirely as they were guaranteed to be.

22. Drug company manager: Our newest product is just not selling. One way to save it would be a new marketing campaign. This would not guarantee success, but it is one chance to save the product, so we should try it.

Which one of the following, if true, most seriously weakens the manager's argument?

(A) The drug company has invested heavily in its newest product, and losses due to this product would be harmful to the company's profits.

(B) Many new products fail whether or not they are supported by marketing campaigns.

(C) The drug company should not undertake a new marketing campaign for its newest product if the campaign has no chance to succeed.

(D) Undertaking a new marketing campaign would endanger the drug company's overall position by necessitating cutbacks in existing marketing campaigns.

(E) Consumer demand for the drug company's other products has been strong in the time since the company's newest product was introduced.

23. Consumer advocate: TMD, a pesticide used on peaches, shows no effects on human health when it is ingested in the amount present in the per capita peach consumption in this country. But while 80 percent of the population eat no peaches, others, including small children, consume much more than the national average, and thus ingest disproportionately large amounts of TMD. So even though the use of TMD on peaches poses minimal risk to most of the population, it has not been shown to be an acceptable practice.

Which one of the following principles, if valid, most helps to justify the consumer advocate's argumentation?

(A) The possibility that more data about a pesticide's health effects might reveal previously unknown risks at low doses warrants caution in assessing that pesticide's overall risks.

(B) The consequences of using a pesticide are unlikely to be acceptable when a majority of the population is likely to ingest it.

(C) Use of a pesticide is acceptable only if it is used for its intended purpose and the pesticide has been shown not to harm any portion of the population.

(D) Society has a special obligation to protect small children from pesticides unless average doses received by the population are low and have not been shown to be harmful to children's health.

(E) Measures taken to protect the population from a harm sometimes turn out to be the cause of a more serious harm to certain segments of the population.

24. Legal commentator: The goal of a recently enacted law that bans smoking in workplaces is to protect employees from secondhand smoke. But the law is written in such a way that it cannot be interpreted as ever prohibiting people from smoking in their own homes.

The statements above, if true, provide a basis for rejecting which one of the following claims?

(A) The law will be interpreted in a way that is inconsistent with the intentions of the legislators who supported it.

(B) Supporters of the law believe that it will have a significant impact on the health of many workers.

(C) The law offers no protection from secondhand smoke for people outside of their workplaces.

(D) Most people believe that smokers have a fundamental right to smoke in their own homes.

(E) The law will protect domestic workers such as housecleaners from secondhand smoke in their workplaces.

GO ON TO THE NEXT PAGE.

25. University president: Our pool of applicants has been shrinking over the past few years. One possible explanation of this unwelcome phenomenon is that we charge too little for tuition and fees. Prospective students and their parents conclude that the quality of education they would receive at this institution is not as high as that offered by institutions with higher tuition. So, if we want to increase the size of our applicant pool, we need to raise our tuition and fees.

The university president's argument requires the assumption that

(A) the proposed explanation for the decline in applications applies in this case
(B) the quality of a university education is dependent on the amount of tuition charged by the university
(C) an increase in tuition and fees at the university would guarantee a larger applicant pool
(D) there is no additional explanation for the university's shrinking applicant pool
(E) the amount charged by the university for tuition has not increased in recent years

26. Editorial: It has been suggested that private, for-profit companies should be hired to supply clean drinking water to areas of the world where it is unavailable now. But water should not be supplied by private companies. After all, clean water is essential for human health, and the purpose of a private company is to produce profit, not to promote health.

Which one of the following principles, if valid, would most help to justify the reasoning in the editorial?

(A) A private company should not be allowed to supply a commodity that is essential to human health unless that commodity is also supplied by a government agency.
(B) If something is essential for human health and private companies are unwilling or unable to supply it, then it should be supplied by a government agency.
(C) Drinking water should never be supplied by an organization that is not able to consistently supply clean, safe water.
(D) The mere fact that something actually promotes human health is not sufficient to show that its purpose is to promote health.
(E) If something is necessary for human health, then it should be provided by an organization whose primary purpose is the promotion of health.

S T O P

IF YOU FINISH BEFORE TIME IS CALLED, YOU MAY CHECK YOUR WORK ON THIS SECTION ONLY.
DO NOT WORK ON ANY OTHER SECTION IN THE TEST.

3   **3**

Directions: Each group of questions in this section is based on a set of conditions. In answering some of the questions, it may be useful to draw a rough diagram. Choose the response that most accurately and completely answers each question and blacken the corresponding space on your answer sheet.

Questions 1–6

A motel operator is scheduling appointments to start up services at a new motel. Appointments for six services—gas, landscaping, power, satellite, telephone, and water—will be scheduled, one appointment per day for the next six days. The schedule for the appointments is subject to the following conditions:

The water appointment must be scheduled for an earlier day than the landscaping appointment.

The power appointment must be scheduled for an earlier day than both the gas and satellite appointments.

The appointments scheduled for the second and third days cannot be for either gas, satellite, or telephone.

The telephone appointment cannot be scheduled for the sixth day.

1. Which one of the following is an acceptable schedule of appointments, listed in order from earliest to latest?

   (A)   gas, water, power, telephone, landscaping, satellite
   (B)   power, water, landscaping, gas, satellite, telephone
   (C)   telephone, power, landscaping, gas, water, satellite
   (D)   telephone, water, power, landscaping, gas, satellite
   (E)   water, telephone, power, gas, satellite, landscaping

2. If neither the gas nor the satellite nor the telephone appointment is scheduled for the fourth day, which one of the following must be true?

   (A)   The gas appointment is scheduled for the fifth day.
   (B)   The power appointment is scheduled for the third day.
   (C)   The satellite appointment is scheduled for the sixth day.
   (D)   The telephone appointment is scheduled for the first day.
   (E)   The water appointment is scheduled for the second day.

3. Which one of the following must be true?

   (A)   The landscaping appointment is scheduled for an earlier day than the telephone appointment.
   (B)   The power appointment is scheduled for an earlier day than the landscaping appointment.
   (C)   The telephone appointment is scheduled for an earlier day than the gas appointment.
   (D)   The telephone appointment is scheduled for an earlier day than the water appointment.
   (E)   The water appointment is scheduled for an earlier day than the gas appointment.

4. Which one of the following CANNOT be the appointments scheduled for the fourth, fifth, and sixth days, listed in that order?

   (A)   gas, satellite, landscaping
   (B)   landscaping, satellite, gas
   (C)   power, satellite, gas
   (D)   telephone, satellite, gas
   (E)   water, gas, landscaping

5. If neither the gas appointment nor the satellite appointment is scheduled for the sixth day, which one of the following must be true?

   (A)   The gas appointment is scheduled for the fifth day.
   (B)   The landscaping appointment is scheduled for the sixth day.
   (C)   The power appointment is scheduled for the third day.
   (D)   The telephone appointment is scheduled for the fourth day.
   (E)   The water appointment is scheduled for the second day.

6. Which one of the following, if substituted for the condition that the telephone appointment cannot be scheduled for the sixth day, would have the same effect in determining the order of the appointments?

   (A)   The telephone appointment must be scheduled for an earlier day than the gas appointment or the satellite appointment, or both.
   (B)   The telephone appointment must be scheduled for the day immediately before either the gas appointment or the satellite appointment.
   (C)   The telephone appointment must be scheduled for an earlier day than the landscaping appointment.
   (D)   If the telephone appointment is not scheduled for the first day, it must be scheduled for the day immediately before the gas appointment.
   (E)   Either the gas appointment or the satellite appointment must be scheduled for the sixth day.

GO ON TO THE NEXT PAGE.

Questions 7–13

An artisan has been hired to create three stained glass windows. The artisan will use exactly five colors of glass: green, orange, purple, rose, and yellow. Each color of glass will be used at least once, and each window will contain at least two different colors of glass. The windows must also conform to the following conditions:

> Exactly one of the windows contains both green glass and purple glass.
> Exactly two of the windows contain rose glass.
> If a window contains yellow glass, then that window contains neither green glass nor orange glass.
> If a window does not contain purple glass, then that window contains orange glass.

7. Which one of the following could be the color combinations of the glass in the three windows?

   (A)   window 1: green, purple, rose, and orange
         window 2: rose and yellow
         window 3: green and orange
   (B)   window 1: green, purple, and rose
         window 2: green, rose, and orange
         window 3: purple and yellow
   (C)   window 1: green, purple, and rose
         window 2: green, purple, and orange
         window 3: purple, rose, and yellow
   (D)   window 1: green, purple, and orange
         window 2: rose, orange, and yellow
         window 3: purple and rose
   (E)   window 1: green, purple, and orange
         window 2: purple, rose, and yellow
         window 3: purple and orange

8. Which one of the following CANNOT be the complete color combination of the glass in one of the windows?

   (A)   green and orange
   (B)   green and purple
   (C)   green and rose
   (D)   purple and orange
   (E)   rose and orange

9. If two of the windows are made with exactly two colors of glass each, then the complete color combination of the glass in one of those windows could be

   (A)   rose and yellow
   (B)   orange and rose
   (C)   orange and purple
   (D)   green and rose
   (E)   green and orange

10. If the complete color combination of the glass in one of the windows is purple, rose, and orange, then the complete color combination of the glass in one of the other windows could be

   (A)   green, orange, and rose
   (B)   green, orange, and purple
   (C)   orange and rose
   (D)   orange and purple
   (E)   green and orange

11. If orange glass is used in more of the windows than green glass, then the complete color combination of the glass in one of the windows could be

   (A)   orange and purple
   (B)   green, purple, and rose
   (C)   green and purple
   (D)   green and orange
   (E)   green, orange, and rose

12. Which one of the following could be used in all three windows?

   (A)   green glass
   (B)   orange glass
   (C)   purple glass
   (D)   rose glass
   (E)   yellow glass

13. If none of the windows contains both rose glass and orange glass, then the complete color combination of the glass in one of the windows must be

   (A)   green and purple
   (B)   green, purple, and orange
   (C)   green and orange
   (D)   purple and orange
   (E)   purple, rose, and yellow

GO ON TO THE NEXT PAGE.

Questions 14–18

A conference on management skills consists of exactly five talks, which are held successively in the following order: Feedback, Goal Sharing, Handling People, Information Overload, and Leadership. Exactly four employees of SoftCorp—Quigley, Rivera, Spivey, and Tran—each attend exactly two of the talks. No talk is attended by more than two of the employees, who attend the talks in accordance with the following conditions:

Quigley attends neither Feedback nor Handling People.
Rivera attends neither Goal Sharing nor Handling People.
Spivey does not attend either of the talks that Tran attends.
Quigley attends the first talk Tran attends.
Spivey attends the first talk Rivera attends.

14. Which one of the following could be a complete and accurate matching of the talks to the SoftCorp employees who attend them?

(A) Feedback: Rivera, Spivey
Goal Sharing: Quigley, Tran
Handling People: None
Information Overload: Quigley, Rivera
Leadership: Spivey, Tran

(B) Feedback: Rivera, Spivey
Goal Sharing: Quigley, Tran
Handling People: Rivera, Tran
Information Overload: Quigley
Leadership: Spivey

(C) Feedback: Rivera, Spivey
Goal Sharing: Quigley, Tran
Handling People: Tran
Information Overload: Quigley, Rivera
Leadership: Spivey

(D) Feedback: Rivera, Spivey
Goal Sharing: Tran
Handling People: Tran
Information Overload: Quigley, Rivera
Leadership: Quigley, Spivey

(E) Feedback: Spivey
Goal Sharing: Quigley, Tran
Handling People: Spivey
Information Overload: Quigley, Rivera
Leadership: Rivera, Tran

15. If none of the SoftCorp employees attends Handling People, then which one of the following must be true?

(A) Rivera attends Feedback.
(B) Rivera attends Leadership.
(C) Spivey attends Information Overload.
(D) Tran attends Goal Sharing.
(E) Tran attends Information Overload.

16. Which one of the following is a complete and accurate list of the talks any one of which Rivera and Spivey could attend together?

(A) Feedback, Information Overload, Leadership
(B) Feedback, Goal Sharing, Information Overload
(C) Information Overload, Leadership
(D) Feedback, Leadership
(E) Feedback, Information Overload

17. If Quigley is the only SoftCorp employee to attend Leadership, then which one of the following could be false?

(A) Rivera attends Feedback.
(B) Rivera attends Information Overload.
(C) Spivey attends Feedback.
(D) Spivey attends Handling People.
(E) Tran attends Goal Sharing.

18. If Rivera is the only SoftCorp employee to attend Information Overload, then which one of the following could be false?

(A) Quigley attends Leadership.
(B) Rivera attends Feedback.
(C) Spivey attends Feedback.
(D) Tran attends Goal Sharing.
(E) Tran attends Handling People.

GO ON TO THE NEXT PAGE.

Questions 19–23

Exactly six witnesses will testify in a trial: Mangione, Ramirez, Sanderson, Tannenbaum, Ujemori, and Wong. The witnesses will testify one by one, and each only once. The order in which the witnesses testify is subject to the following constraints:

Sanderson must testify immediately before either Tannenbaum or Ujemori.

Ujemori must testify earlier than both Ramirez and Wong.

Either Tannenbaum or Wong must testify immediately before Mangione.

19. Which one of the following lists the witnesses in an order in which they could testify?

   (A)   Ramirez, Sanderson, Tannenbaum, Mangione, Ujemori, Wong
   (B)   Sanderson, Tannenbaum, Ujemori, Ramirez, Wong, Mangione
   (C)   Sanderson, Ujemori, Tannenbaum, Wong, Ramirez, Mangione
   (D)   Tannenbaum, Mangione, Ujemori, Sanderson, Ramirez, Wong
   (E)   Wong, Ramirez, Sanderson, Tannenbaum, Mangione, Ujemori

20. If Tannenbaum testifies first, then which one of the following could be true?

   (A)   Ramirez testifies second.
   (B)   Wong testifies third.
   (C)   Sanderson testifies fourth.
   (D)   Ujemori testifies fifth.
   (E)   Mangione testifies sixth.

21. If Sanderson testifies fifth, then Ujemori must testify

   (A)   first
   (B)   second
   (C)   third
   (D)   fourth
   (E)   sixth

22. Which one of the following pairs of witnesses CANNOT testify third and fourth, respectively?

   (A)   Mangione, Tannenbaum
   (B)   Ramirez, Sanderson
   (C)   Sanderson, Ujemori
   (D)   Tannenbaum, Ramirez
   (E)   Ujemori, Wong

23. Which one of the following pairs of witnesses CANNOT testify first and second, respectively?

   (A)   Sanderson, Ujemori
   (B)   Tannenbaum, Mangione
   (C)   Tannenbaum, Sanderson
   (D)   Ujemori, Tannenbaum
   (E)   Ujemori, Wong

S T O P

IF YOU FINISH BEFORE TIME IS CALLED, YOU MAY CHECK YOUR WORK ON THIS SECTION ONLY. DO NOT WORK ON ANY OTHER SECTION IN THE TEST.

SECTION IV
Time—35 minutes
26 Questions

Directions: The questions in this section are based on the reasoning contained in brief statements or passages. For some questions, more than one of the choices could conceivably answer the question. However, you are to choose the best answer; that is, the response that most accurately and completely answers the question. You should not make assumptions that are by commonsense standards implausible, superfluous, or incompatible with the passage. After you have chosen the best answer, blacken the corresponding space on your answer sheet.

1. Marine biologist: Scientists have long wondered why the fish that live around coral reefs exhibit such brilliant colors. One suggestion is that coral reefs are colorful and, therefore, that colorful fish are camouflaged by them. Many animal species, after all, use camouflage to avoid predators. However, as regards the populations around reefs, this suggestion is mistaken. A reef stripped of its fish is quite monochromatic. Most corals, it turns out, are relatively dull browns and greens.

Which one of the following most accurately expresses the main conclusion drawn in the marine biologist's argument?

(A) One hypothesis about why fish living near coral reefs exhibit such bright colors is that the fish are camouflaged by their bright colors.

(B) The fact that many species use camouflage to avoid predators is one reason to believe that brightly colored fish living near reefs do too.

(C) The suggestion that the fish living around coral reefs exhibit bright colors because they are camouflaged by the reefs is mistaken.

(D) A reef stripped of its fish is relatively monochromatic.

(E) It turns out that the corals in a coral reef are mostly dull hues of brown and green.

2. To discover what percentage of teenagers believe in telekinesis—the psychic ability to move objects without physically touching them—a recent survey asked a representative sample of teenagers whether they agreed with the following statement: "A person's thoughts can influence the movement of physical objects." But because this statement is particularly ambiguous and is amenable to a naturalistic, uncontroversial interpretation, the survey's responses are also ambiguous.

The reasoning above conforms most closely to which one of the following general propositions?

(A) Uncontroversial statements are useless in surveys.

(B) Every statement is amenable to several interpretations.

(C) Responses to surveys are always unambiguous if the survey's questions are well phrased.

(D) Responses people give to poorly phrased questions are likely to be ambiguous.

(E) Statements about psychic phenomena can always be given naturalistic interpretations.

GO ON TO THE NEXT PAGE.

3. A recent study of perfect pitch—the ability to identify the pitch of an isolated musical note—found that a high percentage of people who have perfect pitch are related to someone else who has it. Among those without perfect pitch, the percentage was much lower. This shows that having perfect pitch is a consequence of genetic factors.

Which one of the following, if true, most strengthens the argument?

(A) People who have relatives with perfect pitch generally receive no more musical training than do others.

(B) All of the researchers conducting the study had perfect pitch.

(C) People with perfect pitch are more likely than others to choose music as a career.

(D) People with perfect pitch are more likely than others to make sure that their children receive musical training.

(E) People who have some training in music are more likely to have perfect pitch than those with no such training.

4. Paleontologists recently excavated two corresponding sets of dinosaur tracks, one left by a large grazing dinosaur and the other by a smaller predatory dinosaur. The two sets of tracks make abrupt turns repeatedly in tandem, suggesting that the predator was following the grazing dinosaur and had matched its stride. Modern predatory mammals, such as lions, usually match the stride of prey they are chasing immediately before they strike those prey. This suggests that the predatory dinosaur was chasing the grazing dinosaur and attacked immediately afterwards.

Which one of the following most accurately describes the role played in the argument by the statement that the predatory dinosaur was following the grazing dinosaur and had matched its stride?

(A) It helps establish the scientific importance of the argument's overall conclusion, but is not offered as evidence for that conclusion.

(B) It is a hypothesis that is rejected in favor of the hypothesis stated in the argument's overall conclusion.

(C) It provides the basis for an analogy used in support of the argument's overall conclusion.

(D) It is presented to counteract a possible objection to the argument's overall conclusion.

(E) It is the overall conclusion of the argument.

5. Researchers announced recently that over the past 25 years the incidence of skin cancer caused by exposure to harmful rays from the sun has continued to grow in spite of the increasingly widespread use of sunscreens. This shows that using sunscreen is unlikely to reduce a person's risk of developing such skin cancer.

Which one of the following, if true, most weakens the argument?

(A) Most people who purchase a sunscreen product will not purchase the most expensive brand available.

(B) Skin cancer generally develops among the very old as a result of sunburns experienced when very young.

(C) The development of sunscreens by pharmaceutical companies was based upon research conducted by dermatologists.

(D) People who know that they are especially susceptible to skin cancer are generally disinclined to spend a large amount of time in the sun.

(E) Those who use sunscreens most regularly are people who believe themselves to be most susceptible to skin cancer.

6. University administrator: Any proposal for a new department will not be funded if there are fewer than 50 people per year available for hire in that field and the proposed department would duplicate more than 25 percent of the material covered in one of our existing departments. The proposed Area Studies Department will duplicate more than 25 percent of the material covered in our existing Anthropology Department. However, we will fund the new department.

Which one of the following statements follows logically from the university administrator's statements?

(A) The field of Area Studies has at least 50 people per year available for hire.

(B) The proposed Area Studies Department would not duplicate more than 25 percent of the material covered in any existing department other than Anthropology.

(C) If the proposed Area Studies Department did not duplicate more than 25 percent of the material covered in Anthropology, then the new department would not be funded.

(D) The Anthropology Department duplicates more than 25 percent of the material covered in the proposed Area Studies Department.

(E) The field of Area Studies has fewer than 50 people per year available for hire.

GO ON TO THE NEXT PAGE.

7. Researcher: Over the course of three decades, we kept records of the average beak size of two populations of the same species of bird, one wild population, the other captive. During this period, the average beak size of the captive birds did not change, while the average beak size of the wild birds decreased significantly.

Which one of the following, if true, most helps to explain the researcher's findings?

(A) The small-beaked wild birds were easier to capture and measure than the large-beaked wild birds.

(B) The large-beaked wild birds were easier to capture and measure than the small-beaked wild birds.

(C) Changes in the wild birds' food supply during the study period favored the survival of small-beaked birds over large-beaked birds.

(D) The average body size of the captive birds remained the same over the study period.

(E) The researcher measured the beaks of some of the wild birds on more than one occasion.

8. Storytelling appears to be a universal aspect of both past and present cultures. Comparative study of traditional narratives from widely separated epochs and diverse cultures reveals common themes such as creation, tribal origin, mystical beings and quasi-historical figures, and common story types such as fables and tales in which animals assume human personalities.

The evidence cited above from the study of traditional narratives most supports which one of the following statements?

(A) Storytellers routinely borrow themes from other cultures.

(B) Storytellers have long understood that the narrative is a universal aspect of human culture.

(C) Certain human concerns and interests arise in all of the world's cultures.

(D) Storytelling was no less important in ancient cultures than it is in modern cultures.

(E) The best way to understand a culture is to understand what motivates its storytellers.

9. If a mother's first child is born before its due date, it is likely that her second child will be also. Jackie's second child was not born before its due date, so it is likely that Jackie's first child was not born before its due date either.

The questionable reasoning in the argument above is most similar in its reasoning to which one of the following?

(A) Artisans who finish their projects before the craft fair will probably go to the craft fair. Ben will not finish his project before the fair. So he probably will not go to the craft fair.

(B) All responsible pet owners are likely to be good with children. So anyone who is good with children is probably a responsible pet owner.

(C) If a movie is a box-office hit, it is likely that its sequel will be also. *Hawkman II*, the sequel to *Hawkman I*, was not a box-office hit, so *Hawkman I* was probably not a box-office hit.

(D) If a business is likely to fail, people will not invest in it. Pallid Starr is likely to fail, therefore no one is likely to invest in it.

(E) Tai will go sailing only if the weather is nice. The weather will be nice, thus Tai will probably go sailing.

10. Science journalist: Europa, a moon of Jupiter, is covered with ice. Data recently transmitted by a spacecraft strongly suggest that there are oceans of liquid water deep under the ice. Life as we know it could evolve only in the presence of liquid water. Hence, it is likely that at least primitive life has evolved on Europa.

The science journalist's argument is most vulnerable to criticism on the grounds that it

(A) takes for granted that if a condition would be necessary for the evolution of life as we know it, then such life could not have evolved anywhere that this condition does not hold

(B) fails to address adequately the possibility that there are conditions necessary for the evolution of life in addition to the presence of liquid water

(C) takes for granted that life is likely to be present on Europa if, but only if, life evolved on Europa

(D) overlooks the possibility that there could be unfamiliar forms of life that have evolved without the presence of liquid water

(E) takes for granted that no conditions on Europa other than the supposed presence of liquid water could have accounted for the data transmitted by the spacecraft

GO ON TO THE NEXT PAGE.

11. A bacterial species will inevitably develop greater resistance within a few years to any antibiotics used against it, unless those antibiotics eliminate that species completely. However, no single antibiotic now on the market is powerful enough to eliminate bacterial species X completely.

Which one of the following is most strongly supported by the statements above?

(A) It is unlikely that any antibiotic can be developed that will completely eliminate bacterial species X.

(B) If any antibiotic now on the market is used against bacterial species X, that species will develop greater resistance to it within a few years.

(C) The only way of completely eliminating bacterial species X is by a combination of two or more antibiotics now on the market.

(D) Bacterial species X will inevitably become more virulent in the course of time.

(E) Bacterial species X is more resistant to at least some antibiotics that have been used against it than it was before those antibiotics were used against it.

12. Political scientist: It is not uncommon for a politician to criticize his or her political opponents by claiming that their exposition of their ideas is muddled and incomprehensible. Such criticism, however, is never sincere. Political agendas promoted in a manner that cannot be understood by large numbers of people will not be realized for, as every politician knows, political mobilization requires commonality of purpose.

Which one of the following is the most accurate rendering of the political scientist's main conclusion?

(A) People who promote political agendas in an incomprehensible manner should be regarded as insincere.

(B) Sincere critics of the proponents of a political agenda should not focus their criticisms on the manner in which that agenda is promoted.

(C) The ineffectiveness of a confusingly promoted political agenda is a reason for refraining from, rather than engaging in, criticism of those who are promoting it.

(D) A politician criticizing his or her political opponents for presenting their political agendas in an incomprehensible manner is being insincere.

(E) To mobilize large numbers of people in support of a political agenda, that political agenda must be presented in such a way that it cannot be misunderstood.

13. Many symptoms of mental illnesses are affected by organic factors such as a deficiency in a compound in the brain. What is surprising, however, is the tremendous variation among different countries in the incidence of these symptoms in people with mental illnesses. This variation establishes that the organic factors that affect symptoms of mental illnesses are not distributed evenly around the globe.

The reasoning above is most vulnerable to criticism on the grounds that it

(A) does not say how many different mental illnesses are being discussed

(B) neglects the possibility that nutritional factors that contribute to deficiencies in compounds in the brain vary from culture to culture

(C) fails to consider the possibility that cultural factors significantly affect how mental illnesses manifest themselves in symptoms

(D) presumes, without providing justification, that any change in brain chemistry manifests itself as a change in mental condition

(E) presumes, without providing justification, that mental phenomena are only manifestations of physical phenomena

14. Politician: It has been proposed that the national parks in our country be managed by private companies rather than the government. A similar privatization of the telecommunications industry has benefited consumers by allowing competition among a variety of telephone companies to improve service and force down prices. Therefore, the privatization of the national parks would probably benefit park visitors as well.

Which one of the following, if true, most weakens the politician's argument?

(A) It would not be politically expedient to privatize the national parks even if doing so would, in the long run, improve service and reduce the fees charged to visitors.

(B) The privatization of the telecommunications industry has been problematic in that it has led to significantly increased unemployment and economic instability in that industry.

(C) The vast majority of people visiting the national parks are unaware of proposals to privatize the management of those parks.

(D) Privatizing the national parks would benefit a much smaller number of consumers to a much smaller extent than did the privatization of the telecommunications industry.

(E) The privatization of the national parks would produce much less competition between different companies than did the privatization of the telecommunications industry.

GO ON TO THE NEXT PAGE.

15. Jewel collectors, fearing that their eyes will be deceived by a counterfeit, will not buy a diamond unless the dealer guarantees that it is genuine. But why should a counterfeit give any less aesthetic pleasure when the naked eye cannot distinguish it from a real diamond? Both jewels should be deemed of equal value.

Which one of the following principles, if valid, most helps to justify the reasoning in the argument above?

(A) Jewel collectors should collect only those jewels that provide the most aesthetic pleasure.

(B) The value of a jewel should depend at least partly on market demand.

(C) It should not be assumed that everyone who likes diamonds receives the same degree of aesthetic pleasure from them.

(D) The value of a jewel should derive solely from the aesthetic pleasure it provides.

(E) Jewel collectors should not buy counterfeit jewels unless they are unable to distinguish counterfeit jewels from real ones.

16. All etching tools are either pin-tipped or bladed. While some bladed etching tools are used for engraving, some are not. On the other hand, all pin-tipped etching tools are used for engraving. Thus, there are more etching tools that are used for engraving than there are etching tools that are not used for engraving.

The conclusion of the argument follows logically if which one of the following is assumed?

(A) All tools used for engraving are etching tools as well.

(B) There are as many pin-tipped etching tools as there are bladed etching tools.

(C) No etching tool is both pin-tipped and bladed.

(D) The majority of bladed etching tools are not used for engraving.

(E) All etching tools that are not used for engraving are bladed.

17. A 24-year study of 1,500 adults showed that those subjects with a high intake of foods rich in beta-carotene were much less likely to die from cancer or heart disease than were those with a low intake of such foods. On the other hand, taking beta-carotene supplements for 12 years had no positive or negative effect on the health of subjects in a separate study of 20,000 adults.

Each of the following, if true, would help to resolve the apparent discrepancy between the results of the two studies EXCEPT:

(A) The human body processes the beta-carotene present in foods much more efficiently than it does beta-carotene supplements.

(B) Beta-carotene must be taken for longer than 12 years to have any cancer-preventive effects.

(C) Foods rich in beta-carotene also tend to contain other nutrients that assist in the human body's absorption of beta-carotene.

(D) In the 12-year study, half of the subjects were given beta-carotene supplements and half were given a placebo.

(E) In the 24-year study, the percentage of the subjects who had a high intake of beta-carotene-rich foods who smoked cigarettes was much smaller than the percentage of the subjects with a low intake of beta-carotene-rich foods who smoked.

GO ON TO THE NEXT PAGE.

18. If there are sentient beings on planets outside our solar system, we will not be able to determine this anytime in the near future unless some of these beings are at least as intelligent as humans. We will not be able to send spacecraft to planets outside our solar system anytime in the near future, and any sentient being on another planet capable of communicating with us anytime in the near future would have to be at least as intelligent as we are.

The argument's conclusion can be properly inferred if which one of the following is assumed?

(A) There are no sentient beings on planets in our solar system other than those on Earth.

(B) Any beings that are at least as intelligent as humans would want to communicate with sentient beings outside their own solar systems.

(C) If there is a sentient being on another planet that is as intelligent as humans are, we will not be able to send spacecraft to the being's planet anytime in the near future.

(D) If a sentient being on another planet cannot communicate with us, then the only way to detect its existence is by sending a spacecraft to its planet.

(E) Any sentient beings on planets outside our solar system that are at least as intelligent as humans would be capable of communicating with us.

19. Doctor: Medical researchers recently examined a large group of individuals who said that they had never experienced serious back pain. Half of the members of the group turned out to have bulging or slipped disks in their spines, conditions often blamed for serious back pain. Since these individuals with bulging or slipped disks evidently felt no pain from them, these conditions could not lead to serious back pain in people who do experience such pain.

The reasoning in the doctor's argument is most vulnerable to the criticism that it fails to consider which one of the following possibilities?

(A) A factor that need not be present in order for a certain effect to arise may nonetheless be sufficient to produce that effect.

(B) A factor that is not in itself sufficient to produce a certain effect may nonetheless be partly responsible for that effect in some instances.

(C) An effect that occurs in the absence of a particular phenomenon might not occur when that phenomenon is present.

(D) A characteristic found in half of a given sample of the population might not occur in half of the entire population.

(E) A factor that does not bring about a certain effect may nonetheless be more likely to be present when the effect occurs than when the effect does not occur.

20. Many workers who handled substance T in factories became seriously ill years later. We now know T caused at least some of their illnesses. Earlier ignorance of this connection does not absolve T's manufacturer of all responsibility. For had it investigated the safety of T before allowing workers to be exposed to it, many of their illnesses would have been prevented.

Which one of the following principles most helps to justify the conclusion above?

(A) Employees who are harmed by substances they handle on the job should be compensated for medical costs they incur as a result.

(B) Manufacturers should be held responsible only for the preventable consequences of their actions.

(C) Manufacturers have an obligation to inform workers of health risks of which they are aware.

(D) Whether or not an action's consequences were preventable is irrelevant to whether a manufacturer should be held responsible for those consequences.

(E) Manufacturers should be held responsible for the consequences of any of their actions that harm innocent people if those consequences were preventable.

21. It is virtually certain that the government contract for building the new highway will be awarded to either Phoenix Contracting or Cartwright Company. I have just learned that the government has decided not to award the contract to Cartwright Company. It is therefore almost inevitable that Phoenix Contracting will be awarded the contract.

The argument proceeds by

(A) concluding that it is extremely likely that an event will occur by ruling out the only probable alternative

(B) inferring, from a claim that one of two possible events will occur, that the other event will not occur

(C) refuting a claim that a particular event is inevitable by establishing the possibility of an alternative event

(D) predicting a future event on the basis of an established pattern of past events

(E) inferring a claim about the probability of a particular event from a general statistical statement

GO ON TO THE NEXT PAGE.

22. Researchers have found that children in large families—particularly the younger siblings—generally have fewer allergies than children in small families do. They hypothesize that exposure to germs during infancy makes people less likely to develop allergies.

Which one of the following, if true, most supports the researchers' hypothesis?

(A) In countries where the average number of children per family has decreased over the last century, the incidence of allergies has increased.

(B) Children in small families generally eat more kinds of very allergenic foods than children in large families do.

(C) Some allergies are life threatening, while many diseases caused by germs produce only temporary discomfort.

(D) Children whose parents have allergies have an above-average likelihood of developing allergies themselves.

(E) Children from small families who entered day care before age one were less likely to develop allergies than children from small families who entered day care later.

23. Film preservation requires transferring old movies from their original material—unstable, deteriorating nitrate film—to stable acetate film. But this is a time-consuming, expensive process, and there is no way to transfer all currently deteriorating nitrate films to acetate before they disintegrate. So some films from the earliest years of Hollywood will not be preserved.

Which one of the following is an assumption on which the argument depends?

(A) No new technology for transferring old movies from nitrate film to acetate film will ever be developed.

(B) Transferring films from nitrate to acetate is not the least expensive way of preserving them.

(C) Not many films from the earliest years of Hollywood have already been transferred to acetate.

(D) Some films from the earliest years of Hollywood currently exist solely in their original material.

(E) The least popular films from the earliest years of Hollywood are the ones most likely to be lost.

24. In a recent study of arthritis, researchers tried but failed to find any correlation between pain intensity and any of those features of the weather—humidity, temperature swings, barometric pressure—usually cited by arthritis sufferers as the cause of their increased pain. Those arthritis sufferers in the study who were convinced of the existence of such a correlation gave widely varying accounts of the time delay between the occurrence of what they believed to be the relevant feature of the weather and the increased intensity of the pain. Thus, this study _____.

Of the following, which one most logically completes the argument?

(A) indicates that the weather affects some arthritis sufferers more quickly than it does other arthritis sufferers

(B) indicates that arthritis sufferers' beliefs about the causes of the pain they feel may affect their assessment of the intensity of that pain

(C) suggests that arthritis sufferers are imagining the correlation they assert to exist

(D) suggests that some people are more susceptible to weather-induced arthritis pain than are others

(E) suggests that the scientific investigation of possible links between weather and arthritis pain is impossible

GO ON TO THE NEXT PAGE.

25. Cities with healthy economies typically have plenty of job openings. Cities with high-technology businesses also tend to have healthy economies, so those in search of jobs should move to a city with high-technology businesses.

The reasoning in which one of the following is most similar to the reasoning in the argument above?

(A) Older antiques are usually the most valuable. Antique dealers generally authenticate the age of the antiques they sell, so those collectors who want the most valuable antiques should purchase their antiques from antique dealers.

(B) Antique dealers who authenticate the age of the antiques they sell typically have plenty of antiques for sale. Since the most valuable antiques are those that have had their ages authenticated, antique collectors in search of valuable antiques should purchase their antiques from antique dealers.

(C) Antiques that have had their ages authenticated tend to be valuable. Since antique dealers generally carry antiques that have had their ages authenticated, those collectors who want antiques that are valuable should purchase their antiques from antique dealers.

(D) Many antique collectors know that antique dealers can authenticate the age of the antiques they sell. Since antiques that have had their ages authenticated are always the most valuable, most antique collectors who want antiques that are valuable tend to purchase their antiques from antique dealers.

(E) Many antiques increase in value once they have had their ages authenticated by antique dealers. Since antique dealers tend to have plenty of valuable antiques, antique collectors who prefer to purchase the most valuable antiques should purchase antiques from antique dealers.

26. Sociologist: A recent study of 5,000 individuals found, on the basis of a physical exam, that more than 25 percent of people older than 65 were malnourished, though only 12 percent of the people in this age group fell below government poverty standards. In contrast, a greater percentage of the people 65 or younger fell below poverty standards than were found in the study to be malnourished.

Each of the following, if true, helps to explain the findings of the study cited by the sociologist EXCEPT:

(A) Doctors are less likely to correctly diagnose and treat malnutrition in their patients who are over 65 than in their younger patients.

(B) People over 65 are more likely to take medications that increase their need for certain nutrients than are people 65 or younger.

(C) People over 65 are more likely to suffer from loss of appetite due to medication than are people 65 or younger.

(D) People 65 or younger are no more likely to fall below government poverty standards than are people over 65.

(E) People 65 or younger are less likely to have medical conditions that interfere with their digestion than are people over 65.

S T O P

IF YOU FINISH BEFORE TIME IS CALLED, YOU MAY CHECK YOUR WORK ON THIS SECTION ONLY.
DO NOT WORK ON ANY OTHER SECTION IN THE TEST.

COMPUTING YOUR SCORE

Directions:

1. Use the Answer Key on the next page to check your answers.

2. Use the Scoring Worksheet below to compute your raw score.

3. Use the Score Conversion Chart to convert your raw score into the 120–180 scale.

Scoring Worksheet

1. Enter the number of questions you answered correctly in each section.

	Number Correct
SECTION I.................	_____
SECTION II...............	_____
SECTION III..............	_____
SECTION IV	_____

2. Enter the sum here: _____

This is your Raw Score.

Conversion Chart
For Converting Raw Score to the 120–180 LSAT Scaled Score
LSAT Form 0LSN85

Reported Score	Raw Score Lowest	Raw Score Highest
180	99	102
179	98	98
178	97	97
177	96	96
176	95	95
175	94	94
174	93	93
173	91	92
172	90	90
171	89	89
170	88	88
169	86	87
168	85	85
167	83	84
166	82	82
165	80	81
164	79	79
163	77	78
162	75	76
161	74	74
160	72	73
159	70	71
158	69	69
157	67	68
156	65	66
155	63	64
154	62	62
153	60	61
152	58	59
151	57	57
150	55	56
149	53	54
148	52	52
147	50	51
146	48	49
145	47	47
144	45	46
143	43	44
142	42	42
141	40	41
140	39	39
139	37	38
138	36	36
137	35	35
136	33	34
135	32	32
134	30	31
133	29	29
132	28	28
131	27	27
130	25	26
129	24	24
128	23	23
127	22	22
126	21	21
125	20	20
124	18	19
123	17	17
122	16	16
121	15	15
120	0	14

ANSWER KEY

SECTION I

1.	A	8.	D	15.	A	22.	D
2.	C	9.	A	16.	B	23.	C
3.	E	10.	E	17.	A	24.	B
4.	B	11.	E	18.	B	25.	E
5.	B	12.	D	19.	D	26.	E
6.	E	13.	C	20.	C	27.	C
7.	D	14.	B	21.	D		

SECTION II

1.	D	8.	A	15.	B	22.	D
2.	E	9.	C	16.	E	23.	C
3.	B	10.	B	17.	A	24.	E
4.	E	11.	A	18.	D	25.	A
5.	C	12.	E	19.	D	26.	E
6.	A	13.	D	20.	C		
7.	C	14.	B	21.	E		

SECTION III

1.	D	8.	C	15.	A	22.	A
2.	D	9.	B	16.	A	23.	D
3.	E	10.	B	17.	D		
4.	E	11.	A	18.	E		
5.	B	12.	C	19.	B		
6.	A	13.	E	20.	E		
7.	B	14.	C	21.	A		

SECTION IV

1.	C	8.	C	15.	D	22.	E
2.	D	9.	C	16.	B	23.	D
3.	A	10.	B	17.	D	24.	C
4.	C	11.	B	18.	D	25.	C
5.	B	12.	D	19.	B	26.	D
6.	A	13.	C	20.	E		
7.	C	14.	E	21.	A		

SECTION
ONE

Reading Comprehension

(Or: Breaking the Boredom)

The key to the Reading Comprehension sections of the LSAT is to accept, in advance, that the passages are probably going to be boring as hell.

If I were reading any of these passages in a magazine, I'd probably skip to the next story. Unfortunately, that's not an option on the LSAT. It's critical that we 1) stay awake, and 2) understand as much as possible about the passage from *one* read-through. The absolute enemy here is that sort of "reading" where our eyes glaze over and we spend five minutes looking at the words, only to realize that we haven't the foggiest idea what the passage actually says.

In order to stay as present as possible, I use a little device I call "Why are you wasting my time with this?" It's a very simple concept with powerful results. I pretend that the author of any given passage has stopped me on the street and is telling me a long, rambling, boring story. I just want to pick up my Chinese takeout, so I'm impatiently trying to make them get to the point. I ask the author, repeatedly: "Why are you wasting my time with this?"

For me, taking this nasty attitude helps me focus on what the author is saying. I may not get every single detail; in fact, I'm necessarily tuning out some of the noise in order to try to find the main point. I know that the author is going to say in 60 lines what he could have said in 10. By asking the author why he's wasting my time after every paragraph, I'm able to home in on the author's main thesis and attitude. I'm also able to stay awake. The good news is, if we fake interest for a while, we might find ourselves actually getting interested. Fake it 'til you make it.

Let's dig in ...

Passage One (Questions 1–8)

To study centuries-old earthquakes and the geologic faults that caused them, seismologists usually dig trenches along visible fault lines, looking for sediments that show evidence of having shifted. Using radiocarbon
(5) dating, they measure the quantity of the radioactive isotope carbon 14 present in wood or other organic material trapped in the sediments when they shifted. Since carbon 14 occurs naturally in organic materials and decays at a constant rate, the age of organic
(10) materials can be reconstructed from the amount of the isotope remaining in them. These data can show the location and frequency of past earthquakes and provide hints about the likelihood and location of future earthquakes.

(15) Geologists William Bull and Mark Brandon have recently developed a new method, called lichenometry, for detecting and dating past earthquakes. Bull and Brandon developed the method based on the fact that large earthquakes generate numerous simultaneous
(20) rockfalls in mountain ranges that are sensitive to seismic shaking. Instead of dating fault-line sediments, lichenometry involves measuring the size of lichens growing on the rocks exposed by these rockfalls. Lichens—symbiotic organisms consisting of a fungus
(25) and an alga—quickly colonize newly exposed rock surfaces in the wake of rockfalls, and once established they grow radially, flat against the rocks, at a slow but constant rate for as long as 1,000 years if left undisturbed. One species of North American lichen, for example,
(30) spreads outward by about 9.5 millimeters each century.

Hence, the diameter of the largest lichen on a boulder provides direct evidence of when the boulder was dislodged and repositioned. If many rockfalls over a large geographic area occurred simultaneously, that
(35) pattern would imply that there had been a strong earthquake. The location of the earthquake's epicenter can then be determined by mapping these rockfalls, since they decrease in abundance as the distance from the epicenter increases.

(40) Lichenometry has distinct advantages over radiocarbon dating. Radiocarbon dating is accurate only to within plus or minus 40 years, because the amount of the carbon 14 isotope varies naturally in the environment depending on the intensity of the radiation striking Earth's upper atmosphere. Additionally, this
(45) intensity has fluctuated greatly during the past 300 years, causing many radiocarbon datings of events during this period to be of little value. Lichenometry, Bull and Brandon claim, can accurately date an earthquake to within ten years. They note, however,
(50) that using lichenometry requires careful site selection and accurate calibration of lichen growth rates, adding that the method is best used for earthquakes that occurred within the last 500 years. Sites must be selected to minimize the influence of snow avalanches
(55) and other disturbances that would affect normal lichen growth, and conditions like shade and wind that promote faster lichen growth must be factored in.

Jesus Christ. I cannot think of a topic that could possibly be more boring than "lichenometry." I tried to fake interest as I was reading, but honestly, I failed. This was a struggle for me—see, it's not just you.

Anyway, "lichenometry" is apparently a new alternative to (or supplement for) radiocarbon dating that can be used to figure out when and where earthquakes have happened. My paragraph-by-paragraph summaries are as follows:

Paragraph One: Introduction to radiocarbon dating ... basics of how it works.

Paragraph Two: Introduction to lichenometry ... basics of how it works.

Paragraph Three: Lichenometry's advantages over radiocarbon dating, followed by an acknowledgment of some of the weaknesses or imperfections of lichenometry.

Why is the author wasting our time? Basically, it looks like he's a supporter of lichenometry. He's not completely gung-ho about it—he does acknowledge its imperfections—but he wouldn't be here wasting our time today if he didn't think it was something valuable and interesting that we ought to know about.

QUESTION 1:

Which one of the following most accurately expresses the main idea of the passage?

A) Lichenometry is a new method for dating past earthquakes that has advantages over radiocarbon dating.
B) Despite its limitations, lichenometry has been proven to be more accurate than any other method of discerning the dates of past earthquakes.
C) Most seismologists today have rejected radiocarbon dating and are embracing lichenometry as the most reliable method for studying past earthquakes.
D) Two geologists have revolutionized the study of past earthquakes by developing lichenometry, an easily applied method of earthquake detection and dating.
E) Radiocarbon dating, an unreliable test used in dating past earthquakes, can finally be abandoned now that lichenometry has been developed.

This is a main point question, so the correct answer is going to be the answer to the "Why are you wasting my time?" question above. In short, it's "Lichenometry is good and new." A bit longer, it's "Lichenometry is good, new, and can be used to date earthquakes in place of radiocarbon dating."

A) This seems pretty good. The author came here to tell us a bit about lichenometry, with an emphasis on its advantages over radiocarbon dating.
B) The passage doesn't go this far. The author never claims that lichenometry is better than all other methods of dating earthquakes.
C) The author never says that "most seismologists" have rejected radiocarbon dating in favor of lichenometry. This is out.
D) I think "revolutionized" is too strong. Does the author really say this? Furthermore, the author seems to say that lichenometry is difficult (sites must be selected carefully, growth rates must be calibrated accurately, etc.) The author certainly doesn't say it's easy.
E) The author doesn't say radiocarbon dating is "unreliable" or that it can "finally be abandoned." The best answer is A.

QUESTION 2:

The passage provides information that most helps to answer which one of the following questions?

A) How do scientists measure lichen growth rates under the varying conditions that lichens may encounter?
B) How do scientists determine the intensity of the radiation striking Earth's upper atmosphere?
C) What are some of the conditions that encourage lichens to grow at a more rapid rate than usual?
D) What is the approximate date of the earliest earthquake that lichenometry has been used to identify?
E) What are some applications of the techniques involved in radiocarbon dating other than their use in studying past earthquakes?

We can't answer this question in advance, because the passage is 58 lines long and could conceivably be used to answer a shitload of different questions. No problem though, we'll just go through each answer choice looking for a question that has been specifically addressed by the passage.

A) The passage mentions the importance of measuring lichen growth rates under different growth conditions, but there's nothing in the passage about *how* to do this.
B) The passage mentions that the intensity of radiation striking the Earth's atmosphere varies, but there's nothing in the passage about *how* scientists measure this.
C) The very last line of the passage says shade and wind promote faster lichen growth. So this is probably the answer.
D) The passage says lichenometry is best used for earthquakes that occurred within the last 500 years, but never gives a date (approximate or otherwise) of the earliest earthquake that has been measured with lichenometry.
E) The passage only mentions radiocarbon dating in the context of earthquakes, and never gives any other applications of the technique. The best answer is still C.

QUESTION 3:

What is the author's primary purpose in referring to the rate of growth of a North American lichen species (lines 29–30)?

A) to emphasize the rapidity with which lichen colonies can establish themselves on newly exposed rock surfaces

B) to offer an example of a lichen species with one of the slowest known rates of growth

C) to present additional evidence supporting the claim that environmental conditions can alter lichens' rate of growth

D) to explain why lichenometry works best for dating earthquakes that occurred in the last 500 years

E) to provide a sense of the sort of timescale on which lichen growth occurs

Before going to the answer choices, let's glance back at the paragraph mentioned (not just lines 29–30, but a few lines before as well, to get context) then try to answer the question. It's a good idea to do this because the answer choices are *not* designed to help you. The incorrect answer choices are professionally written to attract and confuse you, and the correct answer is sometimes written in the camouflage of convoluted language. Something in the realm of "The author mentioned the rate of growth in a North American lichen species in lines 29–30 in order to explain how scientists can use lichens to estimate the passage of time" sounds about right. It may not be exactly correct, but it should be close.

A) This doesn't match what we're looking for. And anyway, lichens only grow *after* attaching to a new growing site, so this certainly isn't what the author was talking about.

B) Doesn't seem like this is it either. The author said nothing about whether this specific lichen is relatively slow or fast.

C) Again, not what we're looking for. And the bit about environmental factors changing lichen growth rates didn't happen until much later in the passage.

D) Nah, this isn't what we're looking for either. And the author didn't mention that lichens work best for earthquakes within the last 500 years until much later in the passage.

E) This is the only reasonable answer choice. It's not all that close to our prediction, but it sort of means the same thing. The author presented information about the growth rate of one lichen to give readers a sense of how slowly it grows, so that we'd understand that it can be used to gauge long passages of time. This is our answer.

4

QUESTION 4:

Which one of the following statements is most strongly supported by the passage?

A) Lichenometry is less accurate than radiocarbon dating in predicting the likelihood and location of future earthquakes.
B) Radiocarbon dating is unlikely to be helpful in dating past earthquakes that have no identifiable fault lines associated with them.
C) Radiocarbon dating and lichenometry are currently the only viable methods of detecting and dating past earthquakes.
D) Radiocarbon dating is more accurate than lichenometry in dating earthquakes that occurred approximately 400 years ago.
E) The usefulness of lichenometry for dating earthquakes is limited to geographic regions where factors that disturb or accelerate lichen growth generally do not occur.

Like number 2 above, we can't answer this one in advance. We'll have to tread carefully into the answer choices. Remember the author's main point—"Lichenometry is a good alternative to radiocarbon dating for earthquakes"—and try to find something that was, if possible, explicitly stated or strongly implied by the passage. If we can't find something that was stated or implied, then we'll look for something the author is almost certain to agree with.

A) The author seems to be in favor of lichenometry, and I don't remember him saying it is less accurate than radiocarbon dating.

B) I initially hate this answer, because the passage doesn't specifically say radiocarbon dating is unhelpful when there are no identifiable fault lines. However, the passage does at least *suggest* that this is true, because it says that scientists using radiocarbon dating "usually" dig along existing fault lines. If all the other answers are horrible, we can reconsider this answer. But until we read C-E, I'm hoping for something better.

C) The passage doesn't mention any other methods of detecting and dating earthquakes, but *be careful* here! The LSAT loves to trap the unwary into picking answers like this. If the LSAT doesn't *say* there are no other methods, then you are not allowed to assume it. This is definitely a trap answer, designed to catch folks who leap to unwarranted conclusions.

D) The passage suggests that lichenometry is more accurate than radiocarbon dating when it is available. So I don't think this can be it.

"Best" Doesn't Mean "Perfect"

There are two basic methods for solving LSAT questions: The first is to positively identify the correct answer. Sometimes this can be done even before reading the answer choices. But when this can't be done, you'll have to resort to a process of elimination. Your task is to choose the *best* answer. If none of them are great, then eliminate the four worst and go ahead and choose the best of a bad lot. Sometimes that's just how it goes.

E) The passage says that lichenometrists can calibrate for varying environmental factors, so this is out. After eliminating the rest of the answer choices, I'm forced to reconsider B. My case for it is this: The passage does specifically say that fault lines are "usually" involved when scientists are using radiocarbon dating. Furthermore, answer B is something *bad* about radiocarbon dating, which I like because the author seems to be in favor of lichenometry instead. I'm not completely thrilled about B, but I hate all of the other answers. You're going to run across a couple of these in every section, and you shouldn't sweat it too much. We'll answer the rest of the questions with a lot more certainty than we'll answer this one. Our reluctant choice is B.

QUESTION 5:

The primary purpose of the first paragraph in relation to the rest of the passage is to describe

A) a well-known procedure that will then be examined on a step-by-step basis
B) an established procedure to which a new procedure will then be compared
C) an outdated procedure that will then be shown to be nonetheless useful in some situations
D) a traditional procedure that will then be contrasted with other traditional procedures
E) a popular procedure that will then be shown to have resulted in erroneous conclusions about a phenomenon

The first paragraph gave an introduction to radiocarbon dating. The rest of the passage then focused on lichenometry, an alternative to radiocarbon dating. So, in abstract terms, the purpose of the first paragraph was to "discuss a commonly used tool that the author believes can be replaced or supplemented in some cases by an alternative tool." Something like that anyway.

A) Radiocarbon dating *isn't* examined later on a step-by-step basis, so this is out.
B) This is it. It's very close to our predicted answer. This will be our pick unless something else is really good.
C) The author doesn't go so far as to claim that radiocarbon dating is "outdated." That's enough, by itself, to eliminate this answer choice. (An answer that's 5 percent wrong is 100 percent wrong.) But furthermore, the author also doesn't show "*some situations*" (plural) in which radiocarbon dating is useful—the only (single) situation that is mentioned in which radiocarbon dating works is when there are existing visible fault lines. So for two separate reasons, this isn't it.
D) The passage compares a traditional procedure with a *new* procedure—and only mentions one of those. So "traditional procedures" is out.
E) The passage does not say that radiocarbon dating has resulted in any erroneous conclusions. The best answer is B.

QUESTION 6:

It can be inferred that the statements made by Bull and Brandon and reported in lines 50–58 rely on which one of the following assumptions?

A) While lichenometry is less accurate when it is used to date earthquakes that occurred more than 500 years ago, it is still more accurate than other methods for dating such earthquakes.

B) There is no reliable method for determining the intensity of the radiation now hitting Earth's upper atmosphere.

C) Lichens are able to grow only on the types of rocks that are common in mountainous regions.

D) The mountain ranges that produce the kinds of rockfalls studied in lichenometry are also subject to more frequent snowfalls and avalanches than other mountain ranges are.

E) The extent to which conditions like shade and wind have affected the growth of existing lichen colonies can be determined.

Bull and Brandon are generally favorable toward lichenometry. Still, they also acknowledge that lichenometry requires careful site selection and accurate calibration of growth rates, and is best used for earthquakes within the last 500 years. So they aren't exactly raving fans of lichenometry. They're reasoned advocates.

OK. This is a Necessary Assumption question, because we're asked to find an assumption on which a position relies. This means "find the missing piece of the argument."

A) This is tricky. B&B say that lichenometry is best used on more recent earthquakes, and also say that lichenometry is more accurate than radiocarbon dating. But they don't *assume* these things. Rather, they explicitly state them. Assumptions are unstated. So this can't be our answer.

B) B&B simply take no position on this issue. If it's not true, it doesn't really hurt them at all. This isn't their assumption.

C) It wouldn't hurt B&B's position at all if lichens grew everywhere. This isn't it.

D) B&B probably believe the opposite of this. They say that avalanches and snowfall can be problematic for lichenometrists, so rockfalls studied in lichenometry are probably subject to less snow, not more.

E) Here we go. I was starting to get nervous there for a minute, but this is definitely something that B&B have assumed. In order for their claim that lichenometrists must accurately calibrate lichen growth rates to make any sense, it must be true that lichenometrists can discern the extent to which environmental factors affect growth rates. Otherwise, what kind of "calibration" would be possible? Answer E is a *missing, but necessary*, piece of B&B's position. That's the definition of an assumption.

QUESTION 7:

The passage indicates that using radiocarbon dating to date past earthquakes may be unreliable due to

A) the multiplicity of the types of organic matter that require analysis

B) the variable amount of organic materials caught in shifted sediments

C) the fact that fault lines related to past earthquakes are not always visible

D) the fluctuations in the amount of the carbon-14 isotope in the environment over time

E) the possibility that radiation has not always struck the upper atmosphere

The passage suggests that radiocarbon dating is susceptible to variation in accuracy due to fluctuating radiation hitting the earth's atmosphere. This fluctuation has been particularly high over the past 300 years.

A) The passage doesn't suggest that different types of organic matter cause any problems for radiocarbon dating. So it's not this.
B) The passage doesn't suggest that varying amounts of organic matter cause any problems for radiocarbon dating. Can't be this either.
C) The passage suggests that scientists using radiocarbon dating usually work along visible fault lines, but it doesn't say that radiocarbon dating will suffer accuracy problems in the absence of visible fault lines. This is a tricky one to pass up, but I don't think it's the answer. Let's see what else we've got.
D) The argument says that fluctuation of radiation hitting the atmosphere leads to a variation in the amount of carbon-14 in the atmosphere over time (lines 41–45). This must be it.
E) The passage does specifically say that radiocarbon dating is subject to uncertainty from radiation fluctuations, but it's a bit of a stretch to suppose that the fluctuation could ever have gone all the way to zero. This one could be tempting, but since D is a more sure answer, I can eliminate E.

QUESTION 8:

Given the information in the passage, to which one of the following would lichenometry likely be most applicable?

A) identifying the number of times a particular river has flooded in the past 1,000 years
B) identifying the age of a fossilized skeleton of a mammal that lived many thousands of years ago
C) identifying the age of an ancient beach now underwater approximately 30 kilometers off the present shore
D) identifying the rate, in kilometers per century, at which a glacier has been receding up a mountain valley
E) identifying local trends in annual rainfall rates in a particular valley over the past five centuries

Before we look at the answer choices, let's summarize what we know about lichenometry. First, the author likes it. Second, it's more accurate than radiocarbon dating (when used appropriately). Third, it's best used to date earthquakes within the past 500 years. Finally, lichenometrists must carefully calibrate for different types of lichens and different types of environmental factors. Hopefully this will be enough to answer the question.

A) This wouldn't be the best use of lichenometry because it's best used in the past 500 years.
B) Same as A.
C) The passage doesn't suggest that lichenometry could be used underwater, so I doubt this is it. If they don't say it, we can't assume it.
D) At first I thought this had the same problem as A and B because I didn't think glaciers moved fast enough to produce meaningful data over the past 500 years. However, after eliminating the rest of the answer choices I was forced to give D another chance. A glacier in motion would reveal new rock for lichens to colonize. Scientists would be able to create a map of lichens, measuring how long each lichen had been at each location, to figure out how fast the glacier had moved up the valley. This isn't an easy answer, but it's the best one.
E) Since lichenometry has a margin of error of plus or minus 10 years, it would be useless for gauging annual rainfall rates.

Wow, that passage sucked. Let's agree never to speak of lichenometry again.

Passage Two (Questions 9–14)

While courts have long allowed custom-made medical illustrations depicting personal injury to be presented as evidence in legal cases, the issue of whether they have a legitimate place in the courtroom (5) is surrounded by ongoing debate and misinformation. Some opponents of their general use argue that while illustrations are sometimes invaluable in presenting the physical details of a personal injury, in all cases except those involving the most unusual injuries, illustrations (10) from medical textbooks can be adequate. Most injuries, such as fractures and whiplash, they say, are rather generic in nature—certain commonly encountered forces act on particular areas of the body in standard ways—so they can be represented by (15) generic illustrations.

Another line of complaint stems from the belief that custom-made illustrations often misrepresent the facts in order to comply with the partisan interests of litigants. Even some lawyers appear to share a version (20) of this view, believing that such illustrations can be used to bolster a weak case. Illustrators are sometimes approached by lawyers who, unable to find medical experts to support their clients' claims, think that they can replace expert testimony with such deceptive (25) professional illustrations. But this is mistaken. Even if an unscrupulous illustrator could be found, such illustrations would be inadmissible as evidence in the courtroom unless a medical expert were present to testify to their accuracy.

(30) It has also been maintained that custom-made illustrations may subtly distort the issues through the use of emphasis, coloration, and other means, even if they are technically accurate. But professional medical illustrators strive for objective accuracy and avoid (35) devices that have inflammatory potential, sometimes even eschewing the use of color. Unlike illustrations in medical textbooks, which are designed to include the extensive detail required by medical students, custom-made medical illustrations are designed to (40) include only the information that is relevant for those deciding a case. The end user is typically a jury or a judge, for whose benefit the depiction is reduced to the details that are crucial to determining the legally relevant facts. The more complex details often found (45) in textbooks can be deleted so as not to confuse the issue. For example, illustrations of such things as veins and arteries would only get in the way when an illustration is supposed to be used to explain the nature of a bone fracture.

(50) Custom-made medical illustrations, which are based on a plaintiff's X rays, computerized tomography scans, and medical records and reports, are especially valuable in that they provide visual representations of data whose verbal description would (55) be very complex. Expert testimony by medical professionals often relies heavily on the use of technical terminology, which those who are not specially trained in the field find difficult to translate mentally into visual imagery. Since, for most people, (60) adequate understanding of physical data depends on thinking at least partly in visual terms, the clearly presented visual stimulation provided by custom-made illustrations can be quite instructive.

Personally, I found this passage more manageable than the first because I was able to strongly disagree with the author. If I can be a dick, I can usually answer the questions. (Unfortunately for my friends and family, I'm awful good at doing this.) The main conclusion of the author's argument is "custom-made medical illustrations should be allowed in the courtroom." I had no prior opinion on this issue before reading the passage, but after reading the argument I think this is a position that only a plaintiff-side lawyer could honestly believe. It's not relevant whether I'm right about that. What's relevant is I got interested enough in the passage to *argue*, which will help me better comprehend it.

In the second paragraph, the author acknowledges what I'm guessing would be a huge problem with allowing custom illustrations into court: Custom illustrations could misrepresent the facts in order to comply with the partisan interests of litigants. Imagine a whiplash case where the plaintiff's lawyer hires the most gruesome depiction of the injury possible, instead of using the perfectly adequate depiction available in a medical book. When the author stated "even some lawyers appear to share a version of this view," I laughed out loud because "some" probably includes approximately every defense lawyer ever. The author then says even if such an "unscrupulous" illustrator could be found, there would need to be a medical expert to testify to the accuracy of the drawing. The author seems to think it's not possible to hire an expert to testify to whatever you want him to testify to, but from what I've read, it probably is.

In the third paragraph, the author discusses a subtler version of the same thing. Instead of making the picture look like a horror film, what if a plaintiff's illustrator just subtly made the injury a little bit more red? The author suggests this wouldn't happen, because "professional medical illustrators strive for objective accuracy," but I still think the author is missing the point. A plaintiff could *select* his medical illustrator for the purpose of getting the exact image he wanted for the courtroom!

In the last paragraph the author closes with all the good things that a custom-made medical illustration would supposedly bring. Primarily, the author thinks these illustrations would be "instructive" in that they would translate complicated medical information into an easily understood image. I am not convinced. I think the danger of misleading partisan use outweighs the small likelihood that the custom illustrations would actually bring objective truth to the courtroom. Again, my opinion here isn't the point. The point is that I paid attention to the passage.

QUESTION 9:

Which one of the following is most analogous to the role that, according to the author, custom-made medical illustrations play in personal injury cases?

A) **schematic drawings accompanying an engineer's oral presentation**
B) **road maps used by people unfamiliar with an area so that they will not have to get verbal instructions from strangers**
C) **children's drawings that psychologists use to detect wishes and anxieties not apparent in the children's behavior**
D) **a reproduction of a famous painting in an art history textbook**
E) **an artist's preliminary sketches for a painting**

The custom-made medical illustrations, according to the author, play an educational role. They simplify information and make it easier to understand. So we're looking for something like that.

A) This might be it, but I was hoping for something that conveyed a sense of simplifying information for a lay audience. The word "schematics" sounds a little more complex than what we've already discussed, but this has potential. Let's see what else we've got to work with.
B) The word "strangers" here makes me think this answer must be wrong. There's no analogous role in the courtroom.
C) This isn't what we're looking for. We're looking for "complex information presented more simply."
D) Same as C. Not what we're looking for.
E) Same as C and D—not what we're looking for. The answer must be A, because it's the closest to "complex information presented simply." See how important it is to have a solid summary of the argument before you look at the answer choices? This was a tricky one, but our prediction saved us. (Remember: If you don't stand for something, you'll fall for anything.)

10

QUESTION 10:

Based on the passage, which one of the following is the author most likely to believe about illustrations in medical textbooks?

A) They tend to rely less on the use of color than do custom-made medical illustrations.
B) They are inadmissible in a courtroom unless a medical expert is present to testify to their accuracy.
C) They are in many cases drawn by the same individuals who draw custom-made medical illustrations for courtroom use.
D) They are believed by most lawyers to be less prone than custom-made medical illustrations to misrepresent the nature of a personal injury.
E) In many cases they are more apt to confuse jurors than are custom-made medical illustrations.

Based on my reading of the passage, the author seems to think that the illustrations available in medical textbooks are somehow insufficient to convey the information that needs to be conveyed in court. In the third paragraph, the author says the medical textbook illustrations have *too* much information. Keep your eyes out for something along those lines as we head into the answer choices.

A) This is something an *opponent* of custom-made medical illustrations would say. (I said it myself, above, when I said "let's make it a little bit more red.") This isn't it.
B) The author says custom illustrations require expert medical testimony, but doesn't say whether medical texts can be admitted without expert testimony. So I don't think this is it either.
C) This seems like something the author would believe. The author thinks custom-made illustrations should be admitted alongside medical text illustrations. He talks about the objectivity of professional medical illustrators. He seems to suggest that the medical textbook illustrations and the custom-made medical illustrations could be made by the same people, but he doesn't quite go all the way and say this. Let's keep looking.
D) The author says *some* lawyers believe custom-made illustrations can be used for misrepresentation. The author never says that *most* lawyers hold this or any other view.
E) Yes. The author specifically states that medical text illustrations have too much information, and are therefore more likely to confuse jurors. This is our answer. It's better than C because the author more clearly states the contents of E than the contents of C—the author never says anything, specifically, about the identity of custom illustrators vs. the illustrators of medical textbooks. Answer E is much more strongly supported by the passage.

11

QUESTION 11:

The passage states that a role of medical experts in relation to custom-made medical illustrations in the courtroom is to

A) decide which custom-made medical illustrations should be admissible
B) temper the impact of the illustrations on judges and jurors who are not medical professionals
C) make medical illustrations understandable to judges and jurors
D) provide opinions to attorneys as to which illustrations, if any, would be useful
E) provide their opinions as to the accuracy of the illustrations

The passage states that the testimony of a medical expert is necessary in order to get a custom illustration admitted into court. That's what we're looking for.

A) The medical expert doesn't *decide* what's admissible. The judge would do that.

(This is a slightly stupid question, frankly, because it's easier to answer after you've already gone to law school and taken an Evidence class. But no matter— even without any outside knowledge, we should be able to answer this question by picking the one that has been specifically stated by the passage.)

B) Experts testify for either one side or the other, so while a defense expert might be trying to "temper the impact" of an illustration for the plaintiff, the plaintiff's expert would probably be trying to make the impact as great as possible. This isn't the answer.

C) The passage doesn't say that medical experts are used to explain the drawings. Next!

D) The passage also doesn't say that medical experts are used to provide counsel to the attorneys. We're still looking for something closer to "they are needed to help get illustrations admitted to court."

E) This is the one. The last sentence in the second passage says that experts give their opinions as to whether or not the illustrations are medically accurate. This is our answer, because it's directly supported by the passage.

QUESTION 12:

12

According to the passage, one of the ways that medical textbook illustrations differ from custom-made medical illustrations is that

A) custom-made medical illustrations accurately represent human anatomy, whereas medical textbook illustrations do not

B) medical textbook illustrations employ color freely, whereas custom-made medical illustrations must avoid color

C) medical textbook illustrations are objective, while custom-made medical illustrations are subjective

D) medical textbook illustrations are very detailed, whereas custom-made medical illustrations include only details that are relevant to the case

E) medical textbook illustrations are readily comprehended by nonmedical audiences, whereas custom-made medical illustrations are not

This question is closely related to the main point of the passage. If you can't answer it before looking at the answer choices, you probably can't answer it at all. The author thinks that medical textbook illustrations have too much information, and that custom illustrations are easier to understand. That's our summary and we're sticking to it, so that's what we're looking for.

A) The author never suggests that medical text illustrations are inaccurate.

B) The author never suggests that medical text illustrations use color "freely," nor does he say custom-made illustrations *must* avoid color.

C) The author believes that custom-made medical illustrations are objective (*i.e.*, based on independently verifiable fact, rather than subjective, *i.e.*, based on unverifiable first-person point of view). So this answer has it backward.

D) This is very close to what we're looking for. The author suggests that one of the advantages of custom-made illustrations is that they can be created to include only information that is relevant to the case, whereas medical illustrations have extraneous information (the example of veins and arteries for a case about a bone fracture is given). This is a great answer.

E) This is the exact opposite of what the author believes. D is our guy.

13

QUESTION 13:

The author's attitude toward the testimony of medical experts in personal injury cases is most accurately described as

A) appreciation of the difficulty involved in explaining medical data to judges and jurors together with skepticism concerning the effectiveness of such testimony

B) admiration for the experts' technical knowledge coupled with disdain for the communications skills of medical professionals

C) acceptance of the accuracy of such testimony accompanied with awareness of the limitations of a presentation that is entirely verbal

D) respect for the medical profession tempered by apprehension concerning the tendency of medical professionals to try to overwhelm judges and jurors with technical details

E) respect for expert witnesses combined with intolerance of the use of technical terminology

The author's attitude toward the testimony of medical experts in personal injury cases is the exact opposite of my own. I believe medical experts can be hired who will testify to whatever you want them to testify to. The author, naively (or conveniently, if you're cynical), believes that medical experts are always objective and truthful.

A) This isn't what I'm looking for. The author didn't convey "skepticism" about effectiveness of medical expert testimony. I'm looking for something more like "respectful."

B) The author does not have "disdain" for anyone in the passage.

C) This is close. The author does accept the accuracy of the medical experts, and advocates for illustrated supplements to this testimony. We'll choose C so long as nothing in D or E catches our eyes.

D) The "respect" part is attractive, but the author doesn't give any impression that medical experts try to overwhelm judges and jurors. No way.

E) The author does not have "intolerance" for the use of technical terminology. Our answer is C.

14

QUESTION 14:

The author's primary purpose in the third paragraph is to

A) argue for a greater use of custom-made medical illustrations in court cases involving personal injury

B) reply to a variant of the objection to custom-made medical illustrations raised in the second paragraph

C) argue against the position that illustrations from medical textbooks are well suited for use in the courtroom

D) discuss in greater detail why custom-made medical illustrations are controversial

E) describe the differences between custom-made medical illustrations and illustrations from medical textbooks

Before we go to the answer choices, let's look back at the third paragraph. There, the author started by acknowledging that some people believe that custom-made illustrations can be made to subtly distort the issues through the use of color, *et cetera*. The author doesn't believe this is a fatal problem, of course, and defends against this belief by saying that illustrators strive for objective accuracy. Then the author says that custom illustrations are better than medical text illustrations in that they don't have extraneous detail, and are therefore less likely to confuse.

Ideally, we'll find an answer choice that embodies most of what I just said.

A) The author does not argue for a "greater use" of custom illustrations. Rather, the author simply makes the case that they should be permitted.

B) I bet this is it. The objection in the third paragraph *is* a variant of the objection in the second paragraph. (Second paragraph: custom illustrations might misrepresent the facts; Third paragraph: custom illustrations might subtly distort the facts through use of emphasis and color.) And the author is "replying" to this objection. I like this answer.

C) The author never says medical textbook illustrations aren't suitable for the courtroom. He just thinks custom illustrations can, in some cases, be more useful.

D) This answer doesn't have enough of the author's attitude / main point in it. The author isn't just *discussing* a controversy. The author is arguing for a specific side in the controversy. So this is out.

E) This does happen in the third paragraph, but again the author is not just *describing* something. The author has an axe to grind, and answer B describes the role of the third paragraph most accurately. The author is responding to a specific objection against custom medical illustrations. B is our winner.

That passage wasn't nearly as bad as those goddamned lichens. I'm crossing my fingers for passage #3 to be even less horrible, but I'm sure I'll be disappointed.

Passage Three (Questions 15–21)

Passage A

Because dental caries (decay) is strongly linked to consumption of the sticky, carbohydrate-rich staples of agricultural diets, prehistoric human teeth can provide clues about when a population made the transition
(5) from a hunter-gatherer diet to an agricultural one. Caries formation is influenced by several factors, including tooth structure, bacteria in the mouth, and diet. In particular, caries formation is affected by carbohydrates' texture and composition, since
(10) carbohydrates more readily stick to teeth.

Many researchers have demonstrated the link between carbohydrate consumption and caries. In North America, Leigh studied caries in archaeologically derived teeth, noting that caries rates differed between
(15) indigenous populations that primarily consumed meat (a Sioux sample showed almost no caries) and those heavily dependent on cultivated maize (a Zuni sample had 75 percent carious teeth). Leigh's findings have been frequently confirmed by other researchers, who
(20) have shown that, in general, the greater a population's dependence on agriculture is, the higher its rate of caries formation will be.

Under some circumstances, however, nonagricultural populations may exhibit relatively
(25) high caries rates. For example, early nonagricultural populations in western North America who consumed large amounts of highly processed stone-ground flour made from gathered acorns show relatively high caries frequencies. And wild plants collected by the Hopi
(30) included several species with high cariogenic potential, notably pinyon nuts and wild tubers.

Passage B

Archaeologists recovered human skeletal remains interred over a 2,000-year period in prehistoric Ban Chiang, Thailand. The site's early inhabitants
(35) appear to have had a hunter-gatherer-cultivator economy. Evidence indicates that, over time, the population became increasingly dependent on agriculture.

Research suggests that agricultural intensification
(40) results in declining human health, including dental health. Studies show that dental caries is uncommon in pre-agricultural populations. Increased caries frequency may result from increased consumption of starchy-sticky foodstuffs or from alterations in tooth wear. The
(45) wearing down of tooth crown surfaces reduces caries formation by removing fissures that can trap food particles. A reduction of fiber or grit in a diet may diminish tooth wear, thus increasing caries frequency. However, severe wear that exposes a tooth's pulp
(50) cavity may also result in caries.

The diet of Ban Chiang's inhabitants included some cultivated rice and yams from the beginning of the period represented by the recovered remains. These were part of a varied diet that also included
(55) wild plant and animal foods. Since both rice and yams are carbohydrates, increased reliance on either or both should theoretically result in increased caries frequency.

Yet comparisons of caries frequency in the Early and Late Ban Chiang Groups indicate that overall
(60) caries frequency is slightly greater in the Early Group. Tooth wear patterns do not indicate tooth wear changes between Early and Late Groups that would explain this unexpected finding. It is more likely that, although dependence on agriculture increased, the diet
(65) in the Late period remained varied enough that no single food dominated. Furthermore, there may have been a shift from sweeter carbohydrates (yams) toward rice, a less cariogenic carbohydrate.

Comparative reading is relatively new on the LSAT, and I personally find it slightly more interesting than the other reading comprehension passages because you get two shorter passages rather than one longer one. (Although when we're talking LSAT reading comp, interesting is a very relative term.) As I read, especially as I read passage B, I'm going to consider how passage B relates to passage A. Does it agree? Disagree? *Et cetera*.

Passage A is about the use of dental decay as a tool for figuring out when a population switched from a hunter-gatherer diet to an agricultural one. According to Passage A, carbohydrates stick to the teeth more readily, creating decay. Teeth from pre-agricultural societies that ate mostly meat and few carbs show little decay. Passage A notes, however, in its last paragraph, that some pre-agricultural societies had high levels of carbohydrates in their diets, and therefore had high levels of tooth decay. Because of the last paragraph, it seems that using tooth decay as a tool for dating when a population switched to agriculture is an imperfect tool at best. So my bullshit detector is already tingling.

Passage B is an attempted application of the science discussed in Passage A to a specific population. According to undisclosed "evidence," the people of prehistoric Ban Chiang, Thailand, became increasingly dependent on agriculture over time.

However, the later peoples did not have more dental decay than the early peoples. In fact, the effect was slightly the opposite. To explain this, the author of Passage B says that the people must have kept a balanced diet even after switching to agriculture. Furthermore, according to the last sentence, the later peoples might have switched from sweeter carbohydrates to rice, which does not cause as much decay. So there's definitely a lot of "could haves" and "might haves"—nothing too solid.

QUESTION 15:

15

Both passages are primarily concerned with examining which one of the following topics?

A) evidence of the development of agriculture in the archaeological record
B) the impact of agriculture on the overall health of human populations
C) the effects of carbohydrate-rich foods on caries formation in strictly agricultural societies
D) the archaeological evidence regarding when the first agricultural society arose
E) the extent to which pre-agricultural populations were able to obtain carbohydrate-rich foods

Before we go to the answer choices, let's try to answer this question. My guess is something like "both passages are primarily concerned with examining the effects of diet on tooth decay of prehistoric peoples."

A) I didn't like this at first, but after going through the rest of the answer choices, it feels like this is the best answer. When this answer says "the archaeological record," we can simply substitute the word "prehistoric human teeth" (which are part of the archaeological record) to get a reasonable answer choice. But let's look at the rest of the choices to see where they fail.
B) The passages were not about "overall health" so this can't be the answer.
C) The passages are about the *transition* to agriculture, so the phrase "strictly agricultural societies" rings false.
D) The passages are not about finding the *first* agricultural society, they were about estimating when specific societies switched to agriculture.
E) Both passages touch on this, but neither passage is primarily concerned with discussing the extent to which pre-agricultural populations were able to obtain carbohydrate-rich foods, just dental records. So A is it.

16

QUESTION 16:

Which one of the following distinguishes the Ban Chiang populations discussed in passage B from the populations discussed in the last paragraph of passage A?

A) While the Ban Chiang populations consumed several highly cariogenic foods, the populations discussed in the last paragraph of passage A did not.

B) While the Ban Chiang populations ate cultivated foods, the populations discussed in the last paragraph of passage A did not.

C) While the Ban Chiang populations consumed a diet consisting primarily of carbohydrates, the populations discussed in the last paragraph of passage A did not.

D) While the Ban Chiang populations exhibited very high levels of tooth wear, the populations discussed in the last paragraph of passage A did not.

E) While the Ban Chiang populations ate certain highly processed foods, the populations discussed in the last paragraph of passage A did not.

I don't mind belaboring points that bear belaboring: It's really important to try to answer as many questions as possible before looking at the answer choices. So let's summarize what we know before we proceed. The Ban Chiang populations switched to agriculture but didn't have an increased level of tooth decay. This is possibly because they switched to rice from sweeter carbs, and also possibly because the pre-agricultural society already had access to some carbohydrates. The populations mentioned in the last paragraph of passage B are pre-agricultural populations that ate acorns, nuts and tubers and had high levels of tooth decay. I'm not sure if that "distinguishes" the two populations from each other, but it gives us at least something to work with.

A) No, the populations discussed in the last paragraph of passage A *did* consume highly cariogenic foods.

B) We were asked to find something that "distinguishes" the two populations from each other, which means "find a difference." Answer B does describe a difference between the two populations: the Ban Chiang populations had a "hunter-gatherer-*cultivator*" society, while the populations mentioned in passage A were eating wild acorns and plants. This looks like a good answer.

C) The facts don't say the Ban Chiang ate primarily carbohydrates, so this is out.

D) There is nothing in Passage A that says how much tooth wear those populations exhibited, so this can't possibly be the correct answer.

E) This answer has it backward. The folks mentioned in the last paragraph of Passage A were the ones eating highly processed food, not the Ban Chiang. Our answer is B.

QUESTION 17:

17

Passage B most strongly supports which one of the following statements about fiber and grit in a diet?

A) They can either limit or promote caries formation, depending on their prevalence in the diet.
B) They are typically consumed in greater quantities as a population adopts agriculture.
C) They have a negative effect on overall health since they have no nutritional value.
D) They contribute to the formation of fissures in tooth surfaces.
E) They increase the stickiness of carbohydrate- rich foods.

My prediction is that fiber and grit, according to Passage B, wear down the teeth in a way that minimizes the opportunity for tooth decay (at least until the wear gets all the way into the tooth pulp, ouch).

A) I think this is the answer. According to Passage B, if you have a reasonable amount of fiber and grit in your diet then your teeth are smoothed out some-what and decay is deterred. But if you are constantly eating tree bark and sand, then your teeth wear down to the roots and cavities start to grow again. This is our answer unless something else looks really perfect.
B) Passage B says the opposite of this. Fiber and grit are eaten *less* as a society adopts agriculture.
C) Passage B specifically mentions a health benefit of eating fiber and grit: your teeth smooth out so that cavities have less chance to form.
D) Passage B says eating fiber and grit *removes* fissures in the teeth. (Line 46.)
E) Passage B does not mention any relationship between fiber and grit in the diet and the stickiness of carbohydrate-rich foods. Our answer is A.

QUESTION 18:

18

Which one of the following is mentioned in both passages as evidence tending to support the prevailing view regarding the relationship between dental caries and carbohydrate consumption?

A) the effect of consuming highly processed foods on caries formation
B) the relatively low incidence of caries among nonagricultural people
C) the effect of fiber and grit in the diet on caries formation
D) the effect of the consumption of wild foods on tooth wear
E) the effect of agricultural intensification on overall human health

Can't answer this one in advance, so let's head straight to the answer choices.

A) The two passages don't seem focused on "highly processed" foods. Passage B, especially, is focused on one prehistoric society, which is before foods were highly processed. Feels like a no.
B) Both passages do mention this. I hope the rest of the answers are bad so I can just pick B and move on.
C) Only passage B mentions fiber and grit.
D) Only passage B mentions tooth wear.
E) Neither passage is about "overall human health." The best answer is B,

QUESTION 19:

It is most likely that both authors would agree with which one of the following statements about dental caries?

A) The incidence of dental caries increases predictably in populations over time.
B) Dental caries is often difficult to detect in teeth recovered from archaeological sites.
C) Dental caries tends to be more prevalent in populations with a hunter-gatherer diet than in populations with an agricultural diet.
D) The frequency of dental caries in a population does not necessarily correspond directly to the population's degree of dependence on agriculture.
E) The formation of dental caries tends to be more strongly linked to tooth wear than to the consumption of a particular kind of food.

My prediction to this one is "both authors agree that the incidence of dental caries is associated with the switch to an agricultural diet and/or an increase in carbohydrates in the diet." That may not exactly be the answer, but hopefully it will at least inform the answer.

A) Neither author suggests that tooth decay "increases predictably" over time.
B) Neither author mentions any difficulty in figuring out whether the teeth recovered in archeological finds have dental caries.
C) Both authors would disagree with this statement. (It's backward.)
D) Both authors would agree with this statement, so it's got to be the correct one. Passage A discusses certain populations that had a high degree of carbohydrates in their pre-agricultural diets, and therefore had a high incidence of dental caries. Passage B discusses a population in Thailand that slightly decreased its incidence of dental caries after switching to agriculture. So there you go.
E) Neither author takes the position that dental caries are more strongly linked to tooth wear than to diet. D is our winner.

QUESTION 20:

Each passage suggests which one of the following about carbohydrate-rich foods?

A) Varieties that are cultivated have a greater tendency to cause caries than varieties that grow wild.
B) Those that require substantial processing do not play a role in hunter-gatherer diets.
C) Some of them naturally have a greater tendency than others to cause caries.
D) Some of them reduce caries formation because their relatively high fiber content increases tooth wear.
E) The cariogenic potential of a given variety increases if it is cultivated rather than gathered in the wild.

Each passage suggests that carbohydrate-rich foods can be linked to dental caries.

A) Neither passage takes this position.
B) Passage A disagrees with this, providing evidence in the third paragraph of a hunter-gatherer culture "highly processing" acorns into flour.
C) Passage A refers to highly cariogenic pinyon nuts and wild tubers. Passage B refers to yams being more cariogenic than rice. So both authors believe that some species of plant are inherently more cariogenic than other species of plant. Sounds good.
D) Passage A takes no position on the issue of tooth wear, so this can't be it.
E) Neither passage suggests that particular varieties of plants themselves become more cariogenic when cultivated. Rather, agricultural societies tend to consume more cariogenic varieties. It's got to be C.

QUESTION 21:

21.The evidence from Ban Chiang discussed in passage B relates to the generalization reported in the second paragraph of passage A (lines 20–22) in which one of the following ways?

A) The evidence confirms the generalization.
B) The evidence tends to support the generalization.
C) The evidence is irrelevant to the generalization.
D) The evidence does not conform to the generalization.
E) The evidence disproves the generalization.

21

I had to refer back to Passage A on this one, because of course I didn't remember exactly what was said in lines 20–22. The generalization mentioned there is that the higher a population's dependence on agriculture, the higher (usually) its incidence of dental caries. The Ban Chiang population, I remembered, went slightly against this trend. So the correct answer must be something like "the population acted counter to the generalization."

A) The evidence didn't confirm the generalization. The evidence went the other way.
B) Nope, the evidence didn't support the generalization. The evidence went the other way.
C) The evidence is not irrelevant. It is directly contrary, which is *very* relevant. Unless, of course, you're on Fox News.
D) This is perfect. "Does not conform" indicates that the evidence didn't quite fit the generalization. This is just like we predicted, and it's the correct answer.
E) It's too much to say the evidence "disproves" the generalization. The evidence didn't quite fit the generalization, but that doesn't mean the generalization is patently false.

> ## Provin'
> ## Ain't Easy
> Be careful on the LSAT when you see "proves" or "disproves." This is a very high standard. On the LSAT, pieces of evidence usually "support" or "weaken" a particular position, and very rarely "prove" or "disprove" a particular position.

Passage Four (Questions 22–27)

Recent criticism has sought to align Sarah Orne Jewett, a notable writer of regional fiction in the nineteenth-century United States, with the domestic novelists of the previous generation. Her work does
(5) resemble the domestic novels of the 1850s in its focus on women, their domestic occupations, and their social interactions, with men relegated to the periphery. But it also differs markedly from these antecedents. The world depicted in the latter revolves around children.
(10) Young children play prominent roles in the domestic novels and the work of child rearing—the struggle to instill a mother's values in a child's character—is their chief source of drama. By contrast, children and child rearing are almost entirely absent from the world of
(15) Jewett's fiction. Even more strikingly, while the literary world of the earlier domestic novelists is insistently religious, grounded in the structures of Protestant religious belief, to turn from these writers to Jewett is to encounter an almost wholly secular world.
(20) To the extent that these differences do not merely reflect the personal preferences of the authors, we might attribute them to such historical transformations as the migration of the rural young to cities or the increasing secularization of society. But while such
(25) factors may help to explain the differences, it can be argued that these differences ultimately reflect different conceptions of the nature and purpose of fiction. The domestic novel of the mid-nineteenth century is based on a conception of fiction as part of
(30) a continuum that also included writings devoted to piety and domestic instruction, bound together by a common goal of promoting domestic morality and religious belief. It was not uncommon for the same multipurpose book to be indistinguishably a novel, a
(35) child-rearing manual, and a tract on Christian duty. The more didactic aims are absent from Jewett's writing, which rather embodies the late nineteenth-century "high-cultural" conception of fiction as an autonomous sphere with value in and of itself.
(40) This high-cultural aesthetic was one among several conceptions of fiction operative in the United States in the 1850s and 1860s, but it became the dominant one later in the nineteenth century and remained so for most of the twentieth. On this
(45) conception, fiction came to be seen as pure art: a work was to be viewed in isolation and valued for the formal arrangement of its elements rather than for its larger social connections or the promotion of extraliterary goods. Thus, unlike the domestic novelists, Jewett
(50) intended her works not as a means to an end but as an end in themselves. This fundamental difference should be given more weight in assessing their affinities than any superficial similarity in subject matter.

This is a brutal passage for me because I'm not crazy about fiction, I'm less crazy about "regional" fiction, I'm much less crazy about "domestic" fiction, and somehow I've found a way to be even less crazy about nineteenth-century fiction. I do best on passages where I feel like I'm learning something at least slightly useful. (Who knew that an agricultural diet led to cavities? Fun! I'm pretty sure I'm never going to be at a cocktail party talking about Sarah Orne Jewett, but the cavities thing just might come up. Hell, even the lichens are better than this.) But I know I don't get to choose the topic, and I have to try to do my best to answer the questions correctly. So I'm going to focus even more strongly on "Why are you wasting my time with this?" At the end of the passage, I'm going to do my damndest to be able to at least have understood the author's main point.

At the end of the first paragraph, I think the author came here to tell me that Sarah Orne Jewett's work has similarities to, but is importantly different from its antecedents in two ways: 1) fewer children, and 2) less religion. Because I don't particularly like kids or religion, I've surprisingly become somewhat interested in this passage. This might not be so horrible after all.

The second paragraph is pretty boring, discussing a possible reason for Jewett's differences. Basically, whereas previous work was "indistinguishable" from child-rearing manuals and Christian tracts, Jewett's work fit into the late-nineteenth-century trend of fiction as high culture. According to the author, Jewett considered herself an artist.

The last paragraph expounds on this position. The author says the trend toward high-cultural literature became "dominant" at the same time as Jewett was writing her novels. Jewett, the author says, "intended her works as an end in themselves." Jewett wasn't trying to improve mothering skills or create better citizens with her novels. She was trying to create art. OK, now I think I have a pretty good handle on the main point.

QUESTION 22:

The passage most helps to answer which one of the following questions?

A) Did any men write domestic novels in the 1850s?
B) Were any widely read domestic novels written after the 1860s?
C) How did migration to urban areas affect the development of domestic fiction in the 1850s?
D) What is an effect that Jewett's conception of literary art had on her fiction?
E) With what region of the United States were at least some of Jewett's writings concerned?.

There's no way to answer this one in advance. We just have to dig in and pick the best answer.

A) The passage is not about whether men wrote domestic novels. This isn't it.
B) The passage isn't about what happened after the 1860s. Next, please.
C) The passage dismisses migration to urban areas as one of the factors that may help to explain Jewett's differences, but Jewett's work was not "domestic fiction." So this is out.
D) Yep, this is *exactly* the question that the passage focuses on. Jewett's conception of literary art made her write novels with fewer kids and less religion. She was trying to create art. This is our answer. But let's just skim E to be sure.
E) The passage mentions "regionalism" but doesn't mention any one particular region. So this is out and our best answer is D.

QUESTION 23:

It can be inferred from the passage that the author would be most likely to view the "recent criticism" mentioned in line 1 as

A) advocating a position that is essentially correct even though some powerful arguments can be made against it
B) making a true claim about Jewett, but for the wrong reasons
C) making a claim that is based on some reasonable evidence and is initially plausible but ultimately mistaken
D) questionable, because it relies on a currently dominant literary aesthetic that takes too narrow a view of the proper goals of fiction
E) based on speculation for which there is no reasonable support, and therefore worthy of dismissal

Our prediction here should be that the author disagrees with the criticism. This is because of the "But" that leads off line 7.

A) The author disagrees with the criticism, rather than thinking it is essentially correct.
B) The author also disagrees with the criticism's conclusion, rather than agreeing for different reasons.
C) This is our answer. The author at first acknowledges some of the criticism's legitimate foundations ("Her work does resemble the domestic novels") before disagreeing with it ("But it also differs markedly").
D) The author of the passage doesn't take a stance on what the "proper" goals of fiction might be, so this can't be the answer.
E) The author doesn't think the criticism is "based on speculation for which there is no reasonable support" because the author acknowledges the similarities between Jewett's work and domestic fiction. This is out and our answer is C.

24

QUESTION 24:

In saying that domestic fiction was based on a conception of fiction as part of a "continuum" (line 30), the author most likely means which one of the following?

A) Domestic fiction was part of an ongoing tradition stretching back into the past.
B) Fiction was not treated as clearly distinct from other categories of writing.
C) Domestic fiction was often published in serial form.
D) Fiction is constantly evolving.
E) Domestic fiction promoted the cohesiveness and hence the continuity of society.

In the middle and end of the second paragraph, the author was talking about how books used to blur the line between fiction, child-rearing manual, and religious tract. This is what the author meant when she used the word "continuum" in line 30.

A) The author wasn't talking about a continuum between the present and the past, she was talking about a continuum between different types of written works. This is out.
B) This could be it. "Not clearly distinct from other categories of writing" is pretty similar to our prediction of "blurring the line," so this is probably it. Hopefully nothing else is any good so we can happily choose B.
C) This isn't anywhere close to my prediction, it doesn't strike any unexpected chord, and we've already got a good answer in B. So this is out.
D) Same explanation as C.
E) Same explanation as C and D. The best answer is B. Note that I didn't really bother taking much time figuring out what C, D, and E might mean. Once you have an answer you like, especially if it matches your prediction, read all the rest of the answers but unless one of them really jumps out at you, it's best to go with the answer that immediately made sense.

Don't Make it Hard on Yourself

This question was easy because we LET it be easy. I've heard students say "I would have chosen B, but it seemed too easy. So I chose E, which I didn't really understand but it sounded smart." That's a horrible strategy. If it seems like the answer, it's probably the answer. Read all five, and go with the one that best matches your prediction.

25

QUESTION 25:

Which one of the following most accurately states the primary function of the passage?

A) It proposes and defends a radical redefinition of several historical categories of literary style.
B) It proposes an evaluation of a particular style of writing, of which one writer's work is cited as a paradigmatic case.
C) It argues for a reappraisal of a set of long-held assumptions about the historical connections among a group of writers.
D) It weighs the merits of two opposing conceptions of the nature of fiction.
E) It rejects a way of classifying a particular writer's work and defends an alternative view.

The primary function of the passage, as I read it, was to explain that recent criticism of Sarah Orne Jewett is wrong. The recent criticism aligns her with the "domestic novelists" of the previous generation, but the author says this is wrong because Jewett has fewer kids and less religion in her works. Where previous authors blurred the line between fiction and nonfiction, Jewett was trying to make art. The correct answer isn't going to say exactly all of this, of course. But it's going to be somewhat close.

A) This is nowhere near our prediction. Let's look for something better.
B) The author thinks Jewett was the exception to a previous style, not the paradigm of a particular style that the passage "evaluates." So I don't think this is it.
C) This is probably not it, because while the author is arguing for a reappraisal, it is "recent criticism" that the author wants reappraised, not "long-held assumptions."
D) This is definitely not it, because the author is not comparing the merits of two conceptions of fiction. Rather, the author is trying to place a particular author (Jewett) in one particular tradition of writing.
E) This is it. The author rejects the recent way of classifying Jewett (domestic novelist), and instead argues for a different classification (artist).

QUESTION 26:

Which one of the following most accurately represents the structure of the second paragraph?

A) The author considers and rejects a number of possible explanations for a phenomenon, concluding that any attempt at explanation does violence to the unity of the phenomenon.
B) The author shows that two explanatory hypotheses are incompatible with each other and gives reasons for preferring one of them.
C) The author describes several explanatory hypotheses and argues that they are not really distinct from one another.
D) The author proposes two versions of a classificatory hypothesis, indicates the need for some such hypothesis, and then sets out a counterargument in preparation for rejecting that counterargument in the following paragraph.
E) The author mentions a number of explanatory hypotheses, gives a mildly favorable comment on them, and then advocates and elaborates another explanation that the author considers to be more fundamental.

The second paragraph argues that the differences between Jewett and the domestic novelists are not merely matters of taste, or the effect of historical transformations like migration or secularization, but indicate a fundamental difference in the genre the authors were working in. (Note that this is also, more or less, the main point of the entire passage.)

A) You could argue that there are "a number of possible explanations for a phenomenon" in the second paragraph, but I certainly don't see a conclusion that "any attempt at explanation does violence to the unity of the phenomenon." Quite the opposite: the author explains the phenomenon as "Jewett considered herself an artist rather than a domestic novelist." Pretty sure this isn't the answer.
B) The author offers more than two hypotheses in the second paragraph, and never "shows" (which, on the LSAT, means "proves") that they are incompatible. This is out.
C) The author doesn't say "there are several hypotheses but they are all really the same explanation." No way.
D) The author proposes more than two hypotheses, and never argues for the need for any hypothesis. (This would be like "it is important to put Jewett in some genre because of X, Y, and Z.) I stopped reading this answer halfway through, because that part just can't be right. Remember that if an answer is 1 percent wrong, it's 100 percent wrong.
E) The author does give a number of hypotheses. The author does treat them mildly favorably, stating that "such factors may help to explain the differences." And the author does eventually conclude that a different hypothesis is the correct one. So this is our answer.

27

QUESTION 27:

The differing conceptions of fiction held by Jewett and the domestic novelists can most reasonably be taken as providing an answer to which one of the following questions?

A) Why was Jewett unwilling to feature children and religious themes as prominently in her works as the domestic novelists featured them in theirs?
B) Why did both Jewett and the domestic novelists focus primarily on rural as opposed to urban concerns?
C) Why was Jewett not constrained to feature children and religion as prominently in her works as domestic novelists were?
D) Why did both Jewett and the domestic novelists focus predominantly on women and their concerns?
E) Why was Jewett unable to feature children or religion as prominently in her works as the domestic novelists featured them in theirs?

This is a weird question. Jewett's conception of fiction was "I'm an artist, creating art." The domestic novelists' conception of fiction was something like "I'm a good Christian mother, creating stories that help others be good Christian mothers." This question asks us to identify a question that can be answered by this difference. Very odd.

A) We can answer this question with the above, so this is the correct answer. Jewett was creating art, not tracts on Christian motherhood. That's why she didn't feature kids and God in her works. If this is the correct answer, then the remainder of the answer choices should be questions that are still mysteries to us. Let's see.
B) One can be both an artist and a Christian mother in both rural and urban areas. So we have no idea why Jewett and the domestic novelists both focused on the country. This is out.
C) Uh-oh. This is very similar to A. While A says Jewett was "unwilling" to feature kids and God, this answer choice says Jewett was "not constrained" to feature kids and God. But I don't think the domestic novelists felt "constrained" to feature kids and God. Probably they were just writing about what they wanted to write about. So A still feels like a better answer. (But I won't be shocked, or care all that much, if I miss this question. To finish the test and do your best, you have to take some educated guesses and occasionally go with your gut feeling. Trying for a 180 can be counterproductive. Don't let the perfect be the enemy of the good.)
D) Domestic novelists focused on women and their concerns because they were trying to create tracts on how to be good Christian mothers. Jewett, on the other hand, was an artist. She could have focused on women, or not. The passage gives us no idea why she did. So this is out.
E) The passage doesn't suggest that Jewett was "unable" to feature children or women, so this is out. The best answer is still A.

Editor's note: The correct answer to this question is C.

SECTION
TWO

Logical Reasoning

(Or: Breaking Balls)

Before we begin, two quick lessons on logical reasoning.

First, the questions get harder as each section progresses. Most people can't finish the sections without compromising accuracy. If this is you, then guessing on a few at the end is a perfectly sound strategy. Take your time and get the early—and more answerable—questions right, because the later ones are going to be very difficult no matter how much time you devote to them.

Second, take a supercritical mindset as you read these arguments, because most of them are (intentionally) horribly flawed. You're essentially being tested on your ability to notice when someone is making a foolish or deceitful argument. The stronger the argument is stated, the more likely it is to be total crap. Once when I was young, I heard a preacher shout, "*Obviously* a fish didn't just suddenly have legs pop out its sides and start walking up the beach, so *clearly*, logically, the theory of evolution is wrong!" The problem is that no scientist believes in legs popping out the sides of fish, yet virtually all scientists believe in evolution. Yelling, for the preacher, was easier than reading. From that day on, I have been wary of "logical" arguments, especially those that use words like "clearly" or "obviously." On the LSAT, as in real life, as soon as someone presents an argument as "indisputable" then you would be wise to dispute it. Let's get started.

QUESTION 1:

In a recent study, a group of young children were taught the word "stairs" while walking up and down a flight of stairs. Later that day, when the children were shown a video of a person climbing a ladder, they all called the ladder stairs.

Which one of the following principles is best illustrated by the study described above?

- A) When young children repeatedly hear a word without seeing the object denoted by the word, they sometimes apply the word to objects not denoted by the word.
- B) Young children best learn words when they are shown how the object denoted by the word is used.
- C) The earlier in life a child encounters and uses an object, the easier it is for that child to learn how not to misuse the word denoting that object.
- D) Young children who learn a word by observing how the object denoted by that word is used sometimes apply that word to a different object that is similarly used.
- E) Young children best learn the names of objects when the objects are present at the time the children learn the words and when no other objects are simultaneously present.

The kids in the study all learned to call stairs "stairs" after being taught the word while going up and down them. But when they saw a video of a person climbing a ladder, they called the ladder "stairs" as well. What's happening here? Well, it seems to me that the kids have grasped the idea of climbing up and down as "stairs" but haven't noticed the subtle differences between stairs and a ladder. I imagine that if they saw someone climbing a rock wall, they might also say "stairs" since the person is going up and down. This question asks us to identify a *principle* that the study illustrates. You can't really answer this question in advance. Just make sure that you have a clear understanding of the study. Once you've got that, you can surely pick out the correct answer.

- A) This wouldn't be it, because the children did see the object (the stairs) when being taught the word "stairs." So even though A is probably true, it's not the principle illustrated by the study we learned about in this question. That means it's not our answer.
- B) The study doesn't give us any idea whether children *best* learn words in any particular way. There's only one particular method that was used in the study, and it's not compared to any other method. This is out.
- C) We don't even know how old the kids in this study were, so this can't be it.
- D) This seems pretty good. The kids learning the word "stairs" were using the stairs at the time. So then when they saw a video of someone using a ladder in a similar way, they called the ladder "stairs." This is our answer.
- E) This is just like answer B. Again, the study gives us no idea how children *best* learn words. The best answer is D.

QUESTION 2:

Among people who live to the age of 100 or more, a large proportion have led "unhealthy" lives: smoking, consuming alcohol, eating fatty foods, and getting little exercise. Since such behavior often leads to shortened life spans, it is likely that exceptionally long-lived people are genetically disposed to having long lives.

Which one of the following, if true, most strengthens the argument?

A) There is some evidence that consuming a moderate amount of alcohol can counteract the effects of eating fatty foods.
B) Some of the exceptionally long-lived people who do not smoke or drink do eat fatty foods and get little exercise.
C) Some of the exceptionally long-lived people who exercise regularly and avoid fatty foods do smoke or consume alcohol.
D) Some people who do not live to the age of 100 also lead unhealthy lives.
E) Nearly all people who live to 100 or more have siblings who are also long-lived.

This is a pretty terrible argument. The evidence presented here basically goes as follows: First, there are a significant number of very old folks who have smoked, boozed, *et cetera*. Second, smoking, boozing, *et cetera* often leads to shortened lifespans. From this evidence, the author concludes that *genetics* must be the cause of long lives.

The biggest problem here is that the author has given no reason to believe that genetics actually could be connected to long life. The author could have put literally anything in the place of genetics and the argument would be essentially unchanged. Why didn't the author conclude that getting a lot of sleep is the cause of long life? Or watching television? Or looking at a lot of porn? Who knows! The argument presents just as much support for "genetics promote long life" as he does "looking at porn promotes long life." What's needed here is something— anything—that suggests a connection between genetics and long life.

A) There's no support here for genetics as a cause of long life. The correct answer *must* have something to do with genetics. (I'll only really consider A if I eliminate all five answers and don't find anything that suggests genetics.)
B) Again, no genetics. Next please.
C) Still no genetics.
D) Still no genetics.
E) Siblings! Siblings share ... genetics! This is the only conceivable answer.

QUESTION 3:

Medications with an unpleasant taste are generally produced only in tablet, capsule, or soft-gel form. The active ingredient in medication M is a waxy substance that cannot tolerate the heat used to manufacture tablets because it has a low melting point. So, since the company developing M does not have soft-gel manufacturing technology and manufactures all its medications itself, M will most likely be produced in capsule form.

The conclusion is most strongly supported by the reasoning in the argument if which one of the following is assumed?

A) Medication M can be produced in liquid form.
B) Medication M has an unpleasant taste.
C) No medication is produced in both capsule and soft-gel form.
D) Most medications with a low melting point are produced in soft-gel form.
E) Medications in capsule form taste less unpleasant than those in tablet or soft-gel form.

The first premise in the argument says there are "generally" three ways to package unpleasant-tasting medicine: tablet, capsule, and soft-gel. The second premise says medication M can't be a tablet. The third premise says M can't be a soft-gel. The conclusion, therefore, is that M has to be a capsule.

There are two missing links in this reasoning. The first is that we don't know whether or not medication M is a medication with an unpleasant taste. It might taste like candy, in which case maybe it doesn't have to be produced in tablet, capsule, or soft-gel form.

The second missing link in the reasoning is that the first premise only says medications with an unpleasant taste are "generally" produced only in these three forms. So conceivably, the medication could still taste bad and if the company developing M decided to do something not "generally" done then they could still produce it in some other form.

The first of these missing links is the most important, because the second missing link is only relevant if Medication M does actually taste bad. A perfect answer would be "Medication M has an unpleasant taste and this company always does what is generally done." But a good answer would be simply "Medication M has an unpleasant taste."

A) The possibility that M could be produced as a liquid can't possibly strengthen the conclusion that M will be produced in a capsule form.
B) This matches our prediction, so unless we find another answer that includes both "unpleasant taste" *and* this company always does what is generally done, B will be our answer.
C) We already know M can't be a soft-gel, so this answer is entirely irrelevant. This premise, if true, would neither strengthen nor weaken.
D) This could only weaken because it suggests M should be a soft-gel. (And it's irrelevant since M cannot be a soft-gel.)
E) This doesn't help, because we don't know whether M tastes unpleasant to begin with. The best answer is B.

QUESTION 4:

Carol Morris wants to own a majority of the shares of the city's largest newspaper, The Daily. The only obstacle to Morris's amassing a majority of these shares is that Azedcorp, which currently owns a majority, has steadfastly refused to sell. Industry analysts nevertheless predict that Morris will soon be the majority owner of The Daily.

Which one of the following, if true, provides the most support for the industry analysts' prediction?

A) Azedcorp does not own shares of any newspaper other than The Daily.
B) Morris has recently offered Azedcorp much more for its shares of The Daily than Azedcorp paid for them.
C) No one other than Morris has expressed any interest in purchasing a majority of The Daily's shares.
D) Morris already owns more shares of The Daily than anyone except Azedcorp.
E) Azedcorp is financially so weak that bankruptcy will probably soon force the sale of its newspaper holdings.

There seems to be a paradox here. How can Morris become the majority shareholder in *The Daily* if the current majority owner, Azedcorp, has "steadfastly refused to sell"? Off the top of my head, I can think of a couple of ways. First: Can Morris buy Azedcorp? This is a bit outside the box, but we have no idea how big Azedcorp is or how wealthy Morris is. If Morris could buy Azedcorp outright, then I suppose she would become a majority shareholder in *The Daily*. Second: Can Azedcorp change its mind? Just because Azedcorp has "steadfastly refused" doesn't mean that they will always refuse. What if, for example, they had to file bankruptcy and were forced to sell?

We don't know if either of these will be the correct answer, but we do know that either of them *could* be a correct answer. We're fairly well-armed going into the answer choices looking for one of these or something similar.

A) We need to know how Morris can become a majority shareholder in *The Daily*. Whether or not Azedcorp owns any other newspapers really isn't relevant to that issue.

B) This could only be the answer if none of the answers were any good. If it's true that Morris recently made a big offer, then maybe Azedcorp might change its mind. But how do we know Morris hasn't made such big offers in the past? We are told that Azedcorp has "steadfastly" refused in the past, which might suggest that Morris has made big offers. This answer choice is speculative at best, and seems to require too much effort to explain. We're looking for something that offers a more direct route to Morris becoming the majority shareholder.

C) This can't be it, because we have no indication that Azedcorp wants to sell at all. If Azedcorp doesn't want to sell, then it's irrelevant that Morris is the only apparent buyer. (Furthermore, just because nobody other than Morris has expressed interest doesn't mean that other buyers wouldn't emerge if Azedcorp put the paper up for sale.)

D) This is nice for Morris, but she's still not going to become the majority shareholder unless the current majority shareholder, Azedcorp, decides to sell.

E) Bankruptcy for Azedcorp! This was one of our predictions, and I hated A-D, so this must be the correct answer.

Work Smarter, Not Harder

Any time an answer choice requires you to do a lot of explaining in order to make it the correct answer, it's probably not the one you want. As you practice, you'll start to get a feel for this. You're asked to pick the *best* answer, and usually, the best answer doesn't require a whole lot of work or additional assumptions in order to be correct. Look for the simplest, cleanest path to the conclusion you're trying to prove. Don't put square pegs in round holes.

QUESTION 5:

Area resident: Childhood lead poisoning has declined steadily since the 1970s, when leaded gasoline was phased out and lead paint was banned. But recent statistics indicate that 25 percent of this area's homes still contain lead paint that poses significant health hazards. Therefore, if we eliminate the lead paint in those homes, childhood lead poisoning in the area will finally be eradicated.

The area resident's argument is flawed in that it

A) relies on statistical claims that are likely to be unreliable
B) relies on an assumption that is tantamount to assuming that the conclusion is true
C) fails to consider that there may be other significant sources of lead in the area's environment
D) takes for granted that lead paint in homes can be eliminated economically
E) takes for granted that children reside in all of the homes in the area that contain lead paint

The big clue here is "eradicated." Really? If we eliminate lead paint in homes, then childhood lead poisoning will be completely eradicated? Because I assume that the speakers are trying to bullshit me, an absolute conclusion like this makes me instantly argumentative. In order to disprove "eradicated" all we need to do is come up with *one* case of childhood lead poisoning that would still happen even after there was no more lead paint in homes. Isn't it true that some homes might have lead pipes? Couldn't lead pipes cause childhood lead poisoning? Isn't it true that some homes might have cheap toys made in China that have lead in them? Couldn't cheap toys with lead in them cause childhood lead poisoning? Isn't it true that, even if there is no lead in the home, a child might still contract lead poisoning at school? Or at church? Or at the mall?

The argument asks us to identify a flaw in the argument's reasoning. Even if you can't articulate it exactly, we know that it has something to do with all the other potential causes of childhood lead poisoning other than lead paint in the home.

A) The argument does rely on a statistical claim, but there is no reason shown in the argument to believe that the statistical claim is likely to be unreliable. This is sometimes the correct answer, but *only* choose it when you are given good reason to believe there is a problem with the data.

B) "Relies on an assumption that is tantamount to assuming the conclusion is true" is another way of saying "circular reasoning." An example of circular reasoning is "every word in the Bible is true because it says so in the Bible." These types of questions do appear on the LSAT, but it's not what's happening in this particular question.

C) This looks like the correct answer. Our questioning, above, was all related to other potential causes of lead poisoning. If it's true that there are other significant sources of lead in the area's environment (in the water supply, perhaps?) then eliminating lead paint doesn't seem sufficient to eliminate all childhood lead poisoning. This is a solid answer.

D) Economics is simply irrelevant here. If eliminating lead paint in homes would cost the area's taxpayers eleventy billion dollars per person, that might make eliminating lead paint in homes a bad idea. But it wouldn't weaken the argument that if lead paint in homes could be eliminated then childhood lead poisoning would be eradicated. The area resident never argued, or assumed, that eliminating lead paint was actually economically feasible.

E) The argument didn't assume that all homes with lead paint in the area contain children. The argument assumed that lead paint in homes is the only cause of childhood lead poisoning. Answer C does the best job of pointing out this gap in the reasoning.

Be an Attorney!

You're studying for the LSAT. You're on your way to law school. Start arguing *now*. When I'm answering a logical reasoning question, I'm picturing myself as a trial attorney on cross-examination. No matter what the witness says, I immediately start probing for weaknesses. Be skeptical! If an argument is sound, it should stand up to questioning. Note how the questions I ask here eventually lead directly to the giant flaw in the logic and therefore the correct answer.

QUESTION 6:

Although some nutritional facts about soft drinks are listed on their labels, exact caffeine content is not. Listing exact caffeine content would make it easier to limit, but not eliminate, one's caffeine intake. If it became easier for people to limit, but not eliminate, their caffeine intake, many people would do so, which would improve their health.

If all the statements above are true, which one of the following must be true?

A) The health of at least some people would improve if exact caffeine content were listed on soft-drink labels.
B) Many people will be unable to limit their caffeine intake if exact caffeine content is not listed on soft-drink labels.
C) Many people will find it difficult to eliminate their caffeine intake if they have to guess exactly how much caffeine is in their soft drinks.
D) People who wish to eliminate, rather than simply limit, their caffeine intake would benefit if exact caffeine content were listed on soft-drink labels.
E) The health of at least some people would worsen if everyone knew exactly how much caffeine was in their soft drinks.

The first premise here is "listing exact caffeine content would make it easier to limit caffeine intake." The second premise is "if it became easier to limit caffeine intake, many people would do so." The third premise is "this would improve their health." I don't see a conclusion here. There's no "therefore," or "so," or "consequently," or "clearly" to indicate that the author is going to make a conclusion. It just seems like a series of premises that link up to one another.

The question asks us to identify something that must be true based on the above statements.

There's no explicit conclusion, but we can connect the dots here. Why is the author wasting our time? Well, it seems as if the author came here to tell us that listing exact caffeine content would improve the health of many people. In fact, if all of the author's premises are true, then I think this conclusion *must* be true. So that's our prediction for this question.

A) Boom. This is almost exactly what we predicted, so it's our answer unless one of the other answer choices really knocks our socks off.
B) The author said that listing the caffeine content would be *sufficient* to help people limit their intake. The author did not say that listing caffeine content is *necessary* for people to be able to limit their intake. In other words, there might be plenty of other ways that people could limit their intake. So this is out.
C) Pretty much the same explanation as B. There could be other ways for people to figure out how much caffeine is in their drinks. Listing the exact content is a good way, but not necessarily the only way, according to the author.
D) The argument is really not about what people should do if they want to eliminate caffeine. All the premises are about limiting caffeine. So this is out. (We're provided no information about what people should do if they want to eliminate caffeine, or if this is even possible.)
E) The argument says that eliminating caffeine would be good for the health of many people. It provides no reason whatsoever to believe that some people would have worse health if they knew how much caffeine was in their soft drinks. No way. Answer A is almost exactly what we predicted, and all the remaining answers sucked. So A is our answer.

7

QUESTION 7:

When the famous art collector Vidmar died, a public auction of her collection, the largest privately owned, was held. "I can't possibly afford any of those works because hers is among the most valuable collections ever assembled by a single person," declared art lover MacNeil.

The flawed pattern of reasoning in which one of the following is most closely parallel to that in MacNeil's argument?

A) Each word in the book is in French. So the whole book is in French.
B) The city council voted unanimously to adopt the plan. So councilperson Martinez voted to adopt the plan.
C) This paragraph is long. So the sentences that comprise it are long.
D) The members of the company are old. So the company itself is old.
E) The atoms comprising this molecule are elements. So the molecule itself is an element.

This is the argument of a complete idiot. Seriously. It's like saying "Amazon.com sells a zillion items, and it would cost a bazillion dollars to buy every single one. Therefore I can't afford any single item from Amazon." The question here asks us to identify a similarly ludicrous argument. This should be a breeze.

A) This isn't even flawed. If every word in a book is French, then the whole book is, in fact, in French. So this can't be the answer if we're looking for a flawed argument.

B) This isn't flawed either. If the council was unanimous, and Martinez is on the council, then Martinez voted for the plan. (Unless she was absent that night or something. But even if that's a flaw, it's not the *same* flaw, so this isn't the answer.)

C) This seems pretty good. Just like a very expensive art collection might contain some (or many) affordable items, a long paragraph might contain some (or all) short sentences. This is our answer unless D or E is extremely attractive.

D) This is definitely flawed, because there's nothing stopping a bunch of old dudes from starting up a brand-new dot-com company. But the flaw we were given was "whatever is true of the whole must be true of each of the parts." This is more like "whatever is true of each of the members must be true of the whole company." That's wrong, but it's wrong in a different way. So it's eliminated.

E) Again, this one is "whatever is true of each of the parts must be true of the whole." That's a different flaw. The best answer is C.

Flawed Patterns of Reasoning

The correct answer here must have two characteristics. First, it has to be flawed. Any valid argument cannot be the answer. Second, it has to be flawed *in the same way* as the given argument. You must identify the flaw *before* looking at the answer choices so you can avoid confusion and traps. Ideally, you'll be able to come up with an example, like I've done here with Amazon.

QUESTION 8:

A leading critic of space exploration contends that it would be wrong, given current technology, to send a group of explorers to Mars, since the explorers would be unlikely to survive the trip. But that exaggerates the risk. There would be a well-engineered backup system at every stage of the long and complicated journey. A fatal catastrophe is quite unlikely at any given stage if such a backup system is in place.

The reasoning in the argument is flawed in that the argument

A) infers that something is true of a whole merely from the fact that it is true of each of the parts
B) infers that something cannot occur merely from the fact that it is unlikely to occur
C) draws a conclusion about what must be the case based on evidence about what is probably the case
D) infers that something will work merely because it could work
E) rejects a view merely on the grounds that an inadequate argument has been made for it

Interesting. The author says that even though the trip to Mars is, admittedly, "long and complicated," there would be backup systems in place at every stage of the journey. Since a fatal catastrophe is quite unlikely at any given stage if such backup systems are in place, the author concludes that Mars explorers would be likely to survive the trip.

I think the problem here is that even tiny risks can add up over time. Apologies for going dark here, but imagine if I were to hand you a silver dollar and put a gun to your head. I'll only shoot, I say, if you flip tails 13 unlucky times in a row. Of course this is extremely unlikely. The odds of flipping tails 13 times in a row is .5^13, or barely over .01 percent. (A little over one out of 10,000.) The odds are extremely good that you're going to live through the day. The risk is very small.

But now imagine that I'm going to show up at breakfast every single day, from now on, with my silver dollar and my gun, and force you into the same deal. The odds are roughly 9,999 out of 10,000 that you're going to live through tomorrow. But the odds are only 96% that you're going to make it through the year, and only 69% that you're going to make it through the next 10 years. Small risks add up. The same might hold true for the small risks incurred by Mars explorers every day on a very long journey.

A) This is probably it. The argument assumes that small risks, when added up, are still small. But little bricks can build a very big wall. This matches our prediction, but let's skim B–E to be sure.
B) The argument never goes so far as claiming that disaster *can't* happen to the astronauts. The author never guarantees the astronauts' survival. Rather, the author simply says the explorers would be likely to survive. This isn't the answer.
C) Again, the author never makes an absolute conclusion about what *must* be the case. I like A best so far.
D) This would be like "It's theoretically possible that we could strap a guy to a lawn chair with a bunch of balloons and a six-pack and he would make it to Mars, therefore, it'll work for sure." That's not what the argument does.
E) This would be like "You can't prove there is no God, therefore God is proven to exist." That's not what this argument does. Our answer is A.

How to Become a Good Reader

Sorry for the macabre example here. My twisted imagination is a relic of the dozens of Stephen King novels I read in high school. Call it trash if you like, but King kept me reading constantly throughout the 1990s. This built powerful reading comprehension muscles that now allow me to overpower the LSAT. No matter what anybody tells you, don't be ashamed of reading whatever it is that you like to read. It won't happen overnight, but the more you read (even if it's about sports, celebrities, or bodice-ripping romance) the better reader you'll become. Find something you love and read it. Constantly.

QUESTION 9:

A retrospective study is a scientific study that tries to determine the causes of subjects' present characteristics by looking for significant connections between the present characteristics of subjects and what happened to those subjects in the past, before the study began. Because retrospective studies of human subjects must use the subjects' reports about their own pasts, however, such studies cannot reliably determine the causes of human subjects' present characteristics.

Which one of the following, if assumed, enables the argument's conclusion to be properly drawn?

A) Whether or not a study of human subjects can reliably determine the causes of those subjects' present characteristics may depend at least in part on the extent to which that study uses inaccurate reports about the subjects' pasts.

B) A retrospective study cannot reliably determine the causes of human subjects' present characteristics unless there exist correlations between the present characteristics of the subjects and what happened to those subjects in the past.

C) In studies of human subjects that attempt to find connections between subjects' present characteristics and what happened to those subjects in the past, the subjects' reports about their own pasts are highly susceptible to inaccuracy.

D) If a study of human subjects uses only accurate reports about the subjects' pasts, then that study can reliably determine the causes of those subjects' present characteristics.

E) Every scientific study in which researchers look for significant connections between the present characteristics of subjects and what happened to those subjects in the past must use the subjects' reports about their own pasts.

This is a reasonable argument because people probably can't accurately remember their pasts. Whoops! Sorry for skipping to the end. I'm pretty sure that's going to be the correct answer.

The argument asks us to identify an additional premise that, if true, proves the argument's conclusion. This is a *sufficient* assumption question. (Please contrast my analysis for this question with my analysis on a *necessary* assumption question like number 12.) Sufficient assumption questions ask us to identify an additional premise that would be enough to prove that the author's conclusion is true. You can usually answer this type of question in advance, and I probably already did, above. If it's true that people cannot accurately remember their pasts, then retrospective studies are probably useless for identifying past causes of present characteristics. So that's what we're looking for. Because this is a sufficient assumption question, the answer can be big and overbroad and still be the correct answer. We're not being asked to identify something that the author has actually assumed. (In which case we would be looking for something smaller, because we wouldn't want to overstate the assumption the author made.) Here, we're asked for an additional premise that, if it was true, would force the author's conclusion to be true. So something like "It is impossible for anyone to remember anything that happened more than 30 seconds ago," while not *necessary* to prove the author's conclusion, would still be *sufficient* to prove the author's conclusion, and could be the answer here.

A) If this is true, it strengthens the author's argument. But it could be true and the author's argument could still be false if people are able to remember their pasts accurately. So this might be a necessary assumption, but is not a sufficient assumption. It would be the correct answer if the question had asked, "Which one of the following is an assumption on which the author's argument relies?" But it didn't.

B) Bluh. I just don't think we have time to engage with this answer. We know what we're looking for, so let's not bother trying to figure out what this one means unless we don't find our prediction below.

C) This is more like it. If subjects' reports about their own pasts are unreliable, then how could retrospective studies prove anything? This matches our prediction, and it's much better than A or B. Let's skim D and E quickly before choosing C.

D) This could only weaken the argument, so it's out.

E) This might be true, but even if it is true then the studies could still be valid if people can accurately report their pasts. We were looking for something that forced the author's conclusion to be true, and this isn't it. Our answer is C.

What "Assumption" Means

Consider the following argument:

A equals two. B equals two. Therefore, A plus B equals four.

Sounds pretty good, right? Yeah, I think so too. But believe it or not, for LSAT purposes, something's missing. That missing piece is called an assumption.

The assumption here is something very obvious, but that's OK. The assumption we've made is *two plus two equals four*.

Of course everyone knows two plus two equals four. That's beside the point. On the LSAT, every premise should be made explicit if the argument is going to hold water. The same goes for legal writing. I've always thought that 1) brevity is a virtue and 2) you shouldn't insult the reader by making points that are too obvious. This is not how legal writing works. Less is not more. More is more. As a 1L, I was shocked at how pedantic my Legal Writing instructor wanted my briefs to sound. If your case depends on the proposition that the ocean is wet, you better not leave the words "the ocean is wet" (properly cited to controlling case law, naturally) out of your brief.

Here, the proposition that two plus two equals four is both a necessary and sufficient assumption. I'll explain more about what this means later, but for now, consider this:

"Two plus two equals four" is a necessary assumption of the argument because if it's not true, the argument loses. If I don't prove that "two plus two equals four," then my opponent might put on an expert witness who says that two plus two equals five. And if two plus two equals five, then A plus B does not equal four—it equals five, and I lose my case. (And then I lose my job, for leaving something so elementary out of my case.)

Because "two plus two equals four" must be true in order for my argument to make sense, it is a necessary component of my argument. Since it was unstated, it is a necessary assumption of my argument. If the question had asked "Which one of the following is an assumption on which the argument relies?" or "Which one of the following is an assumption required by the argument?" then two plus two equals four would be a perfect answer.

"Two plus two equals four" is a sufficient assumption of the argument because if it is true, then my argument wins. There are no other holes in the argument: If it is a fact that A equals two, and also a fact that B equals two, and also a fact that two plus two equals four, then it must be true that A plus B equals four, and I win my case. (And then I get promoted.)

Because "two plus two equals four" would make it impossible for my conclusion to be false, it is sufficient (*i.e.*, enough) to prove my argument. Since it was unstated, it is a sufficient assumption of my argument. If the question had asked "Which one of the following, if true, would allow the conclusion to be properly drawn?" or "Which one of the following, if assumed, would allow the conclusion of the argument to be properly inferred?" or "Which one of the following would justify the argument's conclusion?" then two plus two equals four would be a perfect answer.

I used this example to explain this concept to one of my students. He didn't want to buy the proposition that "two plus two equals four" was an "assumption" of the argument, because he felt "two plus two equals four" was "implied" by the argument, and that it was "too obvious." My response was: "Yes, exactly." Anything that is "implied" by the argument is a very good candidate for an "assumption" of the argument. Likewise, anything that seems "obvious" based on the argument, but isn't actually stated by the argument (or proven by the other premises of the argument) is probably an assumption.

A couple final notes:

·Assumptions are sometimes necessary but not sufficient, sometimes sufficient but not necessary, and sometimes both sufficient and necessary, as in this example.

·This "two plus two" example is purposely oversimplified. I doubt a real LSAT question (or a real judge) would ever entertain the proposition that two plus two might actually equal five. But "two plus two equals four" is, by definition, an assumption of the argument I made at the beginning. If you need it, and you didn't explicitly state it, then you've just assumed it. That means there's a weakness in your argument—and a good lawyer isn't going to leave anything to chance.

QUESTION 10:

Gigantic passenger planes currently being developed will have enough space to hold shops and lounges in addition to passenger seating. However, the additional space will more likely be used for more passenger seating. The number of passengers flying the air-traffic system is expected to triple within 20 years, and it will be impossible for airports to accommodate enough normal-sized jet planes to carry that many passengers.

Which one of the following most accurately states the conclusion drawn in the argument?

A) Gigantic planes currently being developed will have enough space in them to hold shops and lounges as well as passenger seating.

B) The additional space in the gigantic planes currently being developed is more likely to be filled with passenger seating than with shops and lounges.

C) The number of passengers flying the air-traffic system is expected to triple within 20 years.

D) In 20 years, it will be impossible for airports to accommodate enough normal-sized planes to carry the number of passengers that are expected to be flying then.

E) In 20 years, most airline passengers will be flying in gigantic passenger planes.

When a question asks you to identify the conclusion of an argument, it's time for "Why are you wasting my time with this?" Confronted with such a question, the speaker would probably take offense at my rudeness. And then, the speaker would attempt to justify his speech by repeating the main conclusion he was trying to make. Here, the response would be something like "Well, you colossal A-hole, I was trying to tell you that even though these new gigantic planes are going to be big enough to have shops and lounges, they will probably end up just carrying more passengers instead."

The reason we know that this is the speaker's main point is that the rest of the argument supports that idea. If I were to ask the speaker how he knows the gigantic planes will be used for stuffing on even more passengers, rather than reserving space for shops and lounges, he would say something like this: "Well, if you would have been listening, you would have heard me say that the number of passengers is expected to triple in upcoming years, and there's not enough room at airports to accommodate enough normal-sized planes."

So the first sentence is an introductory premise (there's a new crop of gigantic planes being developed), the second sentence is the conclusion (the space in the giant planes will be used for more passengers) and the third sentence is an explanatory premise (not enough space at airports to accommodate surge in passengers).

A) This is a premise, but it's not the main conclusion.

B) This is pretty much what we were looking for. It's our answer unless something else really good presents itself.

C) This is a premise, but it's not the main conclusion.

D) This one's also a premise, but it's not the main conclusion either.

E) This is speculative—it's not supported by the argument. Maybe it's true, or maybe "most" passengers will still be flying on the old planes. We don't know how many of the new planes are going to be put into service, or what percentage of passengers will be flying on the new planes. The best answer is B.

QUESTION 11:

11

Scientist: To study the comparative effectiveness of two experimental medications for athlete's foot, a representative sample of people with athlete's foot were randomly assigned to one of two groups. One group received only medication M, and the other received only medication N. The only people whose athlete's foot was cured had been given medication M.
Reporter: This means, then, that if anyone in the study had athlete's foot that was not cured, that person did not receive medication M.

Which one of the following most accurately describes the reporter's error in reasoning?

A) The reporter concludes from evidence showing only that M can cure athlete's foot that M always cures athlete's foot.
B) The reporter illicitly draws a conclusion about the population as a whole on the basis of a study conducted only on a sample of the population.
C) The reporter presumes, without providing justification, that medications M and N are available to people who have athlete's foot but did not participate in the study.
D) The reporter fails to allow for the possibility that athlete's foot may be cured even if neither of the two medications studied is taken.
E) The reporter presumes, without providing justification, that there is no sizeable subgroup of people whose athlete's foot will be cured only if they do not take medication M.

This question is either very easy or very hard. If you engage with the argument and figure out the flaw *before going to the answer choices*, then the question is very easy. If you skim the argument and then hope that the answer choices explain it to you, then the question is very hard. It's your choice. (Psst: Choose the former.)

The reporter has misinterpreted the scientist's data. The data indicates that *only* people in group M were cured. So if you were in group N, you were not cured. And if you were cured, you were in group M. But the reporter mistakenly assumes this means that *all* the people in group M were cured. That's my answer.

A) This is another way of saying what we just said, so it must be the correct answer. We'll quickly scan the rest of the answer choices just to be sure, but I'm 99% certain this will be it.
B) It's OK to draw conclusions about a population based on a representative sample. So this isn't a flaw in the reporter's reasoning.
C) This is a complete non sequitur. The reporter never says anything about anyone who was not involved in the study, or assumes anything about anyone having access to the medication. It's a bizarre answer choice. If you picked this answer, you need to slow down and pay close attention to the arguments that are being made.
D) This is close, but no cigar. I can turn this into a correct answer: "The reporter has failed to allow for the possibility that athlete's foot may not be cured for some people by a medication that cures athlete's foot for some other people." Unfortunately, that's not what the answer choice actually says.
E) This is just a nonsense jumble of words. I stopped reading after "no sizeable subgroup" because it's impossible to make an argument that the reporter assumed anything about any subgroup.

Make a Similar Argument

When presented with a flawed argument, one useful practice technique is to see if you can come up with an argument that shares the same flaw. Sometimes hearing the same logic with a subject you're comfortable with helps you identify the flaw. Here, I came up with "Only professional golfers have won the Masters in the last 50 years. So if you didn't win the Masters in the last 50 years, you must not be a professional golfer." See what you can come up with.

QUESTION 12:

Paleontologist: Plesiosauromorphs were gigantic, long-necked marine reptiles that ruled the oceans during the age of the dinosaurs. Most experts believe that plesiosauromorphs lurked and quickly ambushed their prey. However, plesiosauromorphs probably hunted by chasing their prey over long distances. Plesiosauromorph fins were quite long and thin, like the wings of birds specialized for long-distance flight.

Which one of the following is an assumption on which the paleontologist's argument depends?

A) Birds and reptiles share many physical features because they descend from common evolutionary ancestors.
B) During the age of dinosaurs, plesiosauromorphs were the only marine reptiles that had long, thin fins.
C) A gigantic marine animal would not be able to find enough food to meet the caloric requirements dictated by its body size if it did not hunt by chasing prey over long distances.
D) Most marine animals that chase prey over long distances are specialized for long-distance swimming.
E) The shape of a marine animal's fin affects the way the animal swims in the same way as the shape of a bird's wing affects the way the bird flies.

We're asked to identify an assumption on which the paleontologist's argument depends. This is a *necessary* assumption question. (Please contrast my analysis for this question with my analysis on a *sufficient* assumption question like number 9.) Necessary assumption questions ask us to identify a missing component of the author's argument. The correct answer here *must* be true in order for the paleontologist's argument to make any sense. If we can make an answer choice false without completely spoiling the paleontologist's argument, then it's not necessary for that argument.

You can't always answer necessary assumption questions in advance, but on this one we've got something to work with. The conclusion here is "Plesiosauromorphs probably hunted by chasing their prey over long distances." The only evidence that supports this assertion is the similarity between plesiosauromorph fins and the wings of birds specialized for long-distance flight. This is pretty weak evidence. The paleontologist seems to have assumed that if one animal has a feature similar to the feature of another animal, the two animals must use those characteristics in similar fashion. But that really seems like a stretch, especially when you're comparing an animal that flies to an animal that swims. We need an answer choice that points out this missing piece in the logic.

A) This is nice, and it might be true in real life, but it doesn't have to be true in order for the paleontologist's argument to make sense. If it were false (in other words, if birds and reptiles do not share many features), the paleontologist would say "So what? I'm only talking about one feature that they do, actually, share." So the paleontologist didn't rely on this as part of the argument.
B) If there are other marine reptiles besides plesiosauromorphs that had long, thin fins this wouldn't impact the paleontologist's analysis at all. So the author didn't assume that plesiosauromorphs were the only marine reptiles with long, thin fins.
C) There's simply nothing in the argument about caloric requirements. This doesn't make any difference one way or the other to the argument.
D) The paleontologist didn't make any conclusion about "most marine animals that chase prey," and presented no evidence about creatures being "specialized for long-distance swimming." This can't be it.

E) There we go! We were looking for something about a similarity in form being related to a similarity in function. Answer E spells out, clearly, the missing link in the paleontologist's logic: It connects the birds with long, thin wings to the plesiosauromorophs' long, thin fins. If E is not true, then the shape of a marine animal's fin doesn't affect the way it swims in the same way as the shape of a bird's wing affects the way the bird flies, and the paleontologist's argument is destroyed. In other words, answer E is *necessary* in order for the argument to make sense. This is the correct answer.

13

QUESTION 13:

Buying elaborate screensavers—programs that put moving images on a computer monitor to prevent damage—can cost a company far more in employee time than it saves in electricity and monitor protection. Employees cannot resist spending time playing with screensavers that flash interesting graphics across their screens.

Which one of the following most closely conforms to the principle illustrated above?

A) A school that chooses textbooks based on student preference may not get the most economical package.
B) An energy-efficient insulation system may cost more up front but will ultimately save money over the life of the house.
C) The time that it takes to have a pizza delivered may be longer than it takes to cook a complete dinner.
D) A complicated hotel security system may cost more in customer goodwill than it saves in losses by theft.
E) An electronic keyboard may be cheaper to buy than a piano but more expensive to repair.

The argument here is fairly easy to understand. Screensavers might save on electricity and monitors, but they'll cost you far more than you save because your employees won't be able to stop fiddling with them. I have nothing to argue with here because the logic is pretty sound.

The question asks us to find a similar situation. Tough to answer this one in advance, but we do know that we're looking for another illustration of the same principle. So the correct answer probably isn't going to be about computers, screensavers, employees, or even money necessarily. Rather, it's going to be some totally different illustration of something that might save in one way, but might cost you more than you save because of some unintended consequence.

A) This doesn't seem parallel to me. We need something that saves in one way but costs in another. Let's move on.
B) This is close, but it's about saving in the long run despite higher initial costs. Since the example we were given was about something that ultimately costs more than it saves, this doesn't seem like the correct answer.
C) This could be it. I think I'm going to save time by getting pizza delivered, but by the time it actually shows up I could have already finished cooking. Then again, it's not perfect because while the pizza is being cooked I can get some work done, so it might turn out to be a savings after all. I don't love this answer, but we can pick it if everything else sucks.
D) I like this better. I'm trying to save money on theft by installing a security system, but I end up shooting myself in the foot because my customers hate the hassle of the complicated system. This is better than C because C had the counterargument of "You could do other stuff while waiting for the pizza."
E) This looks like a clever trap to me. It would be the correct answer for sure if it said "but repair costs make it more costly overall"—but that's not what it says. The electronic keyboard, even with more costly repairs, could still be cheaper overall. So my answer is D.

QUESTION 14:

Music professor: Because rap musicians can work alone in a recording studio, they need not accommodate supporting musicians' wishes. Further, learning to rap is not as formal a process as learning an instrument. Thus, rap is an extremely individualistic and nontraditional musical form.

Music critic: But rap appeals to tradition by using bits of older songs. Besides, the themes and styles of rap have developed into a tradition. And successful rap musicians do not perform purely idiosyncratically but conform their work to the preferences of the public.

The music critic's response to the music professor's argument

A) challenges it by offering evidence against one of the stated premises on which its conclusion concerning rap music is based

B) challenges its conclusion concerning rap music by offering certain additional observations that the music professor does not take into account in his argument

C) challenges the grounds on which the music professor generalizes from the particular context of rap music to the broader context of musical tradition and individuality

D) challenges it by offering an alternative explanation of phenomena that the music professor cites as evidence for his thesis about rap music

E) challenges each of a group of claims about tradition and individuality in music that the music professor gives as evidence in his argument

This is a ridiculous conversation because nobody gives a shit what (probably old, probably white) music professors and music critics think about rap. They're both idiots because as everyone knows, Dr. Dre and Snoop Dogg hang out together in the studio and smoke weed while they collaborate on their beats and rhymes. *The Chronic* was hardly the product of just Dr. Dre by himself, so neither of these guys have any clue what they are talking about.

With that off my chest, I can analyze what the old white guys are actually saying. Old white guy number one (professor) concludes that rap is "extremely individualistic and nontraditional" on the thin evidence that rap musicians can work alone in the studio and don't have to use a formal process to learn. Old white guy number two (critic) disagrees with "nontraditional" because 1) rap uses bits of older songs and 2) rap has its own traditions. The critic also disagrees with "individualistic" because rappers conform to the preferences of the public. So the critic seems to completely disagree with the professor, citing different evidence from what the professor cited.

A) The critic doesn't really challenge the professor's evidence. Challenging the evidence would be more like "Actually, they can't work alone in the studio" or "Actually, learning to rap is a quite formal process." That doesn't happen here, so this can't be the answer.

B) This is pretty good. The critic cites evidence that the professor didn't seem to consider in his argument, and seems to disagree with the professor's conclusion since he starts his statement with "but." At first blush I like this answer, so I hope C–E are terrible.

C) I'm not sure exactly what this even means, but I don't think it's present in the arguments that were given. The professor's conclusion was only about rap, so I don't think he tried to "generalize from rap to the broader context of musical tradition and individuality." No way.

D) The critic didn't attempt to explain the "phenomena" that the professor cited as evidence. This would be like "They can work alone in the studio because XYZ." That's not what the critic did.

E) Nah. The music critic doesn't challenge *each* of the music professor's claims. For example, the critic doesn't challenge the claim that rap musicians perform alone in the studio. The best answer is B.

QUESTION 15:

Speaker: Like many contemporary critics, Smith argues that the true meaning of an author's statements can be understood only through insight into the author's social circumstances. But this same line of analysis can be applied to Smith's own words. Thus, if she is right we should be able, at least in part, to discern from Smith's social circumstances the "true meaning" of Smith's statements. This, in turn, suggests that Smith herself is not aware of the true meaning of her own words.

The speaker's main conclusion logically follows if which one of the following is assumed?

A) **Insight into the intended meaning of an author's work is not as important as insight into its true meaning.**
B) **Smith lacks insight into her own social circumstances.**
C) **There is just one meaning that Smith intends her work to have.**
D) **Smith's theory about the relation of social circumstances to the understanding of meaning lacks insight.**
E) **The intended meaning of an author's work is not always good evidence of its true meaning.**

> ## "Connect the Dots" for Lawyers
>
> Sufficient assumption questions can be extremely difficult for LSAT novices and extremely easy for LSAT experts. Don't panic if this question gives you fits at first. Do your best to understand this one, and the next one, and the next one. Eventually it will click. Basically, all we are doing here is connecting the premises to the conclusion. There's a gap in the argument, and we have to bridge that gap. Connecting the dots will get easier with practice.

This is a truly painful argument to read. But it's not a difficult question to answer with lots of practice. The conclusion makes no sense unless Smith does not have insight into her own social circumstances. Scanning down the answer choices, I can tell instantly that the answer is going to be B. Let me break down the argument since intuitively it doesn't make much sense.

Premise one: According to Smith, the true meaning of an author's statements can be understood only through insight into the author's social circumstances. In other words, insight into social circumstances is *necessary* in order to be able to glean an author's true meaning.

Premise two: If Smith is right, then this principle should apply to Smith as well.

Conclusion: Therefore, Smith can't understand her own statements.

No rational person would reach this particular conclusion on the basis of this particular evidence. The argument simply makes no sense. The question asks us to fix the argument. In other words, we are to identify an additional premise that, when added to the evidence, forces the conclusion to be true. To reach an answer, I asked myself "Why the hell would someone make this conclusion on this evidence?" The correct answer then appeared, fully formed, in my brain. The only possible connection between the evidence and the conclusion is that Smith has no insight into her own social circumstances. If that's true, then the premises connect directly to the conclusion. If Smith has no insight into her own social circumstances then, according to Smith's own principle, Smith shouldn't be able to understand her own statements.

A) The argument has nothing to do with whether one factor is more important or less important than another factor. This answer, if true, would not force the conclusion to be true. So it's not the answer on a sufficient assumption question.
B) This is exactly what we were looking for, so it's our answer.
C) The argument has nothing to do with the intent an author has or does not have. This answer, if true, would not force the conclusion to be true. So it's not the answer on a sufficient assumption question.
D) This just puts Smith's theory in a blender and barfs out a nonsensical jumble of words. It's an excellent example of how the answer choices are not your friend— rather, they are there to confuse you if you go in without any pre-consideration. This answer, if true, would not force the conclusion to be true. So it's not the answer on a sufficient assumption question.
E) The argument has nothing to do with the intent an author has or does not have. This answer, if true, would not force the conclusion to be true. So it's not the answer on a sufficient assumption question. B is correct.

16

QUESTION 16:

Tissue biopsies taken on patients who have undergone throat surgery show that those who snored frequently were significantly more likely to have serious abnormalities in their throat muscles than those who snored rarely or not at all. This shows that snoring can damage the throat of the snorer.

Which one of the following, if true, most strengthens the argument?

A) The study relied on the subjects' self-reporting to determine whether or not they snored frequently.

B) The patients' throat surgery was not undertaken to treat abnormalities in their throat muscles.

C) All of the test subjects were of similar age and weight and in similar states of health.

D) People who have undergone throat surgery are no more likely to snore than people who have not undergone throat surgery.

E) The abnormalities in the throat muscles discovered in the study do not cause snoring.

This question has appeared on the LSAT countless times in various forms. The author has taken evidence of a *correlation* between snoring and throat abnormalities and concluded that there must be a *causal* relationship between the two. On a list of the Ten Commandments of the LSAT, this would be very high on the list: **Correlation Does Not Prove Causation!** This principle is tested over, and over, and over on the LSAT. In fact, I don't think I've ever seen a single LSAT that did not have some variation on this flaw.

The author has concluded that snoring causes throat damage, and if I were in court, I would attack that conclusion on two different fronts. First, how does the author know that some other factor isn't confounding his analysis? If any other factor causes throat damage—for example, if smoking causes both snoring and throat damage—then the author's explanation is seriously weakened. Second, how does the author know that throat damage doesn't cause snoring? If throat damage does cause snoring, then the author's argument is backward. Proving this would devastate the argument.

To strengthen the author's argument, I would reverse my two challenges above. (On the LSAT, defense can be the best offense.) If the author can prove that there is no other cause of throat damage besides snoring, then his argument is strengthened because one potential avenue of attack has been closed off. If the author can prove that throat damage does not cause snoring, that closes off a different avenue of attack. Either of these would be great defensive strengtheners.

A) This, if true, could only weaken the argument. We're looking for a strengthener.

B) It's not relevant why people decided to undertake throat surgery. What's relevant is the relationship between snoring and throat abnormalities.

C) This, if true, might only weaken the author's argument because it would indicate that the sample wasn't diverse.

D) The relationship between throat surgery and snoring is not relevant. Everyone in the study had had throat surgery.

E) This exactly matches one of our predictions. If this is true, then the author knows for sure that his argument is not reversed. This is a defensive strengthener, and is the correct answer.

Two Ways to Miss an Easy Question

If you didn't recognize the flaw in the reasoning while you were reading the argument, then one of two things is probably happening: Either you just haven't practiced enough or you're not reading carefully enough.

Preparing for the LSAT consists of falling into all of the common traps a time or two so that you'll learn to recognize them in advance. The flawed pattern of reasoning here is *very* common. If you practice enough, you should see it coming.

If you have been preparing for some time, but you still missed it, you might just not be reading closely enough. Remember that a significant portion of the logical reasoning questions contain their answer in the argument itself. The answer choices are not your friend, so try to answer the questions *before* going to the answer choices.

QUESTION 17:

One should never sacrifice one's health in order to acquire money, for without health, happiness is not obtainable.

The conclusion of the argument follows logically if which one of the following is assumed?

A) Money should be acquired only if its acquisition will not make happiness unobtainable.
B) In order to be happy one must have either money or health.
C) Health should be valued only as a precondition for happiness.
D) Being wealthy is, under certain conditions, conducive to unhappiness.
E) Health is more conducive to happiness than wealth is.

The entire argument consists of one premise and one conclusion. The premise is "without health, happiness is unobtainable." In other words, health is *necessary* for happiness. The conclusion is "one should not sacrifice health in order to acquire money." The question asks us to bridge the gap between the premise and the conclusion. It's yet another *sufficient* assumption question.

So how do we get from the premise to the conclusion? One clue is to look for the new piece of information that is mentioned only in the conclusion and nowhere else. That's right—it's money. What does money have to do with anything? We were talking about health and happiness, but the conclusion then went to money, which seemed totally unrelated.

Let's play along. In order to get from "health is necessary for happiness" to "one should not sacrifice health in order to acquire money" we need to bridge the gap between happiness and money. If we were to say "the only reason to acquire money would be to acquire happiness" then I think that would do it. Because if that is true (and if it is still true that health is necessary for happiness) then sacrificing health to acquire money is completely futile. So that's our prediction: "The only reason to acquire money would be to acquire happiness."

A) This is a bit different from what we predicted, but it does contain the key elements of money and happiness. And with a bit of reflection, we can see that it's exactly what's needed. If Answer A is true, then sacrificing health (which would make happiness impossible) would not be an allowable thing to do in the pursuit of money. This has to be the answer.
B) This has the key terms but it just doesn't connect the dots in the way A does. Even if Answer B is true, we would still be allowed to sacrifice our health (and thereby our happiness) in pursuit of money because there's no premise that says we should be happy.
C) There's nothing about money here, so this can't possibly be it.
D) This is too weakly stated to be the correct answer for a sufficient assumption question. What are the "certain conditions"? Unless we know that, we don't know if this rule even applies.
E) This has the key terms but it doesn't quite get there like A does. Even if Answer E is true, we would still be allowed to sacrifice our health for money because there's nothing that says we should be happy. It's gotta be A.......

QUESTION 18:

Vanessa: All computer code must be written by a pair of programmers working at a single workstation. This is needed to prevent programmers from writing idiosyncratic code that can be understood only by the original programmer.
Jo: Most programming projects are kept afloat by the best programmers on the team, who are typically at least 100 times more productive than the worst. Since they generally work best when they work alone, the most productive programmers must be allowed to work by themselves.

Each of the following assignments of computer programmers is consistent both with the principle expressed by Vanessa and with the principle expressed by Jo EXCEPT:

A) Olga and Kensuke are both programmers of roughly average productivity who feel that they are more productive when working alone. They have been assigned to work together at a single workstation.
B) John is experienced but is not among the most productive programmers on the team. He has been assigned to mentor Tyrone, a new programmer who is not yet very productive. They are to work together at a single workstation.
C) Although not among the most productive programmers on the team, Chris is more productive than Jennifer. They have been assigned to work together at a single workstation.
D) Yolanda is the most productive programmer on the team. She has been assigned to work with Mike, who is also very productive. They are to work together at the same workstation.
E) Kevin and Amy both have a reputation for writing idiosyncratic code; neither is unusually productive. They have been assigned to work together at the same workstation.

Before I even get to Jo's statement, I'm arguing with Vanessa. Why do programmers have to work in pairs to avoid "idiosyncratic code"? Can't properly trained programmers work solo and follow accepted programming procedures? Can't they comment their code so that other programmers can understand what's happening?

Jo, unfortunately, doesn't really address Vanessa's argument. Instead, Jo just says that projects "are kept afloat" by the most productive programmers, who must work alone.

This is a unique question type. Four of the answers (the incorrect ones) are "consistent with" both Vanessa's and Jo's rules. This means that one answer (the correct one) will violate one or both of the rules. There is no way to answer this question in advance. We're forced to evaluate each answer choice and identify the one that breaks a rule.

A) Vanessa would like this because the programmers are working in a pair. Jo wouldn't mind this because she's only concerned with the most productive programmers, and Olga and Kensuke are just average. This one passes both rules, so it's not the answer.
B) Again, Vanessa would be happy because two programmers are working together. Jo wouldn't care, because neither of them are the most productive members of the team. So this one also passes both rules, and is also not the correct answer.
C) Same as A and B.
D) This would cause a problem for Jo, because Jo wants the most productive programmers to work solo. This is the correct answer because it breaks Jo's rule.
E) Same as A, B, and C.

QUESTION 19:

In West Calverton, most pet stores sell exotic birds, and most of those that sell exotic birds also sell tropical fish. However, any pet store there that sells tropical fish but not exotic birds does sell gerbils; and no independently owned pet stores in West Calverton sell gerbils.

If the statements above are true, which one of the following must be true?

A) Most pet stores in West Calverton that are not independently owned do not sell exotic birds.
B) No pet stores in West Calverton that sell tropical fish and exotic birds sell gerbils.
C) Some pet stores in West Calverton that sell gerbils also sell exotic birds.
D) No independently owned pet store in West Calverton sells tropical fish but not exotic birds.
E) Any independently owned pet store in West Calverton that does not sell tropical fish sells exotic birds.

This is a nasty question because it has arbitrary rules that are hard to hold in the head and, simultaneously, it's also a very hard question to diagram. So let's just make some notes that summarize what we know.

Stores that sell exotic birds: most of them also sell tropical fish.
Stores that sell tropical fish but not exotic birds: all of them sell gerbils.
Stores that sell gerbils: none of them are independently owned.
    Combining the second and third premises we can see that no independently owned store can sell tropical fish but not exotic birds. (Because if they did, they'd have to sell gerbils, but no independently owned store sells gerbils.) Hopefully this is one of the answer choices so we can choose it and get the hell out of here: "no independently owned store can sell tropical fish but not exotic birds."

A) Not what we're looking for.
B) Not what we're looking for.
C) Not what we're looking for.
D) Exactly what we were looking for. This is our answer.
E) Guess what? Not what we're looking for.

QUESTION 20:

Astronomer: Earlier estimates of the distances of certain stars from Earth would mean that these stars are about 1 billion years older than the universe itself, an impossible scenario. My estimates of the distances indicate that these stars are much farther away than previously thought. And the farther away the stars are, the greater their intrinsic brightness must be, given their appearance to us on Earth. So the new estimates of these stars' distances from Earth help resolve the earlier conflict between the ages of these stars and the age of the universe.

Which one of the following, if true, most helps to explain why the astronomer's estimates of the stars' distances from Earth help resolve the earlier conflict between the ages of these stars and the age of the universe?

A) The stars are the oldest objects yet discovered in the universe.
B) The younger the universe is, the more bright stars it is likely to have.
C) The brighter a star is, the younger it is.
D) How bright celestial objects appear to be depends on how far away from the observer they are.
E) New telescopes allow astronomers to see a greater number of distant stars.

This is another tough argument to follow. The astronomer starts out by saying that earlier estimates of the distances of certain stars would mean that the stars must be 1 billion years older than the universe itself, which would be impossible. (Nothing can be older than the universe.) So, the astronomer implies in the first sentence, the estimates of these distances must be wrong. In the second sentence, the astronomer says she has made new estimates that indicate that these stars are much farther away than the previous estimates. The third sentence says that since the astronomer's new estimates put the stars at greater distance, they must be brighter than previously thought. (Because they appear at a certain fixed brightness to us here on earth, and presumably brightness would diminish the further a body is from the observer.) I'm still on board with the argument at this point—the astronomer is making logical sense to me so far.

The ultimate conclusion of the argument, however, is "So the new estimates of these stars' distances from Earth help resolve the earlier conflict between the ages of these stars and the age of the universe." Many readers are going to fall off the train at this point—and they should! Why would the astronomer's new estimates about distance and brightness help explain anything about the ages of the stars? There is a big gap in the logic here. The question asks us to bridge this gap.

Remember, the initial problem with the estimates of the stars' ages was that the stars were estimated to be older than the universe itself. To reconcile this impossibility, either the stars have to get younger or the universe has to get older. The astronomer doesn't seem to have presented any evidence that might suggest the universe is older than previously thought. It's the ages of the stars that seem to be in question, not the age of the universe. So we have to use the astronomer's evidence to make the stars get younger. The astronomer said that the stars were farther away and brighter than previously thought. So maybe the missing link is "younger stars are brighter," or "older stars are dimmer." If that were true, and if the astronomer's estimates about the distance and brightness of the stars are correct, then the astronomer's estimates about distance and brightness would help resolve the earlier conflict between the ages of the stars and the age of the universe.

A) This isn't what we're looking for. Until I've seen all five answer choices, I won't even spend time figuring out what this answer choice means.
B) Again, this isn't what we're looking for.
C) This is exactly what we predicted, and it's our answer.
D) Answer C was right on target, so I only read this answer choice to make sure it's not a better version of C. Since it's something different, we can quickly dismiss it.
E) Same as D. Answer C is our guy.

Predicting Answers in Advance

We ended up answering this question the same way we answered number 19. We predicted the answer, almost precisely, before looking at the answer choices. You can't do this on every question—some questions require a process of elimination. But when you see an answer that exactly matches your prediction, trust your intuition. Here, it doesn't matter what the wrong answers say. They are wrong because C is so right.

QUESTION 21:

Most large nurseries sell raspberry plants primarily to commercial raspberry growers and sell only plants that are guaranteed to be disease-free. However, the shipment of raspberry plants that Johnson received from Wally's Plants carried a virus that commonly afflicts raspberries.

Which one of the following is most strongly supported by the information above?

A) If Johnson is a commercial raspberry grower and Wally's Plants is not a large nursery, then the shipment of raspberry plants that Johnson received was probably guaranteed to be disease-free.
B) Johnson is probably not a commercial raspberry grower if the shipment of raspberry plants that Johnson received from Wally's Plants was not entirely as it was guaranteed to be.
C) If Johnson is not a commercial raspberry grower, then Wally's Plants is probably not a large nursery.
D) Wally's Plants is probably not a large, well-run nursery if it sells its raspberry plants primarily to commercial raspberry growers.
E) If Wally's Plants is a large nursery, then the raspberry plants that Johnson received in the shipment were probably not entirely as they were guaranteed to be.

The first thing to notice about this question is that there is no conclusion—it's just a set of premises. The second thing to notice is there's not a lot of certainty here. The entire argument is qualified by the phrase "*most* large nurseries." So even if Wally's Plants is a large nursery, we don't know anything for sure. These premises say a lot, but prove nothing.

The question, fortunately, doesn't ask us to identify anything that has been proven by the premises. Instead, we are asked to identify something that is "strongly supported" by the evidence. I'm not sure we can predict this one in advance, but let's give it a quick try before looking at the answer choices. We know that Wally's has sold plants carrying a virus. Since most large nurseries sell only plants that are guaranteed to be disease-free, the facts seem to suggest that Wally's is probably not a large nursery. That's not certain, but it's at least weakly suggested by the evidence.

A) This answer starts out horribly, because whether or not Johnson is a commercial raspberry grower is pretty much irrelevant. Furthermore, if Wally's is *not* a large nursery then we know less not more (since the first premise was about large nurseries.) I'm having a hard time seeing how this nonsense could be supported by the given facts, so let's move on and look for something better.
B) I don't think this is it either. We can't conclude that Johnson is not a commercial grower based on the behavior of Wally's Plants.
C) This is weakly supported by the evidence. I don't love it though, because maybe Wally's is the one of the large nurseries that does sell to non-commercial growers. And furthermore, just because the plants carried a virus doesn't mean they weren't guaranteed to be disease-free. Let's see if we can find something better.
D) The fatal flaw in this answer choice is the phrase "well-run." The quality of management was not mentioned anywhere in the evidence, so this can't be the answer.
E) This is the best of a bad lot. If Wally's is, in fact, a large nursery, then it's probable that Wally's offers a disease-free guarantee. And the plants Wally's sold to Johnson were definitely diseased, so if Wally's has the guarantee, which is probable, then the plants definitely weren't entirely as they were guaranteed to be. I'm not in love with this answer, but it's a bit less speculative than C was. Our answer is E.

22

QUESTION 22:

Drug company manager: Our newest product is just not selling. One way to save it would be a new marketing campaign. This would not guarantee success, but it is one chance to save the product, so we should try it.

Which one of the following, if true, most seriously weakens the manager's argument?

A) The drug company has invested heavily in its newest product, and losses due to this product would be harmful to the company's profits.
B) Many new products fail whether or not they are supported by marketing campaigns.
C) The drug company should not undertake a new marketing campaign for its newest product if the campaign has no chance to succeed.
D) Undertaking a new marketing campaign would endanger the drug company's overall position by necessitating cutbacks in existing marketing campaigns.
E) Consumer demand for the drug company's other products has been strong in the time since the company's newest product was introduced.

The drug company manager seems to be saying, "We're probably screwed anyway, but we should try anything we can to see if we can save this product." If I were the CEO of the company, I would have some questions for the manager (before I fired him for incompetence). First, how much is this going to cost? Second, even though I understand the marketing campaign is not guaranteed to succeed, I'd at least like to know what the probability of success might be. Third, if it succeeds, how much money would we be likely to make from sales of this product? (Would we recover the costs of the marketing campaign? More?)

We're asked to weaken the manager's argument, so we want something that makes it easier to fire the manager. If we discover that the marketing campaign would cost more than we would possibly make in sales, even if it succeeds, then the manager is clearly fired for recommending we go ahead with the campaign.

A) This might strengthen the argument, but wouldn't weaken it. We need a weakener.
B) This doesn't do anything to the argument one way or the other.
C) This isn't relevant because we don't *know* that the marketing campaign has no chance to succeed.
D) This would suck pretty hard for the manager. If this were true, we could say to the manager, "So you want me to authorize a new campaign that is not guaranteed to succeed, even though it will require cutbacks in our other campaigns, thereby endangering our overall position? You're an idiot and you're fired." This is our answer.
E) This wouldn't change our opinion about whether we should do the new campaign or not, so it can't be the answer.

23

QUESTION 23:

Consumer advocate: TMD, a pesticide used on peaches, shows no effects on human health when it is ingested in the amount present in the per capita peach consumption in this country. But while 80 percent of the population eat no peaches, others, including small children, consume much more than the national average, and thus ingest disproportionately large amounts of TMD. So even though the use of TMD on peaches poses minimal risk to most of the population, it has not been shown to be an acceptable practice.

Which one of the following principles, if valid, most helps to justify the consumer advocate's argumentation?

A) The possibility that more data about a pesticide's health effects might reveal previously unknown risks at low doses warrants caution in assessing that pesticide's overall risks.
B) The consequences of using a pesticide are unlikely to be acceptable when a majority of the population is likely to ingest it.
C) Use of a pesticide is acceptable only if it is used for its intended purpose and the pesticide has been shown not to harm any portion of the population.
D) Society has a special obligation to protect small children from pesticides unless average doses received by the population are low and have not been shown to be harmful to children's health.
E) Measures taken to protect the population from a harm sometimes turn out to be the cause of a more serious harm to certain segments of the population.

The consumer advocate's reasoning here is fairly sound. The advocate acknowledges that TMD shows no effects on human health when it is ingested in "the amount present in the per capita peach consumption in this country." The problem, says the advocate, is that 80% of the population eats no peaches at all, so the other 20% of the population eats much more than the average per capita amount of peaches.

Here's how that works (feel free to skip this paragraph if you already get it): Let's say the average per capita consumption is 10 peaches per year per person. If there are 10 total people in the population, that's a total of 100 peaches. But 80 percent of the population (8 people) eats no peaches at all, which means the remaining 20 percent of the population (2 people) has to eat all 100 peaches. The per capita consumption of peaches is only 10, but the *average person who eats peaches* eats 50.

This worries the consumer advocate. The per capita level of TMD consumed through peaches is OK, but the average consumed per peach eater hasn't yet been proven to be safe. From this, the consumer advocate concludes "the use of TMD on peaches has not been shown to be an acceptable practice."

I'm inclined to go along with the advocate's logic. However, the question tells us that there's a missing principle that, if added to the advocate's logic, will "justify the argumentation." On the LSAT, "justify" means "prove." So we're looking to tighten up the logic even further. The correct answer should *force* the advocate's conclusion to be true. If anything is missing, it's something like "per capita data is not sufficient to prove safety." If that were true, then the use of TMD on peaches would not have been shown to be acceptable. Let's see.

A) The advocate seems to accept that TMD is safe at low doses. It's the people gorging on peaches, and thereby ingesting higher doses of TMD, that worry her. So I don't think this is it.
B) The advocate isn't worried about "a majority of the population" ingesting TMD. She's worried about the minority who actually eat peaches. No way.
C) The first part of this answer, "used for intended purpose" is irrelevant. But the last half of the answer might help the consumer advocate, because it makes it *necessary* that a pesticide has been shown not to harm *any portion* of the population before it can be accepted for use. Since the 20 percent of the population that eat peaches consume a higher dose of TMD than has been proven safe, if C is true then the use of the pesticide is definitely not acceptable. This is a strange answer since the first half is irrelevant, but the second half of the answer is on target. It's the best one so far.
D) The advocate isn't worried about "average doses." The average doses are just fine. The problem is that some people are getting far more than the average dose. So this is out.
E) This might be true, but it doesn't do anything to the advocate's argument. The word "sometimes" here is a big clue. On a "justify" the reasoning question we are looking for something bold and strongly stated. A qualifier like "sometimes" makes answer E ineffectual. The best answer is C.

24

QUESTION 24:

Legal commentator: The goal of a recently enacted law that bans smoking in workplaces is to protect employees from secondhand smoke. But the law is written in such a way that it cannot be interpreted as ever prohibiting people from smoking in their own homes.

The statements above, if true, provide a basis for rejecting which one of the following claims?

A) The law will be interpreted in a way that is inconsistent with the intentions of the legislators who supported it.

B) Supporters of the law believe that it will have a significant impact on the health of many workers.

C) The law offers no protection from secondhand smoke for people outside of their workplaces.

D) Most people believe that smokers have a fundamental right to smoke in their own homes.

E) The law will protect domestic workers such as housecleaners from secondhand smoke in their workplaces.

This is fairly straightforward. The legal commentator offers two premises with no conclusion. The first premise is that a new law bans smoking in workplaces, with a stated purpose of protecting employees from secondhand smoke. The second premise is that the law cannot be interpreted as ever prohibiting people from smoking in their own homes.

Before we look at the answer choices, ask yourself how these two facts fit together. Apparently, there is a conflict between the stated goal of the law and a business owner who smokes in his own home office. Since the law says the law cannot ever prohibit people from smoking at home, it seems as if employees of a smoker who work in that smoker's home are left unprotected by the law.

The question asks us to find a claim that would be "rejected" on the basis of the facts. In other words, we're looking for something that must be false according to the facts. It's probably going to be something about the protection of employees of a smoker who work in that smoker's home, because we've already identified that as a potential sticking point given the premises.

A) There's no evidence that the law will not be interpreted consistently with the intentions of the legislators, so this is out.

B) The given facts don't say anything about what the supporters of the law do or don't believe.

C) The facts didn't tell us anything about whether or not there are protections for people *outside* their workplaces. This could be true or false, and we're looking for something that *must* be false.

D) There's nothing in the facts that indicate what "most people believe." No way.

E) This is exactly what we were looking for. The law cannot protect *domestic* workers such as housecleaners from secondhand smoke in their workplaces, because to do so the law would have to force employers not to smoke in their own homes, which the facts say is not allowed. Our answer is E, and we saw it coming.

QUESTION 25:

University president: Our pool of applicants has been shrinking over the past few years. One possible explanation of this unwelcome phenomenon is that we charge too little for tuition and fees. Prospective students and their parents conclude that the quality of education they would receive at this institution is not as high as that offered by institutions with higher tuition. So, if we want to increase the size of our applicant pool, we need to raise our tuition and fees.

The university president's argument requires the assumption that

A) the proposed explanation for the decline in applications applies in this case

B) the quality of a university education is dependent on the amount of tuition charged by the university

C) an increase in tuition and fees at the university would guarantee a larger applicant pool

D) there is no additional explanation for the university's shrinking applicant pool

E) the amount charged by the university for tuition has not increased in recent years

Yet another stupid argument. The university president concludes that her shrinking applicant pool is the result of tuition and fees that are too LOW?! Yes, yes, I agree that some snobby people might be turned off by low tuition because what they really want to do is pay up for some conspicuous consumption, rather than actually learn anything. (I'm sure that some rich kids end up in a crappy Kaplan LSAT class, rather than one of my better, cheaper classes for this very reason.) Anyway, even if this were true, wouldn't a reasonable person think that perhaps other students would be *attracted* by those same low fees and tuition? The university president's argument only makes sense if more kids are turned off by low fees than are turned on by low fees. This is an assumption required by the argument, (a *necessary* assumption) and I'm confident it's going to be almost exactly the answer.

A) I don't even know what "this case" is supposed to mean. Let's look for something better.

B) The argument doesn't require anything regarding actual quality. Perceived quality is more the issue, and perceived quality may or may not be related to actual quality.

C) This would strengthen the argument, but "guarantee" is way too strong. The university president didn't claim that her genius plan was *sufficient* to attract more applicants. Rather, she said it was *necessary*.

D) This is attractive, but again, it likely proves too much. The university president's argument is compatible with possible other factors. For example, imagine that the school is located in a shitty neighborhood (like my *alma mater*, UC Hastings). Surely this scares away some applicants. This could be true without disproving the university president's argument about the level of fees and tuition. This one doesn't seem likely.

E) What? The tuition could have increased over recent years and still be too low. So there's no way this can be the answer.

So ... that's all of them. What next? Having eliminated all five answers here, we are forced to choose the best of a bad lot. I have articulated fatal flaws on all of B, C, D, and E, so I have to reconsider the only remaining candidate. A didn't make a lot of sense at first blush, but you could argue that it has to be true in order for the argument to make sense. If the proposed explanation (students are scared off by low fees) does *not* apply in this case, then the university president's argument is ruined. Therefore, the president has necessarily assumed that the explanation does apply in this case. A is our answer, but there's no way I would ever have gotten there before eliminating all five answers and reconsidering. Tough question.

26

QUESTION 26:

Editorial: It has been suggested that private, for-profit companies should be hired to supply clean drinking water to areas of the world where it is unavailable now. But water should not be supplied by private companies. After all, clean water is essential for human health, and the purpose of a private company is to produce profit, not to promote health.

Which one of the following principles, if valid, would most help to justify the reasoning in the editorial?

A) A private company should not be allowed to supply a commodity that is essential to human health unless that commodity is also supplied by a government agency.

B) If something is essential for human health and private companies are unwilling or unable to supply it, then it should be supplied by a government agency.

C) Drinking water should never be supplied by an organization that is not able to consistently supply clean, safe water.

D) The mere fact that something actually promotes human health is not sufficient to show that its purpose is to promote health.

E) If something is necessary for human health, then it should be provided by an organization whose primary purpose is the promotion of health.

The conclusion is "water should not be supplied by private companies." We know this because the next sentence seems to be evidence in support of this statement, but here's the trick: The word "should" is a common indicator of a conclusion. The evidence in support of this conclusion is "clean water is essential for human health" and "the purpose of a private company is to produce profit, not to promote health." The problem with this line of reasoning is that capitalism, even if it's really just a bunch of greedy bastards, can still turn out good stuff. Steve Jobs might have been the antichrist, and even if all he wanted to do was make money to fund Armageddon, I wouldn't care because I love my Mac and my iPhone.

The question asks us to "help justify the reasoning in the editorial." So we have to try to help the argument. I'm guessing that something like "If your purpose is not to promote health, then you can't promote health" would definitely do it. But something even broader would also work, like "You can only promote things that you intend to promote," or the even grander "Ends can only match intentions and nothing else."

This "Should" Be the Conclusion

An example of the word "should" being used to indicate the conclusion of an argument: "*You shouldn't go to law school. Law school is insanely expensive. Law school is criminally boring. Most lawyers have miserable jobs and no lives. Most lawyers make way less money than you probably think.*" OK, what was the conclusion of that argument? Yep, the part with the "should."

A) We don't know anything about what government agencies do, so this can't help or hurt the argument. No way.

B) Who said private companies aren't willing to supply water? This is out.

C) Who said private companies can't consistently supply clean, safe water? Maybe that was assumed by the argument, but it wasn't stated. If it was stated as fact, then C would be a great answer. But it was never stated, so there's no way C can be the answer.

D) Not what we're looking for. This is close, but backward. We want "If you don't intend something, then you can't do it." Answer D is kinda the reverse of that.

E) There we go. It's not exactly what we wanted, but it's the closest. If this is true, then we shouldn't let private companies provide our water since their purpose is not to promote health. E is our answer.

SECTION
THREE

Analytical Reasoning (Logic Games)

(Or: Breaking It Down)

On games, just like the rest of the LSAT, you have to slow down in order to speed up. First, the good news: Hardly anybody completes all four games. So our goal here is to slow down and focus on accuracy.

Unlike the rest of the LSAT, where often you have to pick the best of a bad bunch of answers, every question on the logic games has a single, objectively correct answer. There is no picking the "best" answer on the logic games. Rather, there are four terrible answers that you hate and one perfect answer that you love. Focus on answering the questions with 100% certainty. For starters, see if you can just get every answer right on a single game. If you can do this in 35 minutes, you're on the right track. Next, see if you can do two games perfectly in 35 minutes. Believe it or not, that would put you well ahead of the average test taker. If you can do three games perfectly, you'll be in the top 90 percent. But you have to walk before you can run.

My general process for Logic Games is as follows:

1. **Read through the entire scenario and all of the rules before doing anything else.** That lets you get the lay of the land before you start messing up the page. Remember that there is no scratch paper allowed, so have a sharp pencil, write small, and think before you write.

2. **Take plenty of time to understand exactly what each rule means, no more and no less.** Sometimes a single rule will have three pieces of information in it. For example, a rule might say "B must go before A and after C, but can't go fourth." There are really three rules here. (1. B before A; 2. B after C; 3. B can't go fourth.) If you miss any one of these rules, you'll struggle with the game. Conversely, sometimes a rule will mean *less* than you think it means at first blush. For example, the rule might say "A, B, C, D, and E are available for interviews." This does NOT mean that each of these people must interview! Look for another rule that says "Each candidate must interview exactly once," or "there will be five interviews and no candidate can interview twice." If these rules are not present,

then it's possible that one or more of the candidates might not interview at all, and/or one or more candidates might interview more than once. The slightest mistake can ruin the entire game, so read carefully, and absolutely do not rush.

3. **Make a diagram that incorporates as much information about the game as possible.** Sometimes, this will be a diagram that is exactly like something you've seen on a previous game. Frequently, you'll be able to use a diagram similar to a game you've seen before, but you'll have to make some minor tweaks. Occasionally, you'll have to invent something entirely new. But never fear: You'll be equipped to do this once you've practiced these methods.

4. **As you diagram, take the time to consider the rules not only alone, but also in the context of the other rules.** The big prep companies will call this "making inferences" like some kind of magical process. But all we're really doing is writing down shit we know for sure. Usually, the first "inferences" come from simply combining two rules together. For example, if A comes before B and there are only seven spots, then A can't go last, because there would be no room left for B. This isn't rocket science. (Hey, B can't go first either, because where would A go?! I'm a genius.) Any time you learn something for sure, no matter how small, write it down. Like a porta-potty at a rock concert, little things will add up fast.

5. **Remember that more powerful inferences come from combining three rules together, or from combining a rule with an inference, or from combining two inferences together.** Every time you make a new inference, you get to consider that inference in light of everything else you know about the game, and frequently you'll be able to make *another* inference. (Which might lead to another, and another ...) Don't short-circuit this process by going to the questions too soon. Always remember that the questions are designed to confuse you! It's much better to invest the time up front in a solid solution rather than frantically trying to answer the questions without having a good foundation. Some of what you're writing down at this stage will directly answer some of the questions you'll see later.

Be a Pencil Pusher

Don't be afraid to take action. Each mark you make won't be an earth-shattering revelation, especially not at the beginning. The point is to simply start writing down the things you know for sure. Start by writing down your list of variables. Does this solve the game immediately? Of course not. But it gets you moving in the right direction, which is much better than freezing up and doing nothing at all.

6. **Move on to the questions when—and only when—you're ready.** "OK, but how do I know when it's time to go to the questions?" Every class asks me this question, and my answer is always the same: Only you can really tell, through lots and lots of practice. The truth is that every game is different, and some games allow more inferences than others. Sometimes, I'll invest five or six minutes before going to the questions. On other games, I'll feel like I've learned all I can after a minute or two and go ahead to the questions. Personally, if I get stuck for 45-60 seconds without making any new inferences then I'm probably ready to proceed to the questions.

Solitaire Logic

Making inferences is like playing solitaire. You're only stuck in solitaire when you go through the entire deck without doing anything new. Every time you place even a single card, you get to go back through the whole deck to see what new possibilities have opened up. Tiny moves can have huge significance! Don't give up or panic too soon.

I realize this isn't a very satisfactory answer, but it's the truth. The logic games are partially art and partially science. You'll need to practice, practice, practice on the games until you get a feel for it. The payoff can be huge. I've never met a single student who couldn't eventually make a plus-5 or plus-6 question leap on the Logic Games. It's the most learnable section of the test. And it's also the most fun.

Game One

A motel operator is scheduling appointments to start up services at a new motel. Appointments for six services—gas, landscaping, power, satellite, telephone, and water—will be scheduled, one appointment per day for the next six days.

The schedule for the appointments is subject to the following conditions:

The water appointment must be scheduled for an earlier day than the landscaping appointment.
The power appointment must be scheduled for an earlier day than both the gas and satellite appointments.
The appointments scheduled for the second and third days cannot be for either gas, satellite, or telephone.
The telephone appointment cannot be scheduled for the sixth day.

Game One Explanation (Questions 1-6)

By the time you are ready to take the LSAT, your eyes should light up when you see a game like this. All we're asked to do here is to put six things in order. There are no ties, nothing can go twice, and nothing can be left out. So all we have to do is figure out which order the six things go in. It doesn't get simpler than this on the logic games. I'll start by listing my variables and making a picture of where they'll end up going:

G L P S T W __ __ __ __ __ __

The rules aren't much harder to understand. The first rule simply looks like this:

W——L

The second rule:

$$P \diagdown \begin{matrix} G \\ S \end{matrix}$$

If the first and second rules had any variables in common, I'd immediately be looking to link these two rules together. Here, we have no such luck.

The third rule just specifies some placements that will _not_ work. So I'll go ahead and incorporate that into my drawing:

$$\begin{matrix} \_ & \_ & \_ & \_ & \_ & \_ \\ & \cancel{G} & \cancel{G} & & & \\ & \cancel{S} & \cancel{S} & & & \\ & \cancel{T} & \cancel{T} & & & \end{matrix}$$

The fourth rule also tells me a placement that will _not_ work. I'll add that as well:

$$\begin{matrix} \_ & \_ & \_ & \_ & \_ & \_ \\ & \cancel{G} & \cancel{G} & & & \cancel{T} \\ & \cancel{S} & \cancel{S} & & & \\ & \cancel{T} & \cancel{T} & & & \end{matrix}$$

We've made a good start. We've understood all the rules. We haven't missed anything, and we haven't misinterpreted anything. But we haven't learned anything new about how the game works, either. Lots of LSAT books will tell you that what you need to do now is "make inferences." Many students think "making inferences" is some sort of mystical process that involves immense effort, huge leaps of intuition, and possibly jamming yourself into the lotus position. Fortunately, that is not how it works. The logic games are basically just simple games of Solitaire or Sudoku. Relax.

Solitaire and Sudoku are games of baby steps. Same thing here. We're going to make tiny moves, and each tiny move might open up one or more other tiny moves. Let's see.

Now, watch carefully so you don't miss the gigantic intuitive leap I'm about to make. The first rule says W has to go before L. This means L can't go first. No shit, right? But this is something that we know for sure. That means we need to write it down:

$$\underset{\substack{\cancel{L} \\ \cancel{S} \\ \cancel{T}}}{} \quad \underset{\substack{\cancel{G} \\ \cancel{S} \\ \cancel{T}}}{} \quad \underset{\substack{\cancel{G} \\ \cancel{S} \\ \cancel{T}}}{} \quad \underline{} \quad \underline{} \quad \underset{\cancel{T}}{}$$

Believe it or not, that's our first inference. Later inferences will (we hope) build on this first inference. Baby steps. Our next baby step is also a result of the "W before L" rule. Just like L can't go first, W can't go last. Let's add that:

$$\underset{\substack{\cancel{L} \\ \cancel{S} \\ \cancel{T}}}{} \quad \underset{\substack{\cancel{G} \\ \cancel{S} \\ \cancel{T}}}{} \quad \underset{\substack{\cancel{G} \\ \cancel{S} \\ \cancel{T}}}{} \quad \underline{} \quad \underline{} \quad \underset{\substack{\cancel{T} \\ W}}{}$$

OK, let's turn our attention to the "P before G and S" rule. If P has two variables that must go behind it, then how could it go in either of the last two spots? It can't. We know this for sure, so we have to write it down:

$$\underset{\substack{\cancel{L} \\ \cancel{S} \\ \cancel{T}}}{} \quad \underset{\substack{\cancel{G} \\ \cancel{S} \\ \cancel{T}}}{} \quad \underset{\substack{\cancel{G} \\ \cancel{S} \\ \cancel{T}}}{} \quad \underline{} \quad \underset{\cancel{P}}{} \quad \underset{\substack{\cancel{T} \\ W \\ \cancel{P}}}{}$$

Still on the same rule, G can't go first (because it has to go after P) and S also can't go first, for the same reason:

$$\underset{\substack{\cancel{L} \\ \cancel{G} \\ \cancel{S}}}{} \quad \underset{\substack{\cancel{G} \\ \cancel{S} \\ \cancel{T}}}{} \quad \underset{\substack{\cancel{G} \\ \cancel{S} \\ \cancel{T}}}{} \quad \underline{} \quad \underset{\cancel{P}}{} \quad \underset{\substack{\cancel{T} \\ W \\ \cancel{P}}}{}$$

OK, we've made some moves, so now we need to consider those moves in light of the other stuff we already knew. Let's think about G and S for a second. We already knew, because of the third rule, that neither G nor S could go second or third. But we just made an inference that they also can't go first. So where *can* they go? Well, I suppose they have to slide into the fourth through six slots. This doesn't leave a lot of room for maneuvering—and that's a good thing! If we are tasked with figuring out the order, we want less flexibility, not more. We're going to want to keep an eye on G and S going forward, because they don't have many options.

It's also worth noticing that the first, second, third, and last spots all have three variables that can't go in those spots. We'll keep an eye on these spots as well.

I don't see any more moves we can make. Is it time to answer some questions? Possibly. There's a little bit of art mixed in with the science here. You'll need to do *a lot* of practice on the logic games so that you can develop a feel for when you should move on to the questions. On some games, one thing will lead to another and I'll spend 5 or 6 minutes making tons of inferences and sketching out scenarios before I even look at the first question. I like it when this happens, because it usually makes the questions very easy. On other games, like this one, I will make a couple inferences and then get stuck. When I get stuck, it's usually time to answer the questions. Let's see.

QUESTION 1:

Which one of the following is an acceptable schedule of appointments, listed in order from earliest to latest?

A) gas, water, power, telephone, landscaping, satellite
B) power, water, landscaping, gas, satellite, telephone
C) telephone, power, landscaping, gas, water, satellite
D) telephone, water, power, landscaping, gas, satellite
E) water, telephone, power, gas, satellite, landscaping

This is the easiest type of question on the logic games, because it lists out all the variables in order on every answer choice and tells us that only one answer (the correct answer) could work. This means the four other answer choices *cannot* work because they break one or more rules. So all we have to do is use the rules to knock out answer choices.

The simplest and quickest way to do this is to take the rules, one at a time, in order, and eliminate as many answer choices as possible. Note that this is *not* the same thing as evaluating each answer choice, in order, against all the rules. That's a slower process because it allows you to get "stuck" trying to figure out what's wrong with the correct answer, when there is (obviously) nothing wrong with the correct answer. Just trust me on this one. Use the rules, one at a time, to knock out answer choices. Here we go:

Rule 1 says <u>W must go before L.</u> That gets rid of answer C. All the other answers pass this rule, but C is forever eliminated. We don't need to consider C again, because it already breaks a rule.

Rule 2 says <u>P has to go before both G and S.</u> That gets rid of answer A. We're already down to B, D, and E. We're not going to look at answer A or C anymore.

Rule 3 says <u>G, S, and T can't go second or third.</u> That gets rid of answer E. We're down to B and D. Pretty efficient, eh?

Rule 4 says <u>T can't go last.</u> That knocks out B. Answer D has met all the requirements, and answers A, B, C, and E have each broken a rule. Therefore D is our answer. Note that we are answering this question with 100% certainty. You could put a gun to my head here, and I'd still be comfortable telling you that D is our answer. It simply has to be. This is the kind of certainty you should be looking for on the Logic Games. On other sections of the LSAT (Logical Reasoning and Reading Comprehension), you'll sometimes be weighing one answer against another, or choosing the most reasonable answer from a bunch of answers you really don't like very much. On the Logic Games, you should be *loving* your answers. There is no guesswork here. Slow down and answer the questions in this section with certainty. You'll speed up eventually, but you have to start by *knowing* your answers are correct.

2

QUESTION 2:

If neither the gas nor the satellite nor the telephone appointment is scheduled for the fourth day, which one of the following must be true?

A) The gas appointment is scheduled for the fifth day.
B) The power appointment is scheduled for the third day.
C) The satellite appointment is scheduled for the sixth day.
D) The telephone appointment is scheduled for the first day.
E) The water appointment is scheduled for the second day.

This question gives us some new requirements that apply *to this question only*. For question 2, we're told that G, S, and T can't go fourth. We need to incorporate this information with the information we already knew. This is going to require making a new picture.

My first thought is that G and S are going to have some problems here. We already knew G and S have to go in the fourth through sixth slots. If they can't go fourth, then they *must* go fifth and sixth in some order. So we can fill up the fifth and sixth spots with G and S:

$$\underline{\quad}\ \underline{\quad}\ \underline{\quad}\ \underline{\quad}\ \underline{\left(G , S \right)}$$

L G G G P T
G S S S W
S T T T P

Having done this, let's turn our attention to T. We already knew T couldn't go second or third. For question 2, T can't go fourth either. And G and S are taking up the last two spots! Therefore T must go first:

$$\underline{T}\ \underline{\quad}\ \underline{\quad}\ \underline{\quad}\ \underline{\left(G , S \right)}$$

L G G G P T
G S S S W
S T T T P

And since the question asks us for something that MUST be true, that makes D our answer.

QUESTION 3:

Which one of the following must be true?

A) The landscaping appointment is scheduled for an earlier day than the telephone appointment.
B) The power appointment is scheduled for an earlier day than the landscaping appointment.
C) The telephone appointment is scheduled for an earlier day than the gas appointment.
D) The telephone appointment is scheduled for an earlier day than the water appointment.
E) The water appointment is scheduled for an earlier day than the gas appointment.

This question asks us for something that must always be true. We are going to disregard the new rule given to us in Question 2 (since that rule applied only to that question) and return to our main diagram. Again, our main diagram is:

Let's just see if that diagram will help us evaluate the answer choices. Since the correct answer "must be true," that means the incorrect answer choices could be false. Let's see.

A) This can't be the answer, because T can sometimes go first. (T went first in Question 2, for example. Question 2 had an additional restriction, of course, that G, S, and T can't go fourth. That restriction doesn't apply for Question 3. But since it was possible for T go go first, even *with* that restriction, then we know that T can in some cases go first.)
B) This doesn't have to be true, because P could go fourth, with G and S in the fifth and sixth spots. This isn't it.
C) I don't see why this would have to be true. Couldn't T go fifth while P went fourth and G went sixth? Let's not spend too long on this answer choice ... we're better off checking out D and E and see if something jumps out at us.
D) Nope, because W can go first. Still looking.
E) Here we go. W has to go before L, and G has to go somewhere in the last three spots. To try to make Answer E false, we'd have to put G in the fourth spot, W in the fifth spot, and L in the sixth spot. But if we did that, then there would be no room for S, which also has to go in the last three spots. We simply can't make Answer E false. Therefore it must be true. Our answer is E.

4

QUESTION 4:

Which one of the following CANNOT be the appointments scheduled for the fourth, fifth, and sixth days, listed in that order?

A) gas, satellite, landscaping
B) landscaping, satellite, gas
C) power, satellite, gas
D) telephone, satellite, gas
E) water, gas, landscaping

Before we went to the answer choices, we learned that the fourth, fifth, and sixth spots have to include both G and S. Question 4 asks us to identify a group of appointments that *can't* fill those last three spots—so any answer choice that leaves out either G or S would have to be the answer. That would be Answer E, which leaves out S. Therefore E is our answer.

It's not always that easy, but sometimes it is. The test likes to reward us for making inferences, even when those inferences are sometimes not very earth-shattering. We're winning!

5

QUESTION 5:

If neither the gas appointment nor the satellite appointment is scheduled for the sixth day, which one of the following must be true?

A) The gas appointment is scheduled for the fifth day.
B) The landscaping appointment is scheduled for the sixth day.
C) The power appointment is scheduled for the third day.
D) The telephone appointment is scheduled for the fourth day.
E) The water appointment is scheduled for the second day.

Here, like question 2, we're given a new rule. So we have to make a new diagram. Notice that G and S are the key players here (again). We know G and S have to go in the last three spots. If the sixth spot is eliminated, that means G and S have to go fourth and fifth in some order:

$$\underline{} \ \underline{} \ \overset{\displaystyle(G,\ S)}{\underline{}} \ \underline{} \ \underline{} \ \underline{}$$

L̶ G G   P̶ T̶
G S S   W
S̶ T̶ T̶   P̶

Having done that, I'm going to turn my attention to the sixth spot. If it can't be G or S, who can it be? It can't be P, because P has to go before G and S. It can't be W, because W has to go before L. It's can't be T, because the last rule says so. Who's left? Well, L is the only one left. So L must go last. Which makes our answer B.

6

QUESTION 6:

Which one of the following, if substituted for the condition that the telephone appointment cannot be scheduled for the sixth day, would have the same effect in determining the order of the appointments?

A) The telephone appointment must be scheduled for an earlier day than the gas appointment or the satellite appointment, or both.
B) The telephone appointment must be scheduled for the day immediately before either the gas appointment or the satellite appointment.
C) The telephone appointment must be scheduled for an earlier day than the landscaping appointment.

D) If the telephone appointment is not scheduled for the first day, it must be scheduled for the day immediately before the gas appointment.

E) Either the gas appointment or the satellite appointment must be scheduled for the sixth day.

Occasionally, the last question in a game will change the rules somehow. Here, the question asks you to identify a new rule that, if substituted for an existing rule, would lead to the exact same outcome. My first advice for a question like this is very simple: Skip it entirely!

No, seriously. These questions tend to be more difficult and time consuming than the average question. Furthermore, since this is the last question in the game, even if you answer it correctly you haven't increased your knowledge of the game in a way that will benefit you on future questions, because— wait for it—this is the last question! Most students should just bubble something in and move on. If you have time at the end of the section, you can always come back to it.

But since we're all here, let's try to answer this beast. What you're looking for is a new rule that, when substituted for the old rule, leads to the exact same effects. This means the new rule can have no more *and* no less effect than the old rule. So let's go through the answer choices and use a process of elimination to find out which one is left standing.

We have two criteria: First, the new rule can do no more than the old rule. So every answer choice, in order to remain in contention, *must be true* according to the old rules. Any answer choice that does not have to be true according to the old rules has gone too far, and can be eliminated.

Second, the new rule can do no less than the old rule. So every answer choice, in order to remain in contention, can allow no more flexibility than the old rules. Any answer choice that allows for outcomes that were impossible under the old rules can be chopped. Here we go:

Smart Skipping

Most people aren't trying for a perfect games score. The best strategy is to maximize your expected score for the section. (Those aren't the same things.) Don't let the perfect be the enemy of the good! Getting your best score is all that matters, so skip this question if it's best for you to skip it. Only you can possibly know for sure, but I'd say at least 90 percent of all test-takers would score higher if they skipped a final question that changes the rules.

A) I'm not sure I can explain it very well, but I have a good feeling about this answer choice. The old rule was "T can't go last." If, instead, we had a rule that said T has to go before G, S, or both, that would do no less than the old rule, because it would ensure that T can't go last. It might do more than the old rule, but I suspect it doesn't. Let's see if we can eliminate B through E for doing more or less than the old rule. If we can, then A will be our answer.

B) This does more than the old rule. Check out our work for number 2, above. In number 2, T could have gone immediately before either P or W. Answer B would make that impossible. So it's a different rule, and therefore not our answer.

C) This does more than the old rule as well. Under the old rules, it would have been possible for L to go third, for example, while T went fifth. Answer C would make that impossible. So it's a different rule, and therefore not our answer.

D) There's no way this can be the answer because G and S are equivalent according to the rules. This is a very advanced technique, but why would T have to go immediately before G, specifically? What rule would make T have to go immediately before G, instead of immediately before S? There's no difference between G and S. This is out.

E) This does more than the old rules, because under the old rules L could go last. Answer E would make that impossible. So it's a different rule, and therefore not our answer. Our answer is A, because B through E all do more than the old rule did. Note that I didn't even attempt to *prove* that A does exactly the same as the old rule. Rather, I got rid of the four rules that do something different than the old rule. Very tough question.

Game Two

An artisan has been hired to create three stained glass windows. The artisan will use exactly five colors of glass: green, orange, purple, rose, and yellow. Each color of glass will be used at least once, and each window will contain at least two different colors of glass. The windows must also conform to the following conditions:

Exactly one of the windows contains both green glass and purple glass.
Exactly two of the windows contain rose glass.
If a window contains yellow glass, then that window contains neither green glass nor orange glass.
If a window does not contain purple glass, then that window contains orange glass.

Game Two Explanation (Questions 7-13)

When I first read the setup for this game, I thought it would be easy. We only have five colors, which isn't too bad. And we only have three windows. The problem begins with the requirement that we use each color *at least* once. Furthermore, we must have two *or more* colors in each window. The game would be a lot easier if we had to use each color *exactly* once, with *exactly* two colors per window. When it says "at least once" and "two or more," that means there is going to be some flexibility in the game. And flexibility is generally our enemy on the games.

Start by writing out the list of variables and making a picture of the windows we are trying to color in:

$$\textbf{G O P R Y} \ \left(\geq 1 \text{ each} \right)$$

$$\left(\text{Each window} \geq 2 \text{ colors} \right) \quad \frac{}{} \ \frac{}{} \ \frac{}{}$$

$$\frac{}{} \ \frac{}{} \ \frac{}{}$$

$$1 \quad 2 \quad 3$$

The first rule says that exactly one of the windows contains both G and P. Since there is no assigned order to the windows, we can arbitrarily put G and P in the first window:

$$\frac{G}{} \ \frac{}{} \ \frac{}{}$$
$$\frac{P}{} \ \frac{}{} \ \frac{}{}$$
$$1 \quad 2 \quad 3$$

(Once we do this, we need to remember that G and P can't go together in window 2 or 3, because G and P go together *exactly* once and we've already put them in window 1.) Next, let's simply add a "2" next to R in our variable list because of the second rule:

$$\textbf{G O P R}^{=2} \textbf{Y}$$

The third rule is a "conditional" rule. The "condition" that triggers the rule is the use of the color yellow. I diagram the rule like this:

$$Y \begin{array}{c} \nearrow \ \cancel{G} \\ \searrow \ \cancel{O} \end{array}$$

Any time I see a conditional rule, I am always going to write the contrapositive of the rule as well. That looks like this:

$$\begin{array}{c} G \ \searrow \\ \qquad \nearrow \ \cancel{Y} \\ O \end{array}$$

It's critical to know exactly what this rule means ... no more, and no less. What it means to me is that Y and G hate each other, and Y and O hate each other. Any window can have Y or G or neither. Any window can have Y or O or neither. It's not OK to have Y with G or Y with O. But it would be perfectly fine to have none of them at all.

Next, I'll diagram the fourth rule:

$$P\!\!\!/ \rightarrow O$$

And its contrapositive:

$$\emptyset\!\!\!/ \rightarrow P$$

There's a subtle difference between this rule and the previous rule. The third rule was about variables that cannot coexist, whereas this rule is about the *absence* of one variable requiring the *presence* of another. The fourth rule says if a window doesn't have P then it must have O. The contrapositive says that if a window doesn't have O then it must have P. So every window, at a minimum, must have either P or O. The huge difference with the fourth rule is that a window could have both P and O. What a window *can't* have is both P and O missing simultaneously.

Understanding the difference between the third and fourth rule is a critical juncture for most LSAT students. Everyone can understand this eventually, but it blows a lot of minds at first. Keep at it! You'll get there eventually. Ask a friend to try to help you understand it if you're struggling. Or email me and we'll figure it out together.

Next, I'm going to link the third and fourth rules together:

$$Y \begin{array}{c} \nearrow G\!\!\!/ \\ \searrow \emptyset\!\!\!/ \rightarrow P \end{array}$$

In the contrapositive, that looks like this:

$$\begin{array}{c} P\!\!\!/ \rightarrow O \searrow \\ \qquad\qquad Y\!\!\!/ \\ G \nearrow \end{array}$$

Superman's Baby

One way of thinking about this that might be helpful: The third rule was about variables that can't be in the same room together...think Superman and Clark Kent. If one is there, the other is absent.

The fourth rule was about variables that can't both be absent from the room together... think Mom and Dad taking care of a newborn baby. It's OK for both Mom and Dad to be home, but it's not possible for both Superman and Clark Kent to be at your party. On the other hand, it's perfectly possible for both Superman and Clark Kent to be absent from your party. But it's not OK for both Mom and Dad to be away from the baby.

Now, before we go on to the questions let's to try to assimilate everything we know about the game to see if we can learn anything else. This is going to happen in baby steps. The first thing I notice is that Window 1, where I put the PG combo, can't have Y. This is because G and Y hate each other:

$$\begin{array}{c} \underline{P} \quad \underline{} \quad \underline{} \\ \underline{G} \quad \underline{} \quad \underline{} \\ \underline{Y\!\!\!/} \end{array}$$

OK, then where *can* Y go? It has to go somewhere, and we have two identical open windows remaining. So let's go ahead and slap Y in there in one of them:

$$\begin{array}{c} \underline{P} \quad \underline{} \quad \underline{} \\ \underline{G} \quad \underline{Y} \quad \underline{} \\ \underline{Y\!\!\!/} \end{array}$$

Remember, the order of the windows doesn't matter, so we can just put it in either 2 or 3, since 2 and 3 are identical.

Once we do that, things start to happen. Y hates both G and O, so let's block G and O from Window 2:

P   —   —

G   Y   —

Y̶   G̶

Ø̶

And since every window requires either O or P or both, that means P will have to go in Window 2:

P   P   —

G   Y   —

Y̶   G̶

Ø̶

Finally, the fourth rule specifies that P or O (or both) must be in every window. we've already taken care of that with P in windows 1 and 2, but Window 3 is still naked. So we'll put a placeholder for P or O in Window 3:

P   P   P/O

G   Y   —

Y̶   G̶

Ø̶

Awesome. At a minimum, all we're required to use is exactly two Rs, which can go anywhere, and one O which can go anywhere but Window 2. We might also be able to use more of the other colors (a third P? A second O? A second G? A second Y?), but we won't be forced to do that unless a question gives us some additional requirements. At this point, I think we're ready to move on to the questions.

7

QUESTION 7:

Which one of the following could be the color combinations of the glass in the three windows?

A) window 1: green, purple, rose, and orange window 2: rose and yellow window 3: green and orange

B) window 1: green, purple, and rose window 2: green, rose, and orange window 3: purple and yellow

C) window 1: green, purple, and rose window 2: green, purple, and orange window 3: purple, rose, and yellow

D) window 1: green, purple, and orange window 2: rose, orange, and yellow window 3: purple and rose

E) window 1: green, purple, and orange window 2: purple, rose, and yellow window 3: purple and orange

A process of elimination is pretty much always the best tactic on a question that lists out entire combinations and asks which one of the complete combinations could be true. We'll take the rules, one at a time, and knock out as many answer choices as we can with each rule. Here goes:

Rule 1: <u>Exactly one PG together.</u> This gets rid of Answer C, because PG is together twice.

Rule 2: <u>Exactly two Rs.</u> This gets rid of Answer E, because there's only one R.

Rule 3: <u>Y hates both G and O.</u> This gets rid of Answer D, because O and Y are together in Window 2.

Rule 4: <u>Every window must have P or O or both.</u> This gets rid of Answer A, because Window 2 has neither. We've tested B against all the rules and it's the only answer to pass all the tests, so B is our answer.

QUESTION 8:

Which one of the following CANNOT be the complete color combination of the glass in one of the windows?

A) green and orange
B) green and purple
C) green and rose
D) purple and orange
E) rose and orange

This question tests your understanding of the fourth rule. All we really know about every window is that it must, at a minimum, have either P or O (or both). Therefore the answer to Question 8 is C, because no complete window can have only G and R (without P or O). Really understanding that fourth rule made this question a breeze.

QUESTION 9:

If two of the windows are made with exactly two colors of glass each, then the complete color combination of the glass in one of those windows could be

A) rose and yellow
B) orange and rose
C) orange and purple
D) green and rose
E) green and orange

This question is pretty difficult—but with a little patience, it can be beaten. First, you can eliminate both A and D because these windows can't be "complete" without a P or an O (or both). So we're left with B, C, and E. One thing that all these windows have in common is the color O. So we can adapt the diagram as follows:

$$\frac{\text{P}}{\frac{\text{G}}{\cancel{\text{Y}}}} \quad \frac{\text{P}}{\frac{\text{Y}}{\cancel{\text{G}}}} \quad \frac{\text{O}}{\underline{\quad}}$$
$$\cancel{\text{O}}$$

The reason we're able to do this is that Windows 1 and 2 already had two colors without O, so if a complete window was going to have O and one other color, it can only be in window 3. Finally, we need to think about our two Rs, which we haven't yet used. The question specifies that "two of the windows are made with exactly two colors each," which means that we can't put both of the Rs in Windows 1 and 2. (That would be three colors in each of two windows.) Therefore we *must* put one of the Rs in Window 3:

$$\frac{\text{P}}{\frac{\text{G}}{\cancel{\text{Y}}}} \quad \frac{\text{P}}{\frac{\text{Y}}{\cancel{\text{G}}}} \quad \frac{\text{O}}{\text{R}}$$
$$\cancel{\text{O}}$$

This makes B our answer, if we put the remaining R in either Window 1 or Window 2.

$$\text{R}$$
$$\swarrow \text{ or } \searrow$$
$$\frac{\text{P}}{\frac{\text{G}}{\cancel{\text{Y}}}} \quad \frac{\text{P}}{\frac{\text{Y}}{\cancel{\text{G}}}} \quad \frac{\text{O}}{\text{R}}$$
$$\cancel{\text{O}}$$

10

QUESTION 10:

If the complete color combination of the glass in one of the windows is purple, rose, and orange, then the complete color combination of the glass in one of the other windows could be

A) green, orange, and rose
B) green, orange, and purple
C) orange and rose
D) orange and purple
E) green and orange

The only way to have PRO as a complete color combination is to do it in Window 3, since Window 1 already has PG and Window 2 already has PY:

```
              P
   P    P     R
   G    Y     O
```

That makes B our answer, with the remaining R again sliding into Window 1 or Window 2:

```
        R      P
       or      R
   P    P      O
   G    Y
```

11

QUESTION 11:

If orange glass is used in more of the windows than green glass, then the complete color combination of the glass in one of the windows could be

A) orange and purple
B) green, purple, and rose
C) green and purple
D) green and orange
E) green, orange, and rose

Since O can't be used in Window 2, the only way O can be used more than G is for O to be used in both Window 1 and Window 3 and G to be used in Window 1 only. So our diagram looks like this:

```
   O
   P    P    _
   G    Y    O
        G̶    G̶
```

From that point, a process of elimination makes A our answer. Each of B, C, D, and E uses G, which can only go in Window 1, which already has both O and P in it. Since none of B through E list G, O, and P, they are all eliminated. The correct answer, A, could be possible in Window 3.

QUESTION 12:

Which one of the following could be used in all three windows?

A) green glass
B) orange glass
C) purple glass
D) rose glass
E) yellow glass

Which color could be used in all three windows? It can't be Y or G, because Y and G hate each other and they each have to be used once. (If G were in all three windows, where would Y go? If Y were in all three windows, where would G go?) Similarly, it can't be O because it also hates Y. R can't be used in all three windows either, because it must be used exactly twice. Therefore our answer is C, purple.

QUESTION 13:

If none of the windows contains both rose glass and orange glass, then the complete color combination of the glass in one of the windows must be

A) green and purple
B) green, purple, and orange
C) green and orange
D) purple and orange
E) purple, rose, and yellow

If none of the windows contains both R and O, and since we know we have to use two Rs, we can make a new diagram that starts out like this:

R	R	O
Ø	Ø	R̸

Since every window has to have either an O or a P, we can add P to Windows 1 and 2:

P	P	
R	R	O
Ø	Ø	R̸

Since Y hates O, and we have to put a Y somewhere, we can arbitrarily put Y in one of the first two windows (since those two windows are identical up to this point). Once we do that, then G can't go in that window:

Y		
P	P	
R	R	O
G̸	Ø	R̸
Ø		

This makes Window 1 complete, and it makes E our answer.

Game Three

A conference on management skills consists of exactly five talks, which are held successively in the following order: Feedback, Goal Sharing, Handling People, Information Overload, and Leadership. Exactly four employees of SoftCorp—Quigley, Rivera, Spivey, and Tran—each attend exactly two of the talks. No talk is attended by more than two of the employees, who attend the talks in accordance with the following conditions:

Quigley attends neither Feedback nor Handling People.
Rivera attends neither Goal Sharing nor Handling People.
Spivey does not attend either of the talks that Tran attends.
Quigley attends the first talk Tran attends.
Spivey attends the first talk Rivera attends.

Game Three Explanation (Questions 14-18)

This game rewards you hugely for making inferences before continuing on to the questions. I'm not sure they intended to make it *this* easy. But I'm not complaining.

The basic setup is five talks, labeled F, G, H, I, and L, in that order:

$$Q^1 \ldots Q^2$$
$$R^1 \ldots R^2$$
$$S^1 \ldots S^2 \qquad \underline{} \; \underline{} \; \underline{} \; \underline{} \; \underline{}$$
$$T^1 \ldots T^2 \qquad \quad F \quad G \quad H \quad I \quad L$$

It's critical that you catch the phrase "in the following order" in the second line of the setup. If you didn't realize that the talks were always in this order, the game would have been completely bewildering. This is a great example of how *slowing down* on the Logic Games will help you go faster. Avoiding devastating mistakes is the first step.

Each of these talks is attended by two employees *at the most*. The employees are Q, R, S, and T, and each employee attends exactly two talks.

The first and second rules are simply about who can't go where:

$$\underline{} \; \underline{} \; \underline{} \; \underline{} \; \underline{}$$
$$F \quad G \quad H \quad I \quad L$$
$$\cancel{Q} \quad \cancel{R} \quad \cancel{Q}$$
$$\qquad \qquad \cancel{R}$$

The third rule says S can never go with T. Let's write that like this:

The fourth rule is tricky. It says "Q attends the first talk T attends." You've got to be really careful here, and figure out exactly what this means. Does it mean that the first T is always with the first Q? Does it mean that Q and T are always together? No, it doesn't mean either of those. Instead, it says that the *first* T requires *one of* the Qs. So the first T can actually go with the first *or* second Q. (And it's possible, but not necessary, that both Qs go with both Ts.) I would write the rule like this:

$$T^1 \rightarrow Q$$

The last rule is parallel to the fourth rule. The first R requires one of the Ss. Like this:

$$R^1 \rightarrow S$$

OK. We've carefully gone through all the rules, and we've noted exactly what the mean, no more and no less. Now, before we go on to the questions, it's critical that we put in some more time and learn some more stuff about the game. The first thing I notice is that since Q can't attend F, neither can T (because F would be T's first talk, and T's first talk requires the attendance of Q.):

$$F \quad G \quad H \quad I \quad L$$
$$\cancel{Q} \quad \cancel{R} \quad \cancel{Q}$$
$$\cancel{T} \qquad \cancel{R}$$

The variable that interests me the most here is Q. That's because not only is Q required to accompany the first T, but Q also can't go to the first talk (F) or the third talk (H). If Q can only go to three seminars, then there are really only two ways to do it:

Once we've made those two worlds, let's see what would have to happen in each of those two worlds. Let's focus on the second world first (where Q attends the fourth and fifth talk (I and L). The first thing to notice is that since T requires Q's presence at the first talk T attends, T's first talk will have to be I. And if T's first talk is I, then T's second talk will have to be L, since that's the only talk left:

$$\overset{1}{T} \quad \overset{2}{T}$$
$$\overset{1}{Q} \quad \overset{2}{Q}$$
$$F \quad G \quad H \quad I \quad L$$
$$\cancel{Q} \quad \circledR \quad \cancel{Q}$$
$$\cancel{T} \qquad \circledR \rightarrow \text{oops!}$$

If that happens, then we're in trouble. Where can R go? Remember, two employees max can attend each talk. So talks I and L are now full. But R can't attend either talk G or talk H! Employee R could attend the first talk, F, but that's it. And R (like all employees), *must* attend two seminars. Therefore this entire world won't work:

$$\overset{1}{\quad} \quad \overset{2}{Q} \quad \overset{}{Q}$$
$$F \quad G \quad H \quad I \quad L$$

Which leaves us with this:

$$\overset{1}{\underline{\quad}} \; Q \; \underline{\quad} \; \overset{2}{(Q,} \; \underline{\quad})$$
$$F \quad G \quad H \quad I \quad L$$
$$\cancel{Q} \quad \cancel{R} \quad \cancel{Q}$$
$$\cancel{T} \qquad \cancel{R}$$

And that's the big inference in the game. It might not seem like much, but we have learned an additional rule here: The first Q *always* goes to the second talk, G. This additional rule

Better Worlds

This technique, which I call "making worlds" since I don't have a better name for it, can be incredibly powerful on certain games. Don't force it though, because it can be a colossal waste of time in the wrong situation.

Knowing when to do it and when not to do it will take a lot of practice. I look for two things: 1) **A limited number of worlds.** Here, I had only two ways to distribute my Qs. Two worlds is the ideal. 2) **I get to fill stuff out in each of those worlds.** There's no point in making worlds if you can't fill out lots of variables in at least one of the worlds. Here, since Q is related to T, I got to start filling out Ts once I had penciled in my Qs. This led to a chain reaction that eliminated one world entirely, which is a dream result. Practice this powerful technique.

will be a powerful weapon for solving this game's questions. (Imagine how difficult a game would be if you had forgotten a rule entirely. This game will be that much easier, because we have an additional rule to help us eliminate scenarios and answer choices that won't work.) Time to check out some questions:

14

QUESTION 14:

Which one of the following could be a complete and accurate matching of the talks to the SoftCorp employees who attend them?

A) Feedback: Rivera, Spivey Goal Sharing: Quigley, Tran Handling People: None, Information Overload: Quigley, Rivera, Leadership: Spivey, Tran

B) Feedback: Rivera, Spivey Goal Sharing: Quigley, Tran Handling People: Rivera, Tran Information Overload: Quigley Leadership: Spivey

C) Feedback: Rivera, Spivey Goal Sharing: Quigley, Tran Handling People: Tran, Information Overload: Quigley, Rivera, Leadership: Spivey

D) Feedback: Rivera, Spivey Goal Sharing: Tran Handling People: Tran, Information Overload: Quigley, Rivera, Leadership: Quigley, Spivey

E) Feedback: Spivey, Goal Sharing: Quigley, Tran, Handling People: Spivey, Information Overload: Quigley, Rivera, Leadership: Rivera, Tran

This is a list question, which we can attack using the rules.

   Rule 1: <u>Q can't go to either F or H.</u> Unfortunately, none of the answer choices violate this rule. So we'll move on to the next rule.
   Rule 2: <u>R can't go to either G or H.</u> Answer B violates this rule, so Answer B is eliminated.
   Rule 3: <u>S and T hate each other.</u> Answer A violates this rule, so Answer A is eliminated.
   Rule 4: <u>Q has to accompany T to T's first talk.</u> Answer D violates this rule, so that one is eliminated.
   Rule 5: <u>S has to accompany R to R's first talk.</u> Answer E violates this rule, so Answer E is eliminated. Answer C has passed all the rules, and A, B, D, and E have all broken a rule, so C is our answer.

15

QUESTION 15:

If none of the SoftCorp employees attends Handling People, then which one of the following must be true?

A) Rivera attends Feedback.
B) Rivera attends Leadership.
C) Spivey attends Information Overload.
D) Tran attends Goal Sharing.
E) Tran attends Information Overload.

If none of the employees attends the third talk, H, then the four remaining talks must have two employees each. (Since each employee must attend two talks, and each talk can have a maximum of two employees.) Since Q and T can't ever go to the first talk, only S and R are left to attend that talk:

$$S^1$$
$$R^1 \; Q^1 \times (Q^2, \underline{\quad})$$
$$F \quad G \quad H \quad I \quad L$$

So our answer is A. Simple as that.

QUESTION 16:

Which one of the following is a complete and accurate list of the talks any one of which Rivera and Spivey could attend together?

A) Feedback, Information Overload, Leadership
B) Feedback, Goal Sharing, Information Overload
C) Information Overload, Leadership
D) Feedback, Leadership
E) Feedback, Information Overload

Let's use a bit of intuition here. We know that the correct answer can't include either G or H, simply because R can't ever attend those two talks. I don't see any reason why R and S couldn't attend any of the remaining three talks together. Let's test these three talks real quick to make sure it's OK for R and S to attend each talk together.

R and S both attend seminar F:

$$
\begin{array}{ccccc}
S^1 & & & & \\
R^1 & Q^1 & \times & (Q^2, \underline{\hphantom{x}}) & \\
\overline{F} & \overline{G} & \overline{H} & \overline{I} & \overline{L} \\
\cancel{Q} & \cancel{R} & \cancel{Q} & & \\
\cancel{T} & & \cancel{R} & &
\end{array}
$$

R and S both attend seminar I:

$$
\begin{array}{ccccc}
R^1 & T^1 & & R^2 & (T^2?) \\
S^1 & Q^1 & (T^2?) & S^2 & Q^2 \\
\overline{F} & \overline{G} & \overline{H} & \overline{I} & \overline{L}
\end{array}
$$

R and S both attend seminar L:

$$
\begin{array}{ccccc}
S^1 & T^1 & & (T^2?) & R^2 \\
R^1 & Q^1 & (T^2?) & Q^2 & S^2 \\
\overline{F} & \overline{G} & \overline{H} & \overline{I} & \overline{L}
\end{array}
$$

All of these scenarios will work, so our answer is A.

QUESTION 17:

If Quigley is the only SoftCorp employee to attend Leadership, then which one of the following could be false?

A) Rivera attends Feedback.
B) Rivera attends Information Overload.
C) Spivey attends Feedback.
D) Spivey attends Handling People.
E) Tran attends Goal Sharing.

Here, I made a new diagram that incorporated the new rule (which applies to this question only) that Q is the only employee to attend talk L:

$$
\begin{array}{ccccc}
 & & & & \times \\
\overset{1}{Q} & & & & \overset{2}{Q} \\
\hline
F & G & H & I & L \\
\cancel{Q} & \cancel{R} & \cancel{Q} & & \\
\cancel{T} & & \cancel{R} & &
\end{array}
$$

The first thing to notice is that T will now have to attend talk G, because that's the only way T's first talk can be accompanied by Q:

$$
\begin{array}{ccccc}
 & \overset{1}{T} & & & \times \\
\overset{1}{Q} & & & & \overset{2}{Q} \\
\hline
F & G & H & I & L \\
\cancel{Q} & \cancel{R} & \cancel{Q} & & \\
\cancel{T} & & \cancel{R} & &
\end{array}
$$

What about the Rs? Remember R can never attend either G or H. If R can't attend L either (because Q is the *only* employee who attends L), then R has to attend both F and I:

$$
\begin{array}{ccccc}
 & \overset{1}{T} & & & \times \\
\overset{1}{R}\ \overset{1}{Q} & & & \overset{2}{R}\ \overset{2}{Q} & \\
\hline
F & G & H & I & L \\
\cancel{Q} & \cancel{R} & \cancel{Q} & & \\
\cancel{T} & & \cancel{R} & &
\end{array}
$$

And since R's first talk has to include S, we get this:

$$
\begin{array}{ccccc}
\overset{1}{S}\ \overset{1}{T} & & & & \times \\
\overset{1}{R}\ \overset{1}{Q} & & & \overset{2}{R}\ \overset{2}{Q} & \\
\hline
F & G & H & I & L \\
\cancel{Q} & \cancel{R} & \cancel{Q} & & \\
\cancel{T} & & \cancel{R} & &
\end{array}
$$

From there, it's easy to answer the question. A, B, C, and E all have to be true according to our diagram. Therefore D, which could be true or false according to our diagram, must be our answer.

QUESTION 18:

If Rivera is the only SoftCorp employee to attend Information Overload, then which one of the following could be false?

A) Quigley attends Leadership.
B) Rivera attends Feedback.
C) Spivey attends Feedback.
D) Tran attends Goal Sharing.
E) Tran attends Handling People.

Just like the previous question, we'll start by making a new diagram that incorporates the new rule:

This forces the second Q into talk L:

The first R also has to go to talk F, because that's the only spot where R can go and be accompanied by S:

The first T will have to go to talk G:

Answers A, B, C, and D all have to be true according to our diagram, but E could be false. So our answer must be E.

Game Four

Exactly six witnesses will testify in a trial: Mangione, Ramirez, Sanderson, Tannenbaum, Ujemori, and Wong. The witnesses will testify one by one, and each only once. The order in which the witnesses testify is subject to the following constraints:

Sanderson must testify immediately before either Tannenbaum or Ujemori.
Ujemori must testify earlier than both Ramirez and Wong.
Either Tannenbaum or Wong must testify immediately before Mangione.

Game Four Explanation (Questions 19-23)

They saved the easiest for last. Well, maybe the first game was easier than this one. But this one is pretty damn easy. It's a big reward for making it through the first three games.

This game turns out to be another basic sequencing game, just like the first. Once again we are putting six things in order. Once again each thing has to go once, nothing can go twice, nothing can be left out. And once again there are no ties. This is the simplest of all Logic Games setups.

The first thing you should always do on a game like this is write out the variables and the spots they'll go in:

M R S T U W _ _ _ _ _ _

Next, look at each of the rules. The first rule looks like this:

S T/U

Based on the first rule, we know S can't go last:

_ _ _ _ _ S̸

The second rule looks like this:

U < R
    W

Based on the second rule, we know U can't go in the last two spots, and neither R nor W can go first:

R̸ _ _ _ U̸ S
W̸   U̸

The last rule looks like this:

T/W M

Based on the last rule, we know M can't go first:

R̸ _ _ _ _ U̸ S
W̸   U̸
M̸

The most restricted spot is the first one. The only possibilities for this spot are S, T, and U. Let's include that in our diagram, and also notice that these also turn out to be the three variables from the first rule. Interesting, right?

S/T/U __ __ __ __ __ __
R   U̸ S̸
W   U̸
M

I don't think we can go much further here, so let's go ahead and look at the questions.

QUESTION 19:

19

Which one of the following lists the witnesses in an order in which they could testify?

A) Ramirez, Sanderson, Tannenbaum, Mangione, Ujemori, Wong
B) Sanderson, Tannenbaum, Ujemori, Ramirez, Wong, Mangione
C) Sanderson, Ujemori, Tannenbaum, Wong, Ramirez, Mangione
D) Tannenbaum, Mangione, Ujemori, Sanderson, Ramirez, Wong
E) Wong, Ramirez, Sanderson, Tannenbaum, Mangione, Ujemori

A simple list question—use the rules to eliminate answer choices:

Rule 1: <u>S immediately before either T or U.</u> This eliminates Answer D.
Rule 2: <u>U before both R and W.</u> This eliminates Answer A *and* Answer E.
Rule 3: <u>Either T or W immediately before M.</u> This eliminates Answer C. Answer B has passed all the rules, and Answers A, C, D, and E have each broken a rule. So B is our answer.

QUESTION 20:

20

If Tannenbaum testifies first, then which one of the following could be true?

A) Ramirez testifies second.
B) Wong testifies third.
C) Sanderson testifies fourth.
D) Ujemori testifies fifth.
E) Mangione testifies sixth.

If T goes first, then S can't go immediately before T. So S must go immediately before U. The diagram looks like this:

This question is another "could be true." Generally, it's easier to eliminate the four "must be falses" rather than positively identify the single answer that "could" be true. Using the diagram, it's pretty easy to eliminate the incorrect answer choices.

A) This wouldn't work, because there wouldn't be room for SU before R.
B) This wouldn't work, because there wouldn't be room for SU before W.
C) This wouldn't work, because we can't squeeze all three of U, R, and W into the last two spots.
D) This wouldn't work, because we can't squeeze both R and W into the last spot.
E) I don't immediately see anything wrong with this, and we've already proven that A through D won't work. So E is our answer.

21

QUESTION 21:

If Sanderson testifies fifth, then Ujemori must testify

A) first
B) second
C) third
D) fourth
E) sixth

If S goes fifth, then U can't go immediately after S because there would be no room for R and W, each of which must go after U. Therefore T must go immediately after S, like this:

Note that we can also put M immediately after W, because if T is last then only W is left to go immediately before M. The question asks where U must go, and this is pretty easy from this point. Remember that S, T, and U were the only options for the first position. If S goes fifth and T goes sixth, then only U is left for the first spot. So our answer is A.

22

QUESTION 22:

Which one of the following pairs of witnesses CANNOT testify third and fourth, respectively?

A) Mangione, Tannenbaum
B) Ramirez, Sanderson
C) Sanderson, Ujemori
D) Tannenbaum, Ramirez
E) Ujemori, Wong

Here we are asked to identify an answer choice that will *not* work. There's nothing you can do here besides test the answer choices. You don't really need to test all five answer choices, because that would take forever. Just test the answer choices in order and stop as soon as you find one that doesn't work.

Fortunately, the first answer choice causes a problem. If M goes third and T goes fourth, then S will have to go immediately before U (because S won't be able to go immediately before T). So SU will have to take up the first two spots and R and W will take the last two spots. But if SU go in the first two spots, then that puts U immediately before M. This breaks the rule that says either T or W must immediately precede M. My diagram looked like this:

That doesn't work, so our answer is A.

QUESTION 23:

Which one of the following pairs of witnesses CANNOT testify first and second, respectively?

A) Sanderson, Ujemori
B) Tannenbaum, Mangione
C) Tannenbaum, Sanderson
D) Ujemori, Tannenbaum
E) Ujemori, Wong

We can do this question just like we did number 22. The key to a "must be false" or "cannot be true" question is to say "I don't see why not" fairly quickly when you test an answer choice and it seems like it will work. There's no need to try to prove that the incorrect answers will actually work. Instead, look for the correct answer that will conclusively *not* work.

A) SU seems like a perfect starting pair, because it satisfies the first rule (S followed immediately by either T or U), and it also satisfies the third rule (U before both R and W). If it immediately satisfies two rules, why would we suspect it's not going to work? Let's leave this one for now and see if we can find an answer that seems problematic.

B) TM seems like a good starting pair, because it would satisfy the third rule (M immediately preceded by either T or W). Again, I don't see why this would be a problem, so we'll leave it for now.

C) TS in the first spot would require U to go third, because S has to be immediately followed by either T or U. But TSU would seem like a fine opening trio, because it would satisfy the requirement that U has to go before R and W. Looks like it works.

D) Here we go. If we put U and T in the first two spots, then how will we satisfy the rule that says S has to be immediately followed by either U or T? This one won't work, so it's definitely our answer. You don't even have to look at answer E.

<u>U</u> <u>T</u> __ __ __ __

| S U/T | ?!

SECTION
FOUR

Logical Reasoning

(or: Breaking Balls, Part II: The Revenge)

Same strategy in this section as we used in Section Two: Get pissed, and answer the questions before looking at the answer choices whenever possible. You can do this.

QUESTION 1:

Marine biologist: Scientists have long wondered why the fish that live around coral reefs exhibit such brilliant colors. One suggestion is that coral reefs are colorful and, therefore, that colorful fish are camouflaged by them. Many animal species, after all, use camouflage to avoid predators. However, as regards the populations around reefs, this suggestion is mistaken. A reef stripped of its fish is quite monochromatic. Most corals, it turns out, are relatively dull browns and greens.

Which one of the following most accurately expresses the main conclusion drawn in the marine biologist's argument?

A) One hypothesis about why fish living near coral reefs exhibit such bright colors is that the fish are camouflaged by their bright colors.

B) The fact that many species use camouflage to avoid predators is one reason to believe that brightly colored fish living near reefs do too.

C) The suggestion that the fish living around coral reefs exhibit bright colors because they are camouflaged by the reefs is mistaken.

D) A reef stripped of its fish is relatively monochromatic.

E) It turns out that the corals in a coral reef are mostly dull hues of brown and green.

This is a cause-and-effect argument. Or an anti-cause-and-effect argument, anyway. The purported effect is: Coral reef fish are multicolored. The purported cause is: The reef is colorful, so the fish are multicolored for camouflage. The argument says this cause and effect is mistaken, however, because "most colors are relatively dull browns and greens."

The question doesn't ask us to strengthen this argument, or weaken it. Instead, it simply asks us to identify the main conclusion of the argument. On questions like this, the answer is going to be the same as the answer the speaker would give if you asked, "Why are you wasting my time with this?" Here, my guess at the answer is, "Coral reef fish are not multicolored for camouflage." Right or wrong, that's why the marine biologist came here today to waste your time. Right or wrong, that's her main point.

A) This is part of the argument, but it's the hypothesis that the marine biologist set out to *dis*prove, rather than prove. This is not our answer.

B) Again, this is what the argument wants to *dis*prove. No way.

C) This almost exactly matches my prediction. This is probably our answer.

D) Part of the argument—a premise—but not the main point of the argument. Nice try, mofos. Answer C is better.

E) Again, part of the argument but not the main point. Our answer is C.

QUESTION 2:

To discover what percentage of teenagers believe in telekinesis—the psychic ability to move objects without physically touching them—a recent survey asked a representative sample of teenagers whether they agreed with the following statement: "A person's thoughts can influence the movement of physical objects." But because this statement is particularly ambiguous and is amenable to a naturalistic, uncontroversial interpretation, the survey's responses are also ambiguous.

The reasoning above conforms most closely to which one of the following general propositions?

A) Uncontroversial statements are useless in surveys.
B) Every statement is amenable to several interpretations.
C) Responses to surveys are always unambiguous if the survey's questions are well phrased.
D) Responses people give to poorly phrased questions are likely to be ambiguous.
E) Statements about psychic phenomena can always be given naturalistic interpretations.

Wait, what? The conclusion of the argument is, "Because this statement is particularly ambiguous and is amenable to a naturalistic, uncontroversial interpretation, the survey's responses are also ambiguous." The statement in question, just to refresh our memory, was "a person's thoughts can influence the movement of physical objects."

OK then, riddle me this: What the hell is so "ambiguous" about that? I would think any teenager, no matter how hormone-addled his or her brain may be, would be able to understand that statement without any ambiguity, at least enough to be able to offer his or her personal opinion on whether that is true. (My own personal opinion is "Anybody who believes a person's thoughts can influence the movement of physical objects is an idiot. Jedis excepted, naturally.") Since the survey was only about teenagers' opinions on that proposition, I don't think the results of the survey have been tainted in any way. (The argument doesn't even tell us what the results were.) I'm pissed at the speaker. Being pissed is a good thing. There is no way I can miss this question.

The argument asks us to find a "general proposition" that "conforms" to the reasoning in the argument. This sorta means I have to switch teams. The speaker is an idiot, but now I have to be the idiot's attorney. Which one of the answers matches up most closely with the argument?

A) This is wrong because it's stated too strongly. The speaker says that survey questions that are "subject to a naturalistic, uncontroversial interpretation" (whatever the hell that even means) lead to "ambiguous" survey responses. But the speaker does not go so far as to claim that the resulting survey responses are "<u>useless</u>." That's a bit too bold of an allegation, so this answer doesn't "conform" to the speaker's reasoning.

B) This could only weaken the argument, not strengthen it, because the argument is based on one particular interpretation. This isn't the correct answer.

C) This can't be it either, because the author is claiming that the argument is *not* well-phrased. No way.

D) OK, here we go. This statement says that *if* we assume that the question is poorly phrased—again, I sure as hell *don't* agree with this assumption, but *if* we did—then the results are ambiguous. If we make this ridiculous assumption, then this strengthens the argument. This is our answer, even though I'll hate myself in the morning.

E) This isn't it, because the statement on its face is not about "psychic phenomena." This is unrelated to the argument, so I don't see how it can be our answer. In retrospect, even though the argument was easy to understand and argue with—which I love—the answer choices were so nasty that this might be the hardest question #2 I have ever seen. Still, our answer is D.

QUESTION 3:

A recent study of perfect pitch—the ability to identify the pitch of an isolated musical note—found that a high percentage of people who have perfect pitch are related to someone else who has it. Among those without perfect pitch, the percentage was much lower. This shows that having perfect pitch is a consequence of genetic factors.

Which one of the following, if true, most strengthens the argument?

A) People who have relatives with perfect pitch generally receive no more musical training than do others.
B) All of the researchers conducting the study had perfect pitch.
C) People with perfect pitch are more likely than others to choose music as a career.
D) People with perfect pitch are more likely than others to make sure that their children receive musical training.
E) People who have some training in music are more likely to have perfect pitch than those with no such training.

This is another cause-and-effect argument. The purported cause is "genetic factors." The purported effect is having perfect pitch. The evidence provided is a correlation between having perfect pitch and being related to someone else who has perfect pitch.

The problem with this line of reasoning is that a correlation does not necessarily imply causation. I love beer and I love whiskey. There's a correlation there ... the same person likes both things. But that doesn't mean that my love of beer causes my love of whiskey, or that my love of whiskey causes my love of beer. There's a simpler explanation for the observed correlation: I love booze. My *love of booze* causes my love of both beer and whiskey. There's no causal relationship between the beer and the whiskey.

OK, so what's another explanation—besides genetics—for family members sharing perfect pitch? My first thought is that some families sing, and some families don't. Families that sing together might develop perfect pitch together. That's nothing to do with genetics. That's practice. If this were true, the argument's claim that genetics is the cause would make no sense. Note that we haven't even looked at the question part of the argument yet. Instead, we're taking the time to understand and criticize the argument. There's no point in rushing to the answer choices before you understand what the argument is saying, and think about what might be wrong with it.

We're asked to strengthen the argument. So my first thought is that the correct answer might be the opposite of my criticism above. Something like "perfect pitch is always inherent, and never acquired" would strengthen the argument by defending against a potential attack. This isn't guaranteed to be there, but if it were there it would be a great answer. If it's not there, then we'll look for something else that strengthens the argument.

A) This has to be it. This is similar to our prediction in that it suggests that perfect pitch is not acquired. This will be our answer unless something else really knocks our socks off.
B) Whether the researchers have pitch is entirely irrelevant. No way.
C) Whether people with pitch have musical careers or not is also irrelevant. Nope.
D) If this were true, it would weaken the argument by suggesting that the correlation could be caused by children's acquisition of perfect pitch. We're looking for a strengthener, so this isn't it.
E) Just like D, this would weaken the argument by suggesting that pitch can be acquired. We were looking for an answer that suggested pitch can't be acquired. Answer A is the only one that did, so it's our answer.

QUESTION 4:

Paleontologists recently excavated two corresponding sets of dinosaur tracks, one left by a large grazing dinosaur and the other by a smaller predatory dinosaur. The two sets of tracks make abrupt turns repeatedly in tandem, suggesting that the predator was following the grazing dinosaur and had matched its stride. Modern predatory mammals, such as lions, usually match the stride of prey they are chasing immediately before they strike those prey. This suggests that the predatory dinosaur was chasing the grazing dinosaur and attacked immediately afterwards.

Which one of the following most accurately describes the role played in the argument by the statement that the predatory dinosaur was following the grazing dinosaur and had matched its stride?

A) It helps establish the scientific importance of the argument's overall conclusion, but is not offered as evidence for that conclusion.
B) It is a hypothesis that is rejected in favor of the hypothesis stated in the argument's overall conclusion.
C) It provides the basis for an analogy used in support of the argument's overall conclusion.
D) It is presented to counteract a possible objection to the argument's overall conclusion.
E) It is the overall conclusion of the argument.

This strikes me as a sensible argument, so for once I don't need to criticize it. (First time for everything.) The argument examines two sets of dinosaur tracks that share the same stride length and the same turns. One dinosaur seems to have been following the other, and matching its stride. Today's predatory mammals do the same thing while tracking their prey. Therefore, the argument concludes, one dinosaur was probably hunting the other. Seems reasonable to me.

The question then asks us to identify the role played in the argument by the statement that "the predatory dinosaur was following the grazing dinosaur and had matched its stride." The first question to ask yourself on this type of identify-the-role-played question is "Was that the conclusion of the argument?" Here, no, it wasn't. The conclusion of the argument was that "one dinosaur was probably hunting the other." The next question to ask yourself is "Was the statement evidence provided to support the conclusion?" Here, I think it was. Why does the author think one dinosaur was chasing the other? Well, they had similar strides and took similar turns. When we combine that with what we know about today's predatory mammals, we end up at the conclusion. So my prediction is "the statement is a premise of the argument." (Or "the statement is support for the conclusion of the argument.")

A) The statement that one dinosaur was following the other, with a similar stride, was not offered to "establish the scientific importance" of anything. This can't be the answer.
B) The statement wasn't rejected by the author. It was a premise offered by the author in support of the eventual conclusion. No way.
C) This could be it. The evidence that one dinosaur was following the other, with a similar stride, leads to the next premise, which is "This is how today's predatory mammals behave while hunting." The bit about the predatory mammals is a similar situation that was provided to prove a conclusion. In other words, an analogy. This is pretty good.
D) What objection would that be? This makes zero sense to me whatsoever. C's still better.
E) No, we're already sure it wasn't the conclusion of the argument. The conclusion was "One dinosaur was hunting the other." So this is out, and C is our answer.

QUESTION 5:

Researchers announced recently that over the past 25 years the incidence of skin cancer caused by exposure to harmful rays from the sun has continued to grow in spite of the increasingly widespread use of sunscreens. This shows that using sunscreen is unlikely to reduce a person's risk of developing such skin cancer.

Which one of the following, if true, most weakens the argument?

A) Most people who purchase a sunscreen product will not purchase the most expensive brand available.
B) Skin cancer generally develops among the very old as a result of sunburns experienced when very young.
C) The development of sunscreens by pharmaceutical companies was based upon research conducted by dermatologists.
D) People who know that they are especially susceptible to skin cancer are generally disinclined to spend a large amount of time in the sun.
E) Those who use sunscreens most regularly are people who believe themselves to be most susceptible to skin cancer.

This argument is just like saying "Despite the increasingly widespread adoption of ecologically conscious lifestyles, greenhouse emissions continue to climb. Therefore, ecologically conscious lifestyles are unlikely to reduce greenhouse gas emissions." The problem with this argument is that we'd probably be in an even *worse* greenhouse gas situation if it wasn't for conservation. Just because something isn't 100 percent effective doesn't mean it's not working. This is a commonly tested flaw on the LSAT. You're likely to see it again.

Back to sunscreen and cancer. My prediction is "Without sunscreen, many more people would have skin cancer," or "People who don't use sunscreen get skin cancer at much higher rates." Either of these would weaken the claim that sunscreen doesn't reduce risk.

A) Cost is not relevant. Next contestant, please.
B) This would weaken the argument, because it would suggest that sunscreen just hasn't been around long enough to have an effect on skin cancer. I like this answer.
C) Who cares *why* the producers of sunscreen developed sunscreen? This is entirely irrelevant to the issue of whether or not the stuff works. No way.
D) This is probably true, but it has nothing to do with whether sunscreen works. B is still the best answer.
E) This is also probably true, and also says nothing about whether sunscreen works. The best answer is B, because it's the only answer that, if true, calls the conclusion of the argument "sunscreen doesn't work" into question.

QUESTION 6:

University administrator: Any proposal for a new department will not be funded if there are fewer than 50 people per year available for hire in that field and the proposed department would duplicate more than 25 percent of the material covered in one of our existing departments. The proposed Area Studies Department will duplicate more than 25 percent of the material covered in our existing Anthropology Department. However, we will fund the new department.

Which one of the following statements follows logically from the university administrator's statements?

A) The field of Area Studies has at least 50 people per year available for hire.
B) The proposed Area Studies Department would not duplicate more than 25 percent of the material covered in any existing department other than Anthropology.
C) If the proposed Area Studies Department did not duplicate more than 25 percent of the material covered in Anthropology, then the new department would not be funded.
D) The Anthropology Department duplicates more than 25 percent of the material covered in the proposed Area Studies Department.
E) The field of Area Studies has fewer than 50 people per year available for hire.

The Power of Prediction

This question is another great example of how important it is to try to predict the answer in advance. I truly can't stress this enough: *The answer choices are not your friend.* You should be predicting the answer at least half the time on the Logical Reasoning before even looking at the answer choices. If you're not doing that, then you're never going to be as fast or as accurate as you could be.

The first sentence here gives a compound (*i.e.,* two-part) condition that will give us sufficient information to know for certain that a proposal will *not* be funded: Those two elements would include: 1) There are fewer than 50 people per year available for hire in that field and 2) the proposed department would duplicate more than 25 percent of the material covered in one of the existing departments. If both of these conditions are met, then a proposal will not be funded. The second sentence says that one of these conditions is met (duplication of more than 25 percent of the material covered) for the proposed Area Studies Department. (Don't get too excited; on its own, this doesn't mean anything at all.) Finally, we know that the department will be funded. This means that the second condition for not funding a new department can't have been met. There must be more than 50 people available for hire each year in the field, because if there weren't then the proposal wouldn't have been funded.

The question asks us for a statement that "follows logically" from the university administrator's statements. All this means is we're looking for something that must be true according to the facts we have been given. I predict the correct answer is "There are more than 50 people available for hire annually in the field." Seems reasonable given the info at hand, right?

A) Well, this exactly matches our predicted answer, so it's probably going to be our choice. Let's skim the rest of the answer choices to be sure. (We can disrespect the remaining choices a little because A matches the prediction so well. This won't take long.)
B) We don't know (or care) whether the proposed Area Studies department duplicates more than 25 percent of any department other than Anthropology. Once it did duplicate more than 25 percent of Anthropology, any other duplication was made irrelevant.
C) No, non-duplication of material can only be a *good* thing for a proposal. This isn't it.
D) No, the proposed Area Studies Department could be gigantic for all we know. This also isn't it.
E) If this were true, then the department could not be funded. But it *is* going to be funded. So this statement must be *false* according to the administrator's statements. We were looking for a must be true. Answer A definitely must be true. That's our answer.

QUESTION 7:

Researcher: Over the course of three decades, we kept records of the average beak size of two populations of the same species of bird, one wild population, the other captive. During this period, the average beak size of the captive birds did not change, while the average beak size of the wild birds decreased significantly.

Which one of the following, if true, most helps to explain the researcher's findings?

A) The small-beaked wild birds were easier to capture and measure than the large-beaked wild birds.

B) The large-beaked wild birds were easier to capture and measure than the small-beaked wild birds.

C) Changes in the wild birds' food supply during the study period favored the survival of small-beaked birds over large-beaked birds.

D) The average body size of the captive birds remained the same over the study period.

E) The researcher measured the beaks of some of the wild birds on more than one occasion.

There's no conclusion here, just the results of a study without any interpretation as to what the study might mean. Here's what happened in the study: The average beak size of the birds in captivity didn't change over time, but the average beak size of the wild birds decreased significantly. This happened over three decades. That's all we know.

The question asks us to explain this phenomenon. Hmm. Why did captive birds stay the same, but wild birds change over time? What could have been different about the forces that the two groups were subject to? Here's my guess: The captive birds were fed the same thing every day by the scientists. The wild birds, on the other hand, had to take whatever food nature gave them. Perhaps the seeds they ate got smaller, providing an advantage to those birds with smaller, more dexterous beaks. Studies of finches in the Galapagos Islands (among countless other studies around the world proving the same thing over and over and over) all show that populations of animals can change dramatically in size, shape, behavior, et cetera in response to nature's forces. These changes have been documented to occur rather rapidly, over the course of even a single generation. Thirty years is plenty of time. That's my prediction.

Outside the Box

On this type of question, it's perfectly fine to use your outside knowledge of the way the world works. The question is asking us to explain the researcher's study. In order to do so, I'm drawing on books I have read about the way natural selection works. One in particular, actually: _The Beak of the Finch_, by Jonathan Weiner. It's a terrific book, and it details the way that the beaks of finches in the Galapagos changed, in shockingly short periods of time, due to changes in the types and amounts of available food from one season to the next. Read it.

The use of outside information would be a mistake if the question asked, "_Based on the researcher's statement_, which of the following must be true?" If that were the question, then I'd have to confine myself to the researcher's statements. (See number 8 for this type of question.) But that's different from what we're asked to do here. Here, we're asked to _explain_ the phenomenon, which means that the answer could very well contain outside information.

I read a lot. It helped me here.

A) I will be pissed if this turns out to be the correct answer, because it's a naïve, half-assed explanation. Yes, it's true that if the scientists were only able to capture the smaller-beaked birds then at the end of the 30 years their results would skew smaller. But would reputable scientists really let this happen? I seriously doubt it. And wouldn't the scientists have had the same issue at the beginning of the study as well, thus nullifying the effect? This can't possibly be it.

B) Same explanation as A. Can't be the answer.

C) This is exactly what we predicted the answer would be. When it matches that closely, you know you're on the right track.

D) Body size is totally irrelevant, since the study we were asked to explain was only about beaks. No way.

E) This is probably true, but it doesn't explain jack. Our answer is most certainly C.

QUESTION 8:

Storytelling appears to be a universal aspect of both past and present cultures. Comparative study of traditional narratives from widely separated epochs and diverse cultures reveals common themes such as creation, tribal origin, mystical beings and quasi-historical figures, and common story types such as fables and tales in which animals assume human personalities.

The evidence cited above from the study of traditional narratives most supports which one of the following statements?

A) Storytellers routinely borrow themes from other cultures.
B) Storytellers have long understood that the narrative is a universal aspect of human culture.
C) Certain human concerns and interests arise in all of the world's cultures.
D) Storytelling was no less important in ancient cultures than it is in modern cultures.
E) The best way to understand a culture is to understand what motivates its storytellers.

Questions 7 and 8 make a great pair because there are no conclusions in either argument, and both arguments are about scientific/academic studies. But while question 7 asks us to explain a phenomenon—which we did using outside knowledge—this question asks us to find something "most supported" by the evidence provided. Here, we aren't asked to explain anything. Rather, we need to find something that, if the evidence is true, is proven or extremely likely to be true. Here, we can only get in trouble by bringing in outside information. We're just looking for something that has to be true (or has very good support) according to the evidence on the page. You can't really predict anything on questions where you're asked to evaluate statements you haven't seen yet. You just have to take them one by one and find the one that seems to have strong support from the evidence.

A) Diverse cultures have storytelling traditions that carry several common themes. But this doesn't mean that storytellers have borrowed from other cultures. It is possible (even likely) that the common themes were independently created by each culture. This has no support in the evidence provided, and can't possibly be the answer.
B) There's no support for this whatsoever. Storytellers now, and storytellers of past cultures, could have been aware or completely unaware of the universality of narrative. We simply don't know, according to the evidence we've been given. No way.
C) If storytelling is a "human concern and interest," then this proposition has been proven by the evidence provided, since storytelling arose in all of the world's cultures. This is looking like a good answer.
D) We don't know how "important" storytelling was then vs. now. This isn't our answer.
E) This might be true, but it has no support from the evidence provided. Our answer is C.

QUESTION 9:

If a mother's first child is born before its due date, it is likely that her second child will be also. Jackie's second child was not born before its due date, so it is likely that Jackie's first child was not born before its due date either.

The questionable reasoning in the argument above is most similar in its reasoning to which one of the following?

A) Artisans who finish their projects before the craft fair will probably go to the craft fair. Ben will not finish his project before the fair. So he probably will not go to the craft fair.

B) All responsible pet owners are likely to be good with children. So anyone who is good with children is probably a responsible pet owner.

C) If a movie is a box-office hit, it is likely that its sequel will be also. Hawkman II, the sequel to Hawkman I, was not a box-office hit, so Hawkman I was probably not a box-office hit.

D) If a business is likely to fail, people will not invest in it. Pallid Starr is likely to fail, therefore no one is likely to invest in it.

E) Tai will go sailing only if the weather is nice. The weather will be nice, thus Tai will probably go sailing.

Hmm. This is puzzling because we're told that the reasoning is "questionable," but I'm not sure I agree that it is. The logic is similar to "If you lose your first baseball game, you're likely to lose your second game as well; team X did not lose its second game, therefore it is likely that it didn't lose its first game either." This seems at least partially reasonable to me. If you lost, you're probably not good, and likely to lose again. It correlates better than the reverse would, at least.

All we're asked to do here is find an argument that is "most similar" to the argument we were given. We've already come up with one similar argument—the baseball example—so it shouldn't be too hard to find something else that uses similar logic. The basic pattern that we're looking for is "Premise 1: If X then probably Y; Premise 2: Not Y; Conclusion: Therefore, probably not X."

A) The first sentence here matches the general pattern we're looking for. If X (finish before craft fair) then probably Y (go to craft fair). But the second sentence then starts with Not X (finish before craft fair) and in order to stay parallel we're looking for Not Y (not go to craft fair). So this is out before I even read the conclusion.

B) The first sentence here matches the general pattern we're looking for. If X (you're a pet owner), probably Y (good with children). The second sentence should start with Not Y (not good with children), but instead it says if you _are_ good with children ... blah blah blah. This can't be the answer either, and I know this before reading the rest of the answer.

C) This seems exactly parallel to both the argument we were presented, about children being born before the due date, and our baseball example. I'm pretty sure this is it.

D) This is valid logic, for sure, and is nowhere close to the argument presented in the question. This can't be it.

E) This is flawed logic (there could be other requirements for Tai to go sailing besides nice weather; for example, maybe his boat needs to be out of the shop in time to sail), but it's not similar to the argument we were presented. So it's not the answer to this question. Our answer is C.

QUESTION 10:

Science journalist: Europa, a moon of Jupiter, is covered with ice. Data recently transmitted by a spacecraft strongly suggest that there are oceans of liquid water deep under the ice. Life as we know it could evolve only in the presence of liquid water. Hence, it is likely that at least primitive life has evolved on Europa.

The science journalist's argument is most vulnerable to criticism on the grounds that it

A) takes for granted that if a condition would be necessary for the evolution of life as we know it, then such life could not have evolved anywhere that this condition does not hold

B) fails to address adequately the possibility that there are conditions necessary for the evolution of life in addition to the presence of liquid water

C) takes for granted that life is likely to be present on Europa if, but only if, life evolved on Europa

D) overlooks the possibility that there could be unfamiliar forms of life that have evolved without the presence of liquid water

E) takes for granted that no conditions on Europa other than the supposed presence of liquid water could have accounted for the data transmitted by the spacecraft

OK, this is just stupid. The argument says water is *necessary* for life as we know it, and Europa has water, therefore Europa has life. This is a super-basic flaw on the LSAT ... the science journalist has confused a condition *necessary* for life with one *sufficient* for life. This is like saying "For beer to be perfect, it has to be cold. This beer is cold, therefore it is perfect." That's obviously not true if the beer is a Hamm's that's been gathering dust in the back of your grandpa's fridge since 1975. Cold is *necessary*, but it's not *sufficient*.

The question asks us to weaken the argument. The answer could be something specific like "there are other factors necessary for life that are absent on Europa." (Oxygen, perhaps?) Or, the answer could be more broadly stated as "The argument has confused a necessary condition for a sufficient condition." Let's see.

A) This uses the word "necessary," but it uses the word in a nonsensical way. This is garbage. Next, please.

B) That's much better. This is essentially the same as "Here are other factors necessary for life." I bet this is it.

C) This would be the answer if the argument had said, "There's life on Europa, therefore life must have evolved on Europa"—ignoring the possibility that life arrived on Europa from some other source, like a comet or a spaceship. The argument didn't say that though, so this isn't the answer.

D) This would be the answer if the argument had said, "Life on Earth requires water. There's no water on Europa, so there's no life on Europa"—ignoring the possibility that some different form of life might exist on Europa that doesn't require water. But that's not what the argument says.

E) This would be the answer if the argument had said, "Data from the spacecraft suggests there is water on Europa, therefore, there definitely is water on Europa"—ignoring the possibility that the data is wrong somehow. But that's not what the argument says. Our answer is B.

11

QUESTION 11:

A bacterial species will inevitably develop greater resistance within a few years to any antibiotics used against it, unless those antibiotics eliminate that species completely. However, no single antibiotic now on the market is powerful enough to eliminate bacterial species X completely.

Which one of the following is most strongly supported by the statements above?

A) It is unlikely that any antibiotic can be developed that will completely eliminate bacterial species X.

B) If any antibiotic now on the market is used against bacterial species X, that species will develop greater resistance to it within a few years.

C) The only way of completely eliminating bacterial species X is by a combination of two or more antibiotics now on the market.

D) Bacterial species X will inevitably become more virulent in the course of time.

E) Bacterial species X is more resistant to at least some antibiotics that have been used against it than it was before those antibiotics were used against it.

There's no conclusion here, just facts. Fact 1: A bacterial species will develop resistance within a few years to any antibiotics used against it, unless it is completely wiped out first. Fact 2: No single antibiotic now on the market is powerful enough to eliminate bacterial species X completely. You know what this adds up to? Absolutely nothing. The sky is not falling with regard to species X! Sure, there's no single antibiotic on the market now that can do the job. But maybe a *combination* of antibiotics would get it done. Or maybe there's a new antibiotic coming out soon that will do it. Let's not panic.

The question asks us to find something that is "strongly supported" by the statements given. Tread very carefully here. Remember, the sky isn't falling. Not much has been proven about species X.

A) The facts said nothing about what might be developed in the future. This isn't even slightly supported. We're looking for something strongly supported by the evidence provided. This ain't it.

B) This is tricky, but looks like it's got some flaws. It's possible that we could use a combination of antibiotics currently available that would wipe out species X. Still looking.

C) This ignores the possibility that a new antibiotic might come out tomorrow that would completely eliminate species X by itself. This can't be the answer.

D) This is *way* too strong. The sky isn't falling. Let's move on.

E) I don't think this is the answer, because we don't know for sure that any antibiotic was ever used against species X.

OK, so ... oops, we've eliminated all five answers. This is OK! In fact, if you don't do this occasionally then you're probably not being critical enough. On further review, the arguments against A, C, D, and E were all pretty fatal. But B can be the answer if we read it as "if any *single* antibiotic now on the market is used ... " Please note that the answer did say "antibiotic," in the singular, not "antibiotics." I'm not 100% certain, but we've got evidence in our favor here. I'd choose B and move on rather than spend any more time worrying about it—and I'd be correct.

QUESTION 12:

Political scientist: It is not uncommon for a politician to criticize his or her political opponents by claiming that their exposition of their ideas is muddled and incomprehensible. Such criticism, however, is never sincere. Political agendas promoted in a manner that cannot be understood by large numbers of people will not be realized for, as every politician knows, political mobilization requires commonality of purpose.

Which one of the following is the most accurate rendering of the political scientist's main conclusion?

A) People who promote political agendas in an incomprehensible manner should be regarded as insincere.
B) Sincere critics of the proponents of a political agenda should not focus their criticisms on the manner in which that agenda is promoted.
C) The ineffectiveness of a confusingly promoted political agenda is a reason for refraining from, rather than engaging in, criticism of those who are promoting it.
D) A politician criticizing his or her political opponents for presenting their political agendas in an incomprehensible manner is being insincere.
E) To mobilize large numbers of people in support of a political agenda, that political agenda must be presented in such a way that it cannot be misunderstood.

The first sentence is basically "Criticism X exists." The second sentence is "Criticism X is not sincere." The third sentence is the trickiest. It's basically a half-assed and poorly worded justification for the second sentence. I think what it's trying to say is "This criticism wouldn't make any sense because politicians would be stupid if they intentionally did what they were supposedly doing." I hate this argument. It sucks.

Fortunately, all we're asked to do is identify the conclusion. We can do that. The conclusion of this argument is "Such criticism is never sincere." We know this because the rest of the argument seems to support this statement. The first sentence says the criticism exists, and the third sentence attempts (poorly) to show why such criticism is not sincere. The second sentence requires the first and third for support. So it's the conclusion.

A) No, the conclusion is that the *critics* are insincere. This answer says the *politicians* who are being criticized are insincere. That's not the same thing. This isn't the answer.
B) This is much bigger and broader than the narrow, specific argument that was actually made. Nobody is saying we shouldn't pay any attention to the way agendas are promoted. This isn't it.
C) Yeah, OK, I can at least see how this could be the answer. This basically says, "There's no point in criticizing your opponent for using a stupid strategy," which is somewhat in the neighborhood of "The critics are insincere." We can pick this if both D and E are bad.
D) This is much better than C. C was more like "The critics are stupid." This says more clearly "The critics are insincere." Odds are, this is our answer.
E) Answer E was a premise of the argument, not the conclusion. D is our answer.

QUESTION 13:

Many symptoms of mental illnesses are affected by organic factors such as a deficiency in a compound in the brain. What is surprising, however, is the tremendous variation among different countries in the incidence of these symptoms in people with mental illnesses. This variation establishes that the organic factors that affect symptoms of mental illnesses are not distributed evenly around the globe.

The reasoning above is most vulnerable to criticism on the grounds that it

A) does not say how many different mental illnesses are being discussed
B) neglects the possibility that nutritional factors that contribute to deficiencies in compounds in the brain vary from culture to culture
C) fails to consider the possibility that cultural factors significantly affect how mental illnesses manifest themselves in symptoms
D) presumes, without providing justification, that any change in brain chemistry manifests itself as a change in mental condition
E) presumes, without providing justification, that mental phenomena are only manifestations of physical phenomena

On the LSAT, the word "establishes" means "proves." And the standard for "proving" something on the LSAT is a very high one. So when you see the word "establishes," you should be very skeptical. Here the argument goes as follows. Premise 1: "organic factors" affect many symptoms of mental illness. Premise 2: Symptoms vary tremendously across different countries. Conclusion: Therefore, "organic factors" aren't distributed evenly across the globe. Is that conclusion really proven by the evidence? No, no it's not.

The problem, of course, is that "organic factors" might be just one of many contributing causes of mental illness symptoms. What about drug and alcohol dependency? What about abuse during childhood? What about poverty? What about homelessness? Are all of these factors distributed evenly across the globe? Of course not. So how can we conclude that organic factors must be causing the discrepancy in mental illness factors in different locations? Couldn't it be one or more of these, and infinite other causes? I didn't really understand this argument until I got pissed and started arguing. Now I've got it.

The question asks us to criticize the argument—which, of course, I've already done. I'm guessing the answer is something like "There are many other factors that contribute to mental illness."

A) I'm looking for multiple causes of mental illness, not multiple mental illnesses. This isn't it.
B) This looks like a trap to me. If "nutritional factors" caused "organic factors" then this could be true and still not weaken the argument. We're looking for something totally unrelated to organic factors—nutrition is too close. Give me poverty or homelessness. That would be ideal. (That's possibly the only time you'll ever read that particular statement, huh?)
C) OK, I'll take "cultural factors." That's certainly not biological. And if it's true that cultural factors affect mental illness symptoms, then that suggests an alternative to the argument's organic explanation. This is pretty solid.
D) The argument doesn't do this. This isn't the answer.
E) The argument doesn't do this either (whatever this even means). Our answer is C.

QUESTION 14:

Politician: It has been proposed that the national parks in our country be managed by private companies rather than the government. A similar privatization of the telecommunications industry has benefited consumers by allowing competition among a variety of telephone companies to improve service and force down prices. Therefore, the privatization of the national parks would probably benefit park visitors as well.

Which one of the following, if true, most weakens the politician's argument?

A) It would not be politically expedient to privatize the national parks even if doing so would, in the long run, improve service and reduce the fees charged to visitors.

B) The privatization of the telecommunications industry has been problematic in that it has led to significantly increased unemployment and economic instability in that industry.

C) The vast majority of people visiting the national parks are unaware of proposals to privatize the management of those parks.

D) Privatizing the national parks would benefit a much smaller number of consumers to a much smaller extent than did the privatization of the telecommunications industry.

E) The privatization of the national parks would produce much less competition between different companies than did the privatization of the telecommunications industry.

Proposal: Privatize the national parks. Why? Because this was good for consumers when the same thing happened in the telecom industry and companies were forced to compete. Conclusion: Privatization of national parks would benefit consumers as well.

OK, so, do you buy this? You are probably not surprised to learn that I do not. Sorry, but what the hell do phone companies and national parks have in common? Do Yosemite and Yellowstone really "compete" in any meaningful way? I doubt it.

We're asked to weaken the argument. I'm hoping for something like, "National parks and telecom companies don't have anything in common."

A) Whether the proposal is "politically expedient" is not relevant to the argument. We aren't asked to evaluate whether the proposal is good or bad. We're evaluating *the argument provided in support of the proposal*. The argument concludes that this proposal would be good for consumers. I'm looking for an answer that weakens that conclusion. Nothing more, nothing less. Who cares about the politicians?

B) This is conceivably the answer, because it points out some of the bad stuff that happened when the telecoms were privatized. Do "consumers" have jobs? Yeah, probably. Cheaper phone bills are probably not worth losing your job. This is a decent answer. But let's see what else is out there.

C) Who cares whether a bunch of idiots are aware of the proposal? You can still be helped by a change, even if you pay zero attention to the news. This does nothing to the argument.

D) This is a weak answer, because something that helps even a small number of consumers, even to a tiny extent, still does help consumers. B was better.

E) OK, now this is a good answer. This basically says "National parks aren't going to compete," which was exactly what we were looking for. If E is true, then the telecom analogy isn't good any more. Since the telecom analogy was the only evidence provided in the argument, without it the argument is destroyed. Our answer is E. (I would have taken B if E wasn't here. But E is a cleaner, more direct answer.)

QUESTION 15:

Jewel collectors, fearing that their eyes will be deceived by a counterfeit, will not buy a diamond unless the dealer guarantees that it is genuine. But why should a counterfeit give any less aesthetic pleasure when the naked eye cannot distinguish it from a real diamond? Both jewels should be deemed of equal value.

Which one of the following principles, if valid, most helps to justify the reasoning in the argument above?

A) Jewel collectors should collect only those jewels that provide the most aesthetic pleasure.
B) The value of a jewel should depend at least partly on market demand.
C) It should not be assumed that everyone who likes diamonds receives the same degree of aesthetic pleasure from them.
D) The value of a jewel should derive solely from the aesthetic pleasure it provides.
E) Jewel collectors should not buy counterfeit jewels unless they are unable to distinguish counterfeit jewels from real ones.

The problem with this argument is that maybe jewel collectors aren't collecting for "aesthetic pleasure." Why else might they be collecting? Well, they might be collecting for financial gain, for one thing. Maybe they keep the jewels in a safe deposit box at a bank anyway, and don't actually give a shit what they look like. If this is true, then the argument really makes no sense because the argument relied on a premise about aesthetic pleasure.

The question asks us to identify a principle that, if true, would "justify," *i.e.*, prove or strengthen, the argument. I'm thinking it might be something like "Jewels should be deemed of equal value if the naked eye cannot distinguish between the two." If that's true, then regardless of whether people are going to be taking it out of the safe deposit box to look at it or not, the conclusion of the argument that both jewels should be deemed of equal value would be justified.

A) This is approximately a mile away from being right. The conclusion of the argument is about *value*, not about who should collect what. No way in hell.
B) This is so weakly stated that it can't be the right answer. We're looking for something strong that will support the conclusion. This business about "at least partly" makes this answer choice seem pale and lame. I don't think this will be it.
C) This seems like a weakener, if anything. We're looking for something like "Aesthetic pleasure is all that matters," whereas this is "Aesthetic pleasure is relative to the beholder." Still looking.
D) Boom. What did we predict the answer would be above? I love it when this happens. This is it.
E) Again, the argument is just not about who should or should not buy something. The argument is about valuing jewels. Our answer is D.

QUESTION 16:

All etching tools are either pin-tipped or bladed. While some bladed etching tools are used for engraving, some are not. On the other hand, all pin-tipped etching tools are used for engraving. Thus, there are more etching tools that are used for engraving than there are etching tools that are not used for engraving.

The conclusion of the argument follows logically if which one of the following is assumed?

A) All tools used for engraving are etching tools as well.
B) There are as many pin-tipped etching tools as there are bladed etching tools.
C) No etching tool is both pin-tipped and bladed.
D) The majority of bladed etching tools are not used for engraving.
E) All etching tools that are not used for engraving are bladed.

The conclusion of this argument is "There are more etching tools that are used for engraving than there are etching tools that are not used for engraving." The evidence used to support this assertion is: 1) There are only two types of etching tools (bladed and pin-tipped). 2) Some bladed etching tools are used for engraving, and some are not. 3) All pin-tipped etching tools are used for engraving.

OK, so is the conclusion of the argument justified? Hell no. Imagine if there are 10 bladed etching tools, two of which are used for engraving and eight of which are not. Now imagine there are two pin-tipped etching tools, both of which are used for engraving. This scenario is consistent with all the facts we were given, but if this is the case then the conclusion of the argument is *false* because we have four etching tools used for engraving and eight that aren't. The argument has a big hole in it.

The conclusion asks us to find an answer choice that makes the conclusion "follow logically" from its facts. This is a sufficient assumption question. In other words, we need to find an answer choice that, if true, will *prove* the conclusion of the argument.

I think the answer "There are more pin-tipped etching tools than bladed etching tools" would definitely do it, because *all* pin-tipped etching tools are used for engraving. Another answer could be "More bladed etching tools are used for engraving than are not used for engraving." If either of these were true, then there would be no way to avoid having more etching tools used for engraving than not used for engraving.

A) This is totally irrelevant ... all this does is make it impossible to use, say, your lawnmower for engraving. (Which, frankly, sounds rather dangerous, if exciting.) No way.
B) This would do it. Since there are at least *some* bladed etching tools used for engraving, and since *all* pin-tipped etching tools are used for engraving, if B were true then there would always have to be at least slightly more etching tools used for engraving than not used for engraving. Tough question, but I think this is our answer.
C) In my example above, I had already assumed that an engraving tool couldn't be both pin-tipped and bladed. The argument was incomplete even with this assumption, so this answer choice can't possibly help.
D) This would be a weakener. We're looking for a strengthener.
E) This already had to be true, because there are only two types of etching tools (pin-tipped and bladed) and all the pin-tipped tools are used for engraving. Since we already knew this fact, and since the argument was already incomplete even with this fact, this can't be our answer. Our answer is B.

QUESTION 17:

A 24-year study of 1,500 adults showed that those subjects with a high intake of foods rich in beta-carotene were much less likely to die from cancer or heart disease than were those with a low intake of such foods. On the other hand, taking beta-carotene supplements for 12 years had no positive or negative effect on the health of subjects in a separate study of 20,000 adults.

Each of the following, if true, would help to resolve the apparent discrepancy between the results of the two studies EXCEPT:

A) The human body processes the beta-carotene present in foods much more efficiently than it does beta-carotene supplements.
B) Beta-carotene must be taken for longer than 12 years to have any cancer-preventive effects.
C) Foods rich in beta-carotene also tend to contain other nutrients that assist in the human body's absorption of beta-carotene.
D) In the 12-year study, half of the subjects were given beta-carotene supplements and half were given a placebo.
E) In the 24-year study, the percentage of the subjects who had a high intake of beta- carotene-rich foods who smoked cigarettes was much smaller than the percentage of the subjects with a low intake of beta-carotene-rich foods who smoked.

We have two studies here, with no conclusion drawn by the author. The first study found that there was a negative correlation between high intake of foods rich in beta-carotene and death from cancer or heart disease. (The more foods you ate with beta-carotene, the less likely it was that you died from cancer and heart disease.) The second study, on the other hand, found that taking beta-carotene *supplements* had no positive or negative effect on the health of subjects.

The question asks us to find the one answer that *does not* resolve the apparent discrepancy between these two studies. Before we go to the answer choices, we have to at least articulate what the discrepancy is. It's got to be something like "Beta-carotene intake seemed to be good for health in one study, but had no effect on health in another study." Of course, the two studies were far from identical so there are all sorts of potential explanations. Four of the answer choices will provide these explanations, and one of them will not. Let's see.

A) Since the first study was about foods, and the second study was about supplements, if this answer choice is true then it could explain why beta-carotene seemed to have beneficial effects in the first study but not in the second. This is a good explanation, which makes it a bad answer to an *except* question.
B) The second study only treated subjects for 12 years, so if this were true then it would indicate why beta-carotene supplements didn't have a beneficial effect on health. I like the explanation in A better, but this is still at least somewhat of an explanation for the discrepancy, so it's probably not our answer. I'm hoping that our answer will either be entirely irrelevant, or will actually make the discrepancy *harder* to understand.
C) This would explain why the food study suggested beneficial effects from beta-carotene and the supplement study did not. This makes sense, so it's not our answer.
D) Here we go. I'm glad to know that the scientists in the second study used a control group with a placebo in their study (that's good science) but this fun fact does nothing to address the issue of why the first study suggested a beta-carotene health benefit and the second study did not. Because this doesn't help us understand the discrepancy, and because this is an *except* question, this is our answer.
E) If this is true, it suggests that beta-carotene might have been beneficial in the supplement study, but then the supplement takers also smoked, which is obviously bad for the health and could have offset the beta-carotene benefit. This is a good explanation of what might have happened, so it's out. Our answer is D.

QUESTION 18:

If there are sentient beings on planets outside our solar system, we will not be able to determine this anytime in the near future unless some of these beings are at least as intelligent as humans. We will not be able to send spacecraft to planets outside our solar system anytime in the near future, and any sentient being on another planet capable of communicating with us anytime in the near future would have to be at least as intelligent as we are.

The argument's conclusion can be properly inferred if which one of the following is assumed?

A) There are no sentient beings on planets in our solar system other than those on Earth.
B) Any beings that are at least as intelligent as humans would want to communicate with sentient beings outside their own solar systems.
C) If there is a sentient being on another planet that is as intelligent as humans are, we will not be able to send spacecraft to the being's planet anytime in the near future.
D) If a sentient being on another planet cannot communicate with us, then the only way to detect its existence is by sending a spacecraft to its planet.
E) Any sentient beings on planets outside our solar system that are at least as intelligent as humans would be capable of communicating with us.

Hey, cool, aliens! Oh, but—not so cool—dumbass logic!

The conclusion of the argument is "We won't be able to tell if there are aliens unless some of them are at least as smart as us." Why? Well, 1) we can't send spacecraft outside our solar system, and 2) any sentient being on another planet capable of communicating with us would have to be at least as intelligent as we are. What's wrong with this? Well, for starters, why the hell do they need to "communicate" with us in order for us to detect their presence? Let's say the planet Zorb has a bunch of Zorbs on it who are not as smart as us, but they looooooove the NASCAR-style Zorb races, and they have built themselves some giant Zorb racing stadiums where they all stand around hooting and hollering and getting horrible sunburns and drinking Zorb Light. Now, what if we built a really bitchin' telescope, and pointed it at Planet Zorb, and were able to detect the giant Zorb racetracks that cover 90% of the entire planet? There's no communication here, and there are no spacecraft involved, but we've still detected sentient beings outside our solar system. Take *that*, LSAT.

The question asks us to switch teams: "The argument's conclusion can be properly inferred if which one of the following is assumed." This is a sufficient assumption question. It means we have to identify an additional premise that, if added to the existing premises, would prove the conclusion to be true. We were weakening above, but now we have to strengthen.

I think my attack above points out the fatal gap in the logic. Why do we have to *communicate* with the Zorb in order to detect their presence? We can predict the answer here: "In order to detect sentient beings, if we can't travel to them, we have to be able to communicate with them." That seems to be the only way to bridge the gap between the premises (we can't travel to them, we can't communicate with them unless they are as smart as us) to the conclusion (we can't detect them unless they are as smart as us).

A) Our own solar system is entirely irrelevant, since the argument was about aliens *outside* our solar system. No way.
B) The argument is definitely not about whether anybody would *want* to communicate or be communicated with. It's only about what's possible. Nope.
C) This puts all the terms of the argument into a blender and barfs out something that looks relevant, but is really just a crappy gibberish smoothie. Next, please.
D) Boom. This answer choice is very similar to what we predicted. It says that the only two ways we can detect aliens is by 1) communication or 2) travel. My bitchin' telescope hypothesis would be eliminated by this answer choice. Therefore this is almost guaranteed to be the correct answer.
E) If this were true, it wouldn't prove that we wouldn't be able to detect the hooting NASCAR-style aliens that I proposed above. So it wouldn't prove the conclusion that we wouldn't be able to detect aliens less smart than us. So D is our answer.

QUESTION 19:

Doctor: Medical researchers recently examined a large group of individuals who said that they had never experienced serious back pain. Half of the members of the group turned out to have bulging or slipped disks in their spines, conditions often blamed for serious back pain. Since these individuals with bulging or slipped disks evidently felt no pain from them, these conditions could not lead to serious back pain in people who do experience such pain.

The reasoning in the doctor's argument is most vulnerable to the criticism that it fails to consider which one of the following possibilities?

A) A factor that need not be present in order for a certain effect to arise may nonetheless be sufficient to produce that effect.
B) A factor that is not in itself sufficient to produce a certain effect may nonetheless be partly responsible for that effect in some instances.
C) An effect that occurs in the absence of a particular phenomenon might not occur when that phenomenon is present.
D) A characteristic found in half of a given sample of the population might not occur in half of the entire population.
E) A factor that does not bring about a certain effect may nonetheless be more likely to be present when the effect occurs than when the effect does not occur.

Wow. Seriously? I expect question #19 to be much more difficult than this, since the questions usually get harder as the sections progress. This argument about back pain makes a very common error. Just because a disk problem doesn't *always* cause back pain for *every* person doesn't mean that it can't *sometimes* cause back pain for *some* people. (Think: Some people survive gunshot wounds. Does this mean that gunshot wounds can never lead to death? If you just said "yes" you've got bigger problems than passing the LSAT. And you should probably upgrade your health care plan.)

The question asks us to weaken the doctor's argument. Our attack above should suffice. Just because something doesn't always cause a certain outcome doesn't mean it can't sometimes cause that outcome. Give me a break.

A) Hmm. This is close but it feels like a trap because it might be saying, "Just because a factor isn't necessary doesn't mean it's sufficient." The flaw we're looking for is more like, "Just because something isn't always sufficient doesn't mean it's not sometimes sufficient." Let's see if we can find something better.
B) This is close, but it's also not exactly what we're looking for. Slipped or bulging disks can sometimes, by themselves, cause back pain. B seems to indicate they'd need help. I'm still looking. And now—because A and B are both close to right, but also imperfect—I'm thinking this question is going to turn out a lot tougher than I initially thought.
C) I don't even know what this means. A and B were at least relevant. What else you got?
D) This is true. (If you sample my friends, you'd find that half of them are Oakland Athletics fans ... but that's not true of half of all Americans.) But that's not the flaw we're looking for.
E) I don't think this is it either. This answer says, "Just because A doesn't cause B doesn't mean that A and B aren't correlated." That's definitely not what we're looking for. Shit.

After reviewing all five answer choices it's obvious that this is a much harder question than I initially suspected. The argument was stupid, and easy to attack, but the answer choices did a good job of confusing what the actual flaw was. I think C, D, and E are really terrible though. So we can get rid of those three. From there, it's really just a 50–50 guess for me. The first time I did this question, I incorrectly guessed A. Knowing that the answer is B, I can make an argument against A: This answer says disk problems can be "sufficient" to produce back pain. But if this were true, then everyone with disk problems would have back pain. And that's not the case, given the study mentioned. So A has a fatal flaw, leaving only B as a possible answer. Honestly though ... I hate this question. There's not a hell of a lot to be learned from studying this one, because even if you understand the argument, you're still at the mercy of some very tricky answer choices. It's just a tough one. You'll find a couple on every test; don't get discouraged! Just know them when you see them, do your best, and move onto the next with your confidence intact.

20

QUESTION 20:

Many workers who handled substance T in factories became seriously ill years later. We now know T caused at least some of their illnesses. Earlier ignorance of this connection does not absolve T's manufacturer of all responsibility. For had it investigated the safety of T before allowing workers to be exposed to it, many of their illnesses would have been prevented.

Which one of the following principles most helps to justify the conclusion above?

A) Employees who are harmed by substances they handle on the job should be compensated for medical costs they incur as a result.

B) Manufacturers should be held responsible only for the preventable consequences of their actions.

C) Manufacturers have an obligation to inform workers of health risks of which they are aware.

D) Whether or not an action's consequences were preventable is irrelevant to whether a manufacturer should be held responsible for those consequences.

E) Manufacturers should be held responsible for the consequences of any of their actions that harm innocent people if those consequences were preventable.

The first sentence (a premise) sets up a correlation between illness and exposure to substance T. The second sentence (also a premise) sets up a causal relationship between substance T and illness. (Substance T causes some illness.) The third sentence is the conclusion of the argument: Ignorance of the causal relationship does not let the manufacturer of substance T off the hook. Why? The fourth sentence pathetically tries to explain, with "If it had investigated, then many of the illnesses would have been prevented."

Now, I follow what this argument is saying, but if I'm the attorney for the manufacturer I am screaming, "WHY WOULD MY CLIENT BE EXPECTED TO DO ALL THIS TESTING IF THEY DIDN'T SUSPECT IT WAS DANGEROUS? TESTING COSTS A LOT OF MONEY! DOES EVERY MANUFACTURER HAVE TO INVESTIGATE EVERY SINGLE ONE OF ITS PRODUCTS, EVEN BEFORE THERE IS REASON TO SUSPECT DANGER?" *Et cetera*. I'm sure it would make for some very spicy sound bites on Fox News.

If it's not obvious, please note that I'm not *actually* on the side of this fictional company doing fictional damages to fictional employees. I'm just arguing the other side, which is something that you must also do, if you want to do well on the LSAT. Fox LSAT Commandment #1: Thou Shalt Argue.

The question proceeds to ask us to justify, *i.e.*, try to prove the conclusion of the argument. So I'm switching teams. Above, I was the defense. Now, I have to be the plaintiff's attorney. But since I used to be the defense, I already know what the defense is going to say. So as the plaintiff, I'll try to shut down that line of reasoning. My greatest fantasy, were I the plaintiff, would be one fact, followed by one rule of law: "1) The manufacturer of substance T had reason to suspect substance T was dangerous, and 2) The law says that anyone who has reason to suspect a substance is dangerous should always do whatever testing is required to find out." Alternatively, something broader but simpler like "Everyone should always test everything" would work equally well. (That's clumsy, but effective. Like a sledgehammer.) Or something slightly more nuanced would work, like "anyone who causes damages that could have been prevented had safety testing been performed is liable for those damages."

OK, enough. We've predicted three perfect answers—let's see if we make a match with any of the answer choices.

A) I suppose this does make the manufacturer responsible for medical costs, but if I'm the prosecutor I'm not sure I want to let them off that easy. Oh wait—actually, this doesn't even say who should have to pay the injured employees for their damages. Is it the government? Yeah, now that I notice that little wrinkle this can't possibly be the answer. Sneaky, but wrong.

B) The problem with this answer is the word "only" because "only" introduces a necessary condition. The proper diagram of this answer would be "liable→preventable" and the contrapositive of that would be "~~preventable→liable~~." This is a premise that only a defense attorney could love, because it can only be used to prove that someone is NOT liable. "It wasn't preventable? Then they're not liable. Oh, it was preventable? Fine … preventability is a necessary condition for liability, not a sufficient one. My client is still not liable for some other reason." If I'm the plaintiff, this ain't the answer.

C) "Informing" workers is simply not relevant here, because we're not even told whether such disclosure did or did not occur. We need something that would force the manufacturer to open up their checkbook. This isn't it.

D) This could only possibly weaken the argument, since part of the argument was that the damages were preventable. Still looking. (Boy, I hope the answer is E.)

E) Bingo! This very closely matches the last of the three model answers we came up with before diving into the answer choices. As a plaintiff's attorney, who stands to make 1/3 of the eventual settlement, this is the one I want because if this is true, then I am going to get rich. Our answer is E.

21

QUESTION 21:

It is virtually certain that the government contract for building the new highway will be awarded to either Phoenix Contracting or Cartwright Company. I have just learned that the government has decided not to award the contract to Cartwright Company. It is therefore almost inevitable that Phoenix Contracting will be awarded the contract.

The argument proceeds by

A) concluding that it is extremely likely that an event will occur by ruling out the only probable alternative
B) inferring, from a claim that one of two possible events will occur, that the other event will not occur
C) refuting a claim that a particular event is inevitable by establishing the possibility of an alternative event
D) predicting a future event on the basis of an established pattern of past events
E) inferring a claim about the probability of a particular event from a general statistical statement

The logic here seems pretty tight. If it is "virtually certain" that there are only two candidates and one of them is going to win, and if it is known for sure that one of the candidates is *not* going to win, then it seems fair to say that the other candidate will "almost inevitably" win. As much as I'd like to argue, I don't think I can.

The question asks us to identify an abstract (*i.e.*, without detail) description of the method of argumentation used. The argument has "concluded that a certain one of two outcomes is very likely to occur, given that one or the other outcome is very likely to occur, and one of the particular outcomes is certain *not* to occur." I know that's kinda hard to follow. Things without detail are hard to follow. The important thing is that <u>we</u> know what it means, because it's going to help us identify the correct answer. Let's see.

A) This sounds about right. Phoenix is extremely likely (this matches "almost inevitable") because the only other probably alternative (Cartwright) has been ruled out. I like it. A lot.
B) This one has too much certainty in it. The argument never claimed that one of two events *will* occur. ("Virtually certain" is not the same thing as "will occur.") This is out.
C) This is almost the exact opposite of what the argument really does. Our argument concludes a particular outcome is almost certain (not refuted) by establishing the impossibility (not possibility) of an alternative. Laters.
D) This would be the answer if the argument had said something like "Donald Trump has always been a blowhard fraud, therefore The Donald will be a blowhard fraud in the future." But that's not what the argument said. So this is out.
E) This would be the answer if the argument had said 95 percent of preachers don't understand science, therefore this particular preacher has a 95 percent chance of not understanding science. But that's not what this argument actually does. And A did a very good job of describing the logic. So A is our answer.

QUESTION 22:

Researchers have found that children in large families— particularly the younger siblings—generally have fewer allergies than children in small families do. They hypothesize that exposure to germs during infancy makes people less likely to develop allergies.

Which one of the following, if true, most supports the researchers' hypothesis?

A) In countries where the average number of children per family has decreased over the last century, the incidence of allergies has increased.

B) Children in small families generally eat more kinds of very allergenic foods than children in large families do.

C) Some allergies are life threatening, while many diseases caused by germs produce only temporary discomfort.

D) Children whose parents have allergies have an above-average likelihood of developing allergies themselves.

E) Children from small families who entered day care before age one were less likely to develop allergies than children from small families who entered day care later.

The researchers' hypothesis could have merit, but my first thought is that they are making an assumption here: Large families expose their infants to more germs than small families do. If you think this is obvious, then you don't quite understand what the LSAT is all about. In legal reasoning (you'll learn this in your first year legal writing/research class) every seemingly obvious step must be made explicit. Here, the premise "large families expose their infants to more germs than small families do" is unstated, but it must be true in order for the argument to make any sense. If I were the opposing attorney, I would do my damndest to argue that infants get exposed to the same amount of germs no matter whether they come from small or large families. I think this is a problem.

The question asks us to "support the researchers' hypothesis." So the answer is probably the opposite of my objection above. A really good way to strengthen an argument is to make a glaring assumption explicit. My predicted answer is "Large families expose their infants to more germs than small families do." If that's true, it makes the researchers' hypothesis seem a lot more reasonable.

A) Nah, this can't be it. All this does is reinforce the smaller families/more allergies correlation that we have already accepted as fact. We're looking to *explain* that correlation, not just reinforce it. We're looking for something that directly connects smaller families to fewer germs.

B) This seems like a trap, because it ignores the idea of smaller families/less germ exposure. I don't think this can be it.

C) This is absolutely irrelevant. What does this have to do with small families/large families/more germs/fewer germs? No way.

D) Again, no relation whatsoever to small families/large families/more germs/less germs. Nope.

E) Because I hated all the previous answers, I can give this one a bit more attention than I normally would. Initially, I didn't think daycare was relevant, but then I remembered that daycare is one germy effing place. So here we have a study of only children from small families, who the researchers propose had little exposure to germs at home, and the kids who go to daycare early (and therefore get exposed to a shitload of germs) have fewer allergies than kids who go to daycare late (and therefore get exposed to fewer germs)—BOOM. This answer isn't exactly what I predicted, but it does reinforce the more germs/fewer allergies hypothesis. This is our answer.

23

QUESTION 23:

Film preservation requires transferring old movies from their original material—unstable, deteriorating nitrate film—to stable acetate film. But this is a time-consuming, expensive process, and there is no way to transfer all currently deteriorating nitrate films to acetate before they disintegrate. So some films from the earliest years of Hollywood will not be preserved.

Which one of the following is an assumption on which the argument depends?

A) No new technology for transferring old movies from nitrate film to acetate film will ever be developed.
B) Transferring films from nitrate to acetate is not the least expensive way of preserving them.
C) Not many films from the earliest years of Hollywood have already been transferred to acetate.
D) Some films from the earliest years of Hollywood currently exist solely in their original material.
E) The least popular films from the earliest years of Hollywood are the ones most likely to be lost.

The first sentence, by using the word "requires," indicates that transferring old movies from their original material to acetate is *necessary* if one wants to preserve a film. So if we can't move a film to acetate, we know we can't preserve it. The next sentence says transferring to acetate is a "time consuming, expensive process," and there is no way to transfer *all* currently deteriorating films to acetate before they disintegrate. These two sentences, taken together, indicate that we are going to fail to preserve *some* films. But the conclusion says, "Some films from the earliest years of Hollywood will not be preserved." OK, now wait a minute. Couldn't it be true that there are garages full of home movies across the country that are disintegrating? How about we let those crappy old home movies disintegrate, while saving all of Hollywood's old movies? (Sorry, I like watching Charlie Chaplin more than I like watching your first puppy play fetch.) Couldn't this be true, and still be compatible with the premises? If so, then the conclusion really sucks.

The question asks us to identify "an assumption on which the argument depends," *i.e.,* a *necessary* assumption. I think I already have, above. Let's restate it before looking at the answer choices: The argument has assumed that there is no way to transfer all currently deteriorating films from Hollywood's earliest years to acetate. If this isn't true, then the argument fails. That's how we know this is a necessary assumption of the argument.

A) The argument doesn't assume that no new preservation technology will *ever* be developed. The argument does assume that no new preservation technology will be developed in time to save all of Hollywood's earliest films. But that's not what the answer says. So this is out.
B) What? The argument doesn't care whether transfer to acetate is the least expensive, most expensive, or somewhere in between. That's not the point. The point is that transfer to acetate is *necessary*, regardless of cost, if we want to preserve a film. So this can't be it.
C) The number of films that have already been preserved is entirely irrelevant. The argument is about films that have not yet been preserved. No way.
D) Yeah, this is required. It doesn't match my prediction, but the argument does assume that at least some of Hollywood's earliest films are still solely in their original material and are deteriorating. If not, then the argument makes absolutely no sense. I think this is the answer.
E) Popularity is completely irrelevant to the argument. Our answer is D.

QUESTION 24:

In a recent study of arthritis, researchers tried but failed to find any correlation between pain intensity and any of those features of the weather—humidity, temperature swings, barometric pressure—usually cited by arthritis sufferers as the cause of their increased pain. Those arthritis sufferers in the study who were convinced of the existence of such a correlation gave widely varying accounts of the time delay between the occurrence of what they believed to be the relevant feature of the weather and the increased intensity of the pain. Thus, this study _____.

Of the following, which one most logically completes the argument?

A) indicates that the weather affects some arthritis sufferers more quickly than it does other arthritis sufferers
B) indicates that arthritis sufferers' beliefs about the causes of the pain they feel may affect their assessment of the intensity of that pain
C) suggests that arthritis sufferers are imagining the correlation they assert to exist
D) suggests that some people are more susceptible to weather-induced arthritis pain than are others
E) suggests that the scientific investigation of possible links between weather and arthritis pain is impossible

Hmm. The study seems to provide evidence—not conclusive proof—that arthritis pain has no consistent link with, and might be completely unrelated to, the weather. Usually on a question like this I'll try to fill in the blank before looking at the answer choices, but here if we were going to do that we would basically just repeat the beginning of the first sentence: The study shows a lack of correlation between weather and arthritis. Let's see what the answer choices have for us.

A) "More quickly"? No way. The study showed no link. This can't be it.
B) This could be the answer if all the other answers were horrendous, but I don't like it. This is possible, but very speculative. The data never shows that "intensity" is different for any one sufferer vs. any other. We want something more closely related to the facts we were given.
C) Again, this is speculative. "Imagining"? That's pretty harsh. It's possible that the weather really does affect arthritis sufferers, but the problem with the study is that weather affects each sufferer in a completely different way, so the study appears to show that there is no *consistent* effect. This could be the answer, but hopefully we'll find something more solidly supported by the facts.
D) Again, this seems speculative. Maybe each sufferer is affected the same amount, just differently. Still looking. I hope the answer is E.
E) OK, there is no way in hell this is the correct answer. In fact, I don't think this would _ever_ be the correct answer on the LSAT. Scientific investigation is never impossible. No way.

Here, I hated all five answers. But I hated A ("more quickly" is completely unsupported by the evidence), B ("intensity" is unsupported), D ("more susceptible" is unsupported), and E ("scientific investigation is impossible" could never be the answer) the most. So I'd be forced to choose C here. Of the five answers, I think the evidence cited best supports the hypothesis that an arthritis-weather link is simply imagined by arthritis sufferers. This is far from proven, but it's more consistent with the evidence than the rest of the shitty answer choices. I'm not happy here, but we have no choice but to choose C. I would call this a 9.5 out of 10 difficulty question.

QUESTION 25:

Cities with healthy economies typically have plenty of job openings. Cities with high-technology businesses also tend to have healthy economies, so those in search of jobs should move to a city with high-technology businesses.

The reasoning in which one of the following is most similar to the reasoning in the argument above?

A) Older antiques are usually the most valuable. Antique dealers generally authenticate the age of the antiques they sell, so those collectors who want the most valuable antiques should purchase their antiques from antique dealers.

B) Antique dealers who authenticate the age of the antiques they sell typically have plenty of antiques for sale. Since the most valuable antiques are those that have had their ages authenticated, antique collectors in search of valuable antiques should purchase their antiques from antique dealers.

C) Antiques that have had their ages authenticated tend to be valuable. Since antique dealers generally carry antiques that have had their ages authenticated, those collectors who want antiques that are valuable should purchase their antiques from antique dealers.

D) Many antique collectors know that antique dealers can authenticate the age of the antiques they sell. Since antiques that have had their ages authenticated are always the most valuable, most antique collectors who want antiques that are valuable tend to purchase their antiques from antique dealers.

E) Many antiques increase in value once they have had their ages authenticated by antique dealers. Since antique dealers tend to have plenty of valuable antiques, antique collectors who prefer to purchase the most valuable antiques should purchase antiques from antique dealers.

Superhard, superlong question. Most students, assuming time is limited when reaching this point in the section, should skip this one in favor of the much shorter #26.

The logic here isn't watertight, but it's not patently unreasonable either. If I were going to object, I'd say something like, "Can't I just pick a city that actually has a lot of job openings? Why should I go to all the trouble of looking for high-tech businesses, as an *indicator* of a healthy economy, which in turn is an *indicator* of a lot of job openings? It seems like just going to Craigslist and counting job openings would be simpler."

The general pattern is something like "Most A are B, and most B are C, therefore if you want C you should look for A." The problem with this reasoning is that *most* implies there could be exceptions. Perhaps San Jose has a lot of tech companies, but it is the rare city with tech companies that does not have a good economy. Or perhaps it does have a good economy, but it still doesn't have a lot of job openings. Again, it seems like looking at Craigslist would be a lot more reliable.

We're asked to find a similar pattern of reasoning, and since I think the reasoning above is flawed, let's look for that same flaw in our correct answer. Let's see what we've got.

A) This one doesn't really follow the pattern I'm looking for. After reading the first sentence, "older antiques are usually valuable," I wanted the second sentence to say "most X are older," or "most valuable antiques are X," in order to match the pattern we were given. I doubt this can be the answer.

B) I don't like how this answer said something about "typically have plenty of antiques for sale" in the first sentence and then never picked up that thread again. The argument we were given didn't do that, so I have a bad feeling about B.

C) OK, this one does it. Antique dealers usually authenticate, authenticated antiques are usually valuable, therefore if you want valuable antiques you should go through a dealer. The problem with this reasoning is that maybe this particular antique dealer is the exception that doesn't authenticate, or maybe he does authenticate but sells antiques that still aren't valuable. Wouldn't it be easier to just make sure that the antique was valuable in advance, instead of just trusting the dealer? I like this answer because my objection to the reasoning matches my objection to the reasoning in the argument we were given. This could be it.

D) This one never even makes a recommendation about what somebody should do. This one is just about what collectors "tend" to do. Doesn't seem like a good match. Answer C was better.

E) This one brings up authentication in the first sentence, and then never mentions it again. That's kind of what B did, and it makes me uncomfortable. C was the best match, so that's our answer.

Note that this type of question is extremely difficult (it's asking to match a pattern of reasoning, which can't be predicted in advance) and time consuming (just look how long it is—it has its own column!) so skipping it is the best strategy for almost everyone. Do it only after you've already done the rest of the questions in the section.

QUESTION 26:

Sociologist: A recent study of 5,000 individuals found, on the basis of a physical exam, that more than 25 percent of people older than 65 were malnourished, though only 12 percent of the people in this age group fell below government poverty standards. In contrast, a greater percentage of the people 65 or younger fell below poverty standards than were found in the study to be malnourished.

Each of the following, if true, helps to explain the findings of the study cited by the sociologist EXCEPT:

A) Doctors are less likely to correctly diagnose and treat malnutrition in their patients who are over 65 than in their younger patients.
B) People over 65 are more likely to take medications that increase their need for certain nutrients than are people 65 or younger.
C) People over 65 are more likely to suffer from loss of appetite due to medication than are people 65 or younger.
D) People 65 or younger are no more likely to fall below government poverty standards than are people over 65.
E) People 65 or younger are less likely to have medical conditions that interfere with their digestion than are people over 65.

The study shows that twice as many people over 65 are malnourished than are poor. But more people 65 and younger are poor than are malnourished. The question asks us to explain this discrepancy ... why are old folks different from young folks?

This is an *except* question, so the four incorrect answers will provide an explanation, while the correct answer will not.

A) This, if true, would explain why the malnutrition/poverty ratio is higher for old folks than for younger folks. This isn't the answer.
B) This would provide an explanation why old folks have a higher-than-normal rate of malnutrition. So it's not the answer.
C) This would explain it, so it's not the answer.
D) This certainly does not explain it. All D does is say the old folks and young folks are similar. How could that possibly explain a difference between the two groups? I bet this is it.
E) This would explain it. Our answer is D.

Epilogue

Whether you think the LSAT is easy or hard, you're right. Mindset is at least half the battle. What I do for a living is convince students like you that the test is actually quite a bit easier than they initially thought. Really, there are just three types of questions:

1) **Questions that are basically easy.** Example: The correlation-equals-causation flaw. Maybe you get these right away, or maybe they trip you up a few times, but after you've done a moderate amount of practice you'll see these questions coming a mile away. This level of difficulty probably makes up a quarter of the test.

2) **Questions that look hard on the surface, but eventually become very easy.** Example: Logic games that require you to understand complex rules and link them together. These will take a lot of practice, but you can become expert at them. This is probably half the test. If you master types one and two, you can score in the 160s.

3) **Questions that are actually hard.** Example: Very long match-the-pattern-of-reasoning questions. These questions are difficult even for experts, and they generally appear toward the end of each section. You can make them incredibly easy by skipping them outright and filling in an answer bubble at random. Or, you can get very good at types one and two so that you have plenty of extra time to devote to these questions. This is probably a quarter of the test. It's not the difference between going to law school and not going to law school, but it does impact what kinds of offers you'll receive.

Start with types one and two. Do a little bit every day. I've never met anyone who couldn't improve his or her LSAT score dramatically by following this simple plan. And as always, let me know if I can help: nathan@foxlsat.com.

APPENDIX:
Logical Reasoning Question Types

What you need to do first, foremost, and always is *argue with the speaker,* and you'll be fine no matter what type of question you're looking at.

But certain question types *do* prefer certain types of answers, so after you've already done your best to understand the argument, it's definitely useful to think about what type of question you're dealing with. Here are some of the common question types, and here's how I like to break them down:

Strategy of Argumentation: (Example: "Mal's response to Zoe proceeds by … ")

Some questions of this type simply ask you to identify the type of reasoning used by an argument. In this case, you must find the answer choice that best describes the logic of the argument as a whole. Note that the correct answer will probably not contain any of the specific details from the argument. Instead, the answer will contain an abstract, or general, description of the method of argumentation used. Since there are frequently several different ways to abstractly describe an argument, it's difficult to predict the correct answer before looking at the answer choices.

A common variation on this type is a question that asks you to identify the role played in an argument by a particular phrase or sentence. **(Example: "Jayne's assertion that Vera is his most favorite gun plays which one of the roles in his argument?")** On these questions, I always ask myself, "Is it the main conclusion of the argument?" If the answer is no, then I ask a follow-up question: "Does it support the main conclusion of the argument?" Sometimes, you will be able to exactly predict the correct answer in advance. If not, then you will almost certainly be able to narrow down the answer choices by simply understanding whether the phrase in question was the conclusion, a premise that supports the conclusion, or something else. Once you've got that down, you're in good shape.

Main Conclusion (Example: "Which one of the following most accurately expresses the conclusion of Wash's argument?")

Questions that ask you to identify the main conclusion are among the easiest questions on the LSAT, since you should always be looking for the conclusion of an argument anyway. (How can you be arguing with the speaker if you don't understand their main point?) On this type of question, you absolutely should predict the correct answer before looking at the answer choices. If you're having any trouble, try asking the speaker, "Why are you wasting my time with this?" to see if it helps you zero in on the speaker's main point.

Must Be True (Example: "Which one of the following must be true, if Kaylee's statements above are correct?")

This question type can be tricky when you first start studying for the LSAT, because you might be inclined to pass up answer choices that seem "too obvious." Don't do that! Be open to the possibility that you're actually plenty smart enough to punch this test in the face. On a question of this type, all you're looking for is the one answer that has been *proven* by the speaker's statements (and nothing more than the speaker's statements … outside information is not allowed.) The correct answer does not have to be the speaker's main point, nor does the speaker's entire statement have to be related to the correct answer. If any part of the speaker's statement *proves* that an answer choice has to be true, then that's your answer. This question type is pretty easy once you get the hang of it.

A common variation on this type of question is the slightly more fluid, and therefore slightly trickier, question that asks you to find something that might not *necessarily* be true based on the given statement, but is at least partially supported by the statement. **(Example: "Which one of the** following is most strongly supported by Kaylee's statements?") The general idea is the same, and this is still a pretty manageable type of question. Pick the answer that is best supported by Kaylee's statement—and no more than Kaylee's statement. (Again, outside information is not allowed.) The correct answer here might not be *proven* true by what Kaylee has said, but ideally it will be pretty damn close to proven.

Agree/Disagree (Example: "Simon and River have committed to disagreeing on which of the following?")

This is another very manageable question type once you know what to look for. (Sensing a theme here? Practice, practice, practice and you'll be in good shape.) Here, we are asked to identify the answer that Simon and River have *actually, already, in their statements*, disagreed upon. Easily dismissed incorrect answer choices might give a statement that Simon and River agree on—there are usually one or two of these. But trickier incorrect answers will frequently be something that Simon and River *probably* disagree on. One common trap on this type of question is an answer choice that the second speaker clearly takes a position on, and which might seem contrary to the first speaker's position, but the first speaker didn't actually address. Don't fall for that crap! You should be able to show me, in Simon's statement, where he said "yes" to a particular answer choice, and then show me, in River's statement, where she said "no" to that same statement. Or vice versa.

A common variation on this type of question is a question that asks you to identify a statement that the two speakers *agree* on. This is easy, as long as you don't make the tragic mistake of reading too fast and thinking you're supposed to be looking for a point of disagreement. It's devastating when that happens.

Weaken (Example: "Which one of the following, if true, most weakens Shepherd Book's argument?")

My primary piece of advice on the Logical Reasoning is "always be attacking," no matter what type of question you're looking at. So a question that asks you to undermine an argument's reasoning shouldn't be too much of a problem. As you read each question, you should always be coming up with weakeners. For me, this takes the form of "Oh yeah, well you're full of shit, because what about this? Or what about that? Or what about this other thing?" I'm constantly barraging the speaker with skepticism. Ideally, by the time the speaker comes around to his conclusion, I'm armed with at least a couple potential holes in the argument. The answer might very well be exactly one of these predictions, or it might be something similar. Even if it's not something I've already thought of, being in that skeptical state of mind helps me spot a kindred argument.

If you're having trouble on weaken questions, you probably aren't quite clear about what it means to "weaken" an argument on the LSAT. Here it is: You weaken an argument by showing that its evidence doesn't justify its conclusion. There are many ways to do this, but at a minimum you *must* know what the conclusion is, and you also must know what evidence was used to reach that conclusion.

Once you understand the argument, there are countless ways to attack it. Maybe Shepherd Book's premises simply don't add up to his conclusion, leaving a big hole in the argument. Or maybe Shepherd Book's conclusion and his evidence can't simultaneously be true. Or maybe he made a sufficient vs. necessary error. (More on that ahead.) Or maybe he made a correlation-equals-causation error. Pick the answer that, if true, causes the argument to be faulty, nonsensical, or just plain stupid. Ask yourself: "Which one of these facts, if I were an attorney arguing *against* Shepherd Book, would I most like to be true?"

Incorrect answer choices on Weaken questions will either strengthen the argument, or, more commonly, simply be irrelevant. One trap to look out for is an answer choice that seems to go against Shepherd Book's position, but doesn't really address his argument. (For example, if Shepherd's argument was about one particular group of people, and the answer choice talks about a different group of people.)

Unlike Must Be True questions, it's totally acceptable to use outside information to answer a Weaken question.

Strengthen (Example: "Which one of the following, if true, most strengthens Shepherd Book's argument?")

Arguments can be strengthened in just as many ways as they can be weakened. You're really just doing the reverse of the process described above. Pick the answer that strengthens the connection between the premises and the conclusion. If there is a big hole in the argument, then fill that gap as best you can. The correct answer on this type of question won't always prove that the conclusion is true, but you should pick the one that gets you the furthest toward that goal. Ask yourself: "Which one of these facts, if I were an attorney *for* Shepherd Book, would I most like to be true?" Again, outside information is fully acceptable here.

Which Fact Would be Most Useful (Example: "Which one of the following would be most useful in determining the validity of Shepherd Book's claim?")

This isn't a very common type of question—it appears maybe once, on average, on each test. Each answer choice is itself a question, and you are asked to pick the one that has the most bearing on the argument. I find that if I read the argument to weaken (which I always do) then I can do a pretty good job of predicting what the missing information is. Ask yourself: "If I were a police officer evaluating Shepherd Book's story, which one of these questions would I ask?" Pick the question that, if answered one way, makes Shepherd guilty, but if answered another way, makes Shepherd innocent.

Necessary Assumptions (Example: "Which one of the following is an assumption on which Inara's argument depends?")

Note the subtle, but very important, distinction between this question type (Necessary Assumption) and the one that follows (Sufficient Assumption). The Necessary Assumption question means, "Which one of the following *must be true in order for Inara's argument to make sense*?" Pick the answer that, if untrue, would make Inara's argument ridiculous. Another way of thinking about this is "Which one of the following is an assumption that Inara actually made?" Avoid answers that are stronger, or more absolute, than the minimum required for Inara's conclusion to make sense. If Badger is on the planet Persephone, and Inara concludes that Badger is a dick, then she has necessarily assumed that at least one person on Persephone is a dick. She has *not* assumed that everyone on Persephone is a dick.

Sufficient Assumptions (Example: "Which one of the following, if assumed, would allow Inara's conclusion to be properly drawn?")

This question means, "Which one of the following, *if true, would prove Inara's conclusion*? Pick the answer that, if true, would force Inara's conclusion to be true. Here, unlike a Necessary Assumption question, there is no limit on the strength or absoluteness of the correct answer. In fact, the bigger the better. If Inara had concluded that Badger is a dick, the correct answer might be something extreme like "Everyone on Persephone is a dick" (if Badger is on Persephone) or even simply "everyone is a dick." If either of these statements were true, then Inara's conclusion would be proven. It might be useful to think of Sufficient Assumption questions as "Super-Strengthen" questions. Conversely, Necessary Assumption questions might be considered more closely related to Weaken questions, because you're picking the answer that, if false, would destroy the argument.

Applying a Principle that is Given (Example: "Which one of the following would be a proper application of the principle stated by Niska?")

Here, all you have to do is 1) understand the principle and 2) pick the answer that conforms to the principle. Suppose Niska's principle is "I never let anyone damage my reputation without getting revenge." Incorrect answers might include people damaging Niska's reputation without Niska getting revenge, or Niska getting revenge on people who did not damage his reputation. The correct answer would most likely include someone doing something damaging to Niska's reputation, and Niska then exacting his revenge.

Identifying a Guiding Principle (Example: "Which one of the following principles best justifies Niska's actions?")

This is the reverse of the "Applying a Principle" question discussed above. The prompt would include a story, and you would be asked to identify a principle that would "justify" or "make acceptable" Niska's actions. For example, the story might include someone damaging Niska's reputation, and Niska then getting revenge. The correct answer would say something like "It is always acceptable to get revenge if someone damages your reputation."

Flaw (Example: "Which one of the following illustrates a flaw in Saffron's reasoning?")

With enough practice, you should get really good at these questions. They are similar to Weaken questions, in that you're asked to identify a problem with the argument. Flaw questions make actual errors of logic. Suppose Saffron had attacked the character of a speaker, rather than addressing the speaker's facts and reasoning. This is the "source attack," or "ad hominem" flaw. The same flaws appear over and over and over on the LSAT, and with practice you will start to see them coming a mile away. (You're not going to fall for the same bad logic more than two or three times, right?) There are way too many flaws to fit in this appendix, but Wikipedia's "fallacy" page is a great resource if you feel like doing some reading.

Matching Pattern (Example: "Which one of the following arguments is most similar to the reasoning in Patience's argument above?")

These are among the most time consuming and difficult questions on the LSAT. Most students (let's say, roughly, anyone regularly scoring 160 or below on their practice tests) should be skipping these questions and coming back to them at the end of the section if there's time. This is especially true on the extremely long Matching Pattern questions. Why would we waste our time on a question that takes up its own column on the page, when we could answer two other questions in the same amount of time? Make sure you've harvested all the low-hanging fruit before you break out the 40-foot ladder.

Because Matching Pattern questions are so tough to nail and are often time-consuming, I end up trusting my gut more than anything else. First, I read the argument carefully and see if I can get a feel for the general pattern of reasoning. Then, I ask myself if the logic in the argument is generally good or generally bad. If the logic in the argument is good, then the logic in the correct answer should also be good. If the logic is generally bad, then the logic in the correct answer should also be bad—and bad in the exact same way. If the beginning of an answer choice is wrong, I won't even bother reading the rest of it. (Example: The given argument says nothing about cause and effect, and an answer choice starts out with something about causation.) Sometimes it's impossible to be 100 percent sure that I have chosen the correct answer on a Matching Pattern question. I'm OK with that. But that's also why they're good candidates to skip.

Matching Flaw (Example: "Which one of the following arguments is most similar to the flawed pattern of reasoning used by Patience?")

This is a slightly easier variation on the Matching Pattern question, because there is something specifically *wrong* with the argument. The correct answer will have the exact same flaw. Make sure you identify the flaw before you look at the answer choices.

Explanation (Example: "Which of the following, if true, contributes most to an explanation of the puzzling situation described above?")

These questions are fun, because they set up a mystery and then ask you to explain that mystery. For example, the argument might go something like "*Firefly* was a bitchin' space western TV series on Fox. The show had great characters, fun stories, and a rabid fan base. Fox canceled the show after one season." Make sure you understand the mystery before looking at the answer choices. Why the hell would Fox cancel a show with so much going for it? That's the mystery.

The correct answer on an Explanation question should, obviously, *explain* that mystery. The correct answer should, ideally, make you say "Aha!" One type of common incorrect answer for an Explanation question is something simply irrelevant, like "Fox is owned by Rupert Murdoch." That's true, but it doesn't explain anything. Another type of common incorrect answer on an Explanation question will actually make the mystery even harder to understand, like "Fox executives claim to want to produce great shows." Here, the correct answer could be something like "Fox executives don't like shows with great characters." Or "Fox executives don't like fans." Or something broader, like "Fox executives are just plain stupid."

About the author

Nathan Fox didn't figure out what he wanted to be when he grew up until he was well past grown. He has been an undergrad economics student, a stockbroker, a half-assed computer programmer, a pro*ject* manager, a pro*duct* manager (and he can't really tell you the difference between the two), a graduate journalism student, an editor, a graduate business student, a law student, and finally an LSAT teacher. He still has nightmares about the first nine things, and loves the last thing so much that he can't believe he gets paid to do it.

He encourages you to keep searching until you find the thing that 1) you are good at, 2) you enjoy doing, and 3) you can get paid to do. There is no reason to settle for less.

Acknowledgments

Most of this book was written with a drink in my hand—the words come out easier that way. My editor, Mike Krolak, promises me that he will censor anything too obscene. I'm very grateful for his watchful eye. This insurance, in turn, just frees me up to be even more obscene than usual. But now that I think of it, Mike has just as foul a sense of humor as I do. So I should probably thank you, the reader, for your thick skin.

Chris Imlay took Mike's edited text and turned it into an actual book. The manuscript would have been unpublishable without his elegant design work. The touches that make this book easy to work with are primarily his.

Los Angeles's Avocado Books gave me a shot before I'd published a single page, and didn't make me feel like I needed to see an attorney before doing business with them. I really only learned one thing in law school, and that's "contracts are for suing each other, so only do business with people you really trust." I couldn't be more comfortable with Avocado, even though we've never put a word of our agreement into writing.

When I was in law school, I bitched nonstop for three years. But my fiancée Christine, who is just about to finish her final year of law school, does not bitch. Instead, she takes time out from far more important work to help me through Fox LSAT's growing pains. She apologizes that she can't do more. But my business, and this book, would not exist without her.

My dad dragged me along to work when I was a kid and taught me everything I know about business. My mom asks eagerly when she'll get to see a copy of my book—funny how rare it is to hear that when you're writing about the LSAT. Christine's mom, Petronella, has also been a great help. I love you all.

NEED A LITTLE HELP?
Call me.

I'M HERE TO HELP

Stop banging your head against the wall! The LSAT and law school admissions aren't as mind-boggling as you might think. If there's a type of LSAT question that's bothering you, or you're really confused by the whole "sufficient vs. necessary" thing, or you want to know how to negotiate for law school scholarships... please let me help! I'm a nerd about this stuff, and I love to show students how easy it can be. Email me any time at **nathan@foxlsat.com**, or just pick up the phone. I'm generally available to talk between 9 am and 7 pm PST.

ONLINE LSAT COURSE

If you like my books, I think you'll love my online LSAT class. It includes the exact same tests, quizzes, and lectures as my 12-week "Extended-Length" Class in San Francisco. Students pay $1495 for the 12-week classroom experience, but the class video is yours to watch and rewatch at your own pace from anywhere in the world for just $595. All materials included. And you're always encouraged to call or email me directly if you have any questions during the course. Like I said, I'm a nerd.

www.foxlsat.com/online-lsat-course

No confusing jargon, no pulled punches, no bullshit.
LSAT made simple.